Loose Connections

Loose
Connections

From Narva Maantee to
Great Russell Street

ESTHER MENELL

First published in 2014 by West Hill Books
westhillbooks@yahoo.com

The first two chapters of this book were published in 2008 by
Inleaf Press, South Portland, Maine, USA
under the title *Remembering Tallinn*

References to André Deutsch Limited are to the firm as it existed
during the period of the author's employment there, 1962–1993.
No reference is intended to the present imprint André Deutsch Books
as it exists under the aegis of Carlton Books.

Book design by Janette Revill
Printed and bound by Smith Settle, Yeadon, West Yorkshire

A CIP catalogue record for this book is available from the British Library

ISBN 978-0-9930087-0-2

For my mother
Zosia Menell (née Gutkin)
b. Tallinn 1905
d. London 1966

Contents

Preface

❦

T HERE COMES A TIME in life – a sure marker of the onset of
middle age – when one begins to prefer evenings in and to take
an interest in gardening. Old age, following all too swiftly, may then
announce itself with a sudden interest in Family and the Past. It is
too late to rectify mistakes but they are distant enough to appear to
have been done by someone else, by this person who was once you.

A wish to re-visit the past before life shuts down for good must
surely be why so many people sit down to write about themselves.
So it was with me, though I came to realise there were more reasons
than one and almost stopped before I had begun, for I could not
decide what to call this person who was me and yet no longer me.

Should I use the grown-up version of my Christian name, which
had begun as Esta, and what about my surname which began as
Menell and became Whitby? 'Esta' was tempting because it was the
way my mother spelt my name; 'Whitby' less so for my marriage
ended more than thirty years ago. But I enjoy seeing WHITBY on
signposts now that I spend part of every year in a cottage on the
edge of the North Yorkshire moors.

And what about other people? It seems, somehow, impertinent
to use real names, but made up names for real people – often recognisable – seem absurd, and the initials which I used at first soon
became a quagmire. One solution someone suggested was very
appealing. Apparently, George Seferis balked at using real people's

real names and substituted the names of streets in Athens: I like the idea of calling my long-term employers, André Deutsch and Tom Rosenthal, Finchley Road and Grosvenor Square. But, clearly, this could be carried too far and, by degrees, adding names first in pencil, then in ink, I have bowed to the inevitable.

So, too, in taking it for granted that memories are unreliable and I will have got a lot of things wrong. But on the same principle as the ignoramus who insists 'I know what I like', I can say 'I know this is how I remember it', and I have made no revisions to the text itself: but there are some pages at the end of the book – not essential reading – which correct some memories and introduce others. It doesn't seem important what colour Anthony Blond's Bentley was and I have made no effort to find out, but it does matter how many British soldiers were hanged by the Irgun or how many people died on the *Estonia* when it sank. On such issues, I have done my best to get things right.

In a newspaper article 'Whose Life Is It Anyway?' which became a seminal text for me, both warning me of the dangers of what I was doing and helping me to understand why I was doing it, the novelist Julie Myerson, who had learnt to her cost how angry people can be at finding themselves or not finding themselves or thinking they have found themselves in a book, ends with the reason for doing it anyway: 'Truth or fiction, fact or fantasy, all we really want is to feel we are part of a story worth remembering . . .'

For me, it is my mother and my Estonian relatives, many of whom were murdered in the first years of the war, who I am most glad to resurrect in these pages. Beside these lives and deaths, the goings-on in a publisher's office are paltry stuff indeed, but I have only my own life to tell.

North Yorkshire, 2002

Eleven years later

The reason for the writing of this book hasn't changed. The reason for publishing it, in its entirety, so many years after it was written – the first two chapters have already appeared under the title *Remembering Tallinn* – is not dissimilar. Those first two chapters were a memorial to my parents, long dead. The remainder (or much of it) is a kind of memorial to book publishing as it once was.

There are still publishers who employ editors and allow them the long hours it takes to read and re-read and read again the books they are working on, but they are rare. And, though it riled André Deutsch – of legendary meanness – that I kept my window open when he was paying to heat the room, he did not think first about Money and Sales when it came to the books themselves. Nor did he or his successor, Tom Rosenthal, think of the slow procedures of editing and copy-editing in terms of cost-effectiveness which seems to be the guiding principle in most areas of publishing now and can be seen back-firing in those monstrous sales-led celebrity advances which so often remain unearned.

It is true that the advances paid to our authors were minuscule but attention to the text was unstinting and many writers who began with us often went on to better things. One such author was Nadeem Aslam. Not many years after we had paid a thousand pounds for his first novel, Faber & Faber paid a six-figure sum for his second.

Whereas computers have changed the production of books beyond recognition, and I remain forever thankful that my typewriter didn't answer back at me during my working life, it is the globalisation of the industry which makes present-day publishing seem so alien. What was more like a cottage industry, fuelled by a love of books, appears to have become a vast money-making machine.

How could today's conglomerate afford to nurture a writer like NBA winner William T. Vollmann who was unlikely ever to repay, in copies sold, the hours spent on him. Of course, one should also ask, Would any of today's CEOs behave with the same disregard for their workers as was so often shown by those book-loving entrepreneurs who preceded them? Life for employees in those days was not always rosy.

The endless hours spent working on Bill Vollmann's fabulous *Seven Dreams*, during the late '80s and early '90s, cemented my friendship with Howard Davies who worked with me as Bill's copy-editor, a truly daunting task, and it was Howard, now a publisher, who suggested it was perhaps time to get my long-abandoned manuscript into print.

He and many of my colleagues at Deutsch, including Diana Athill who I worked alongside for almost thirty years, read the manuscript at the time it was written, with varying degrees of pleasure. For some, it seemed a big muddle: they would have preferred a graspable chronology* and had no time at all for the Notes – this meta text perhaps fall-out from the Vollmann years. But others, including Diana, whose opinion I valued the most, seemed to like it. So, here, as I enter my eighty-first year, it is.

One more word: over the course of the years much has happened. I have made no attempt to up-date the main text of which the final words were written in 2002, though the Notes have grown sevenfold in the intervening years. As for the use of initials – R, M and A – for my husband, ex-husband and son, I felt unable to do otherwise.

Kentish Town, 2013

---

* For an outline of main events, see page xv

Chronology

1934   Conceived, Tallinn. Born, London

1936–39   Tallinn, Estonia

1939–45   Yorkshire and London

1954–57   Oxford

1957–59   Secretary at Methuen

1959–61   Secretary to Anthony Blond

1960   Married first time

1962–93   Editor at André Deutsch

1964   First return to Tallinn

1967   Son, Aaron, born

1970   Divorced

1984   André Deutsch sells firm to Tom Rosenthal

1993   Leave Deutsch

1994   Collect Bus Pass

2006   Married second time

2009   Grandson, Zachariah Hawk, born in Brooklyn, NY

❧ I ❧

Starting in Viljandi

IRST, THE MENELLS. Who have nothing to do with the Meynells, a landed English family in whose territory – Staffordshire, I think – I once stayed with a schoolfriend on a military base of which her father was in command and where hunting, fishing, churchgoing, even a touch of Bohemia (forty years later I was to try and get a life of Alice Meynell published) were taken for granted.

I visited my friend's family next in Stockholm where Colonel Graves-Morris – a hugely romantic figure for this was not long after the war and he had been absent for six years, fighting alongside Wingate (here my Menells *could* begin to identify for Wingate was a Jewish hero, that is to say, a hero to English Jews) – was now military attaché and I, the blonde and beautiful Dierdre's friend, spent a happy and unaccustomed rural week in a well-appointed log cabin where Dierdre's mother watched over her post-war baby son while we took out a rowboat and spent the days fishing – an activity that turned from dreamy enjoyment to horror when I caught my first fish.

But I wasn't a Meynell or very English or the least bit upper class. Our Menells went back only as far as the day on which my grandfather, newly arrived in England, traded in Mendel Grozinski[n] for the more easily pronounceable but less melodious George Menell. The origin of the new surname isn't hard to spot but I couldn't have guessed that the George was for St George[n] – the English St

George, the one with the dragon and the red and white flag. My grandfather had a strong patriotic streak which was to encompass both the land of his landing and the land of his birth.

The land of his landing rather than the land of his choice because it seems he had meant to head on to New York. What stopped him we will never know but it couldn't have been a girl as this sixteen-year-old orphan had already found the girl he wanted to marry back home and, a surprisingly short time later, was able to bring her over. A predictably short time after that, she, the former Esther Hoff of Viljandi, bore her first child, my father, whom they named Alexander Michael and so English had they become that Alex and not Sasha was the name that he carried for the rest of his life.

And Alex suited my father who was to spend almost twenty years of his adult life in the mainly Russian-speaking land of *his* father without ever learning the language and this even though he was to meet there and marry (when they had both managed to get themselves divorced) my mother for whom Russian remained for ever the language of her thoughts and dreams. By the time I came along, providentially born in England, English was what they spoke together – English propped up by German, picked up by my father who knows where but as current as Russian among the middle classes in pre-war Estonia.

But I shouldn't assume my father was stupid just because he was no better at languages than I am and because books played no part in his life whilst the sport at which he so unJewishly excelled remained an abiding passion. QPR, the MCC, and perhaps best loved of all, a rugby team whose name I can no longer recall. There are photos of him as a young man – very slim and athletic – in his black shorts and striped vest posing along with the rest of the team of the Camborne School of Mines. And fifty years later, still wearing his cable-knit V-necked cricket sweater, lost in the sports pages of the *Daily Express*.

I think my father was the only one of four brothers who had this very English passion for sport and who entirely lacked that other kind of drive which was to take at least one of the others to dizzying heights of financial success.

There was Slip – Gordon Simeon. There was Arthur. And there was Eddie – Edward Septimus – the seventh and last child. And then there were the three girls – my aunts Bertha and Freda[n] and Moos – the double o pronounced as in the first syllable of 'bosom'. Apparently there would have been others but they died either in the womb or in infancy or at birth. By all accounts, my grandmother – a formidable-looking lady with a magnificent Edwardian chest – must have been pregnant for much of the time and my slightly built, impish-looking grandfather must have had more energy and nerve than comes across in early photos or later life to mount this battle-axe so often and so successfully.

He must also have been a good tailor for by the time my father was a student and after an inexplicable few years spent in Dublin,[n] he was to open a successful shop in Regent Street, known for its ladies 'costumes' and, later, for its furs.

Regent Street – Upper Regent Street – still has family connections as I found not too long ago. The tailoring shop is long gone but opposite where it once stood are the London offices of Anglo-Transvaal – a modest first or second floor suite belying the immensity of its parent company in Johannesburg. Anglo-Transvaal, the mining conglomerate and creation of my father's younger brother, Slip, whose image in the staid family portrait that hangs on my wall is blurred because, at nine or ten, he was already on the move . . .

In this same picture, taken during the Dublin years, my top-hatted father looks characteristically cheerful; his then youngest brother, Arthur, a future president of the South African Stock Exchange, looks somewhat timid, and the three sisters are already playing themselves: the eldest, Bertha, looks self-possessed and a trifle disdainful, the next in line, Freda, has a sweet, untidy look and, sitting on a cushion like a little princess is Moos, the curly-haired baby of the family and my father's favourite. Like Eddie still to come she was to have a nice disregard for the stuffy conventions of family life and they both knew how to enjoy their wealth – hers acquired by marriage and his through a kind of barrow-boy business sense which could look at a wrecked aeroplane and see it as a stack of aluminium saucepans or, finding himself lumbered with a load of thin rubber sheeting, cut it into petal shapes and stick it on plain old-fashioned bathing caps, turning them into a novel and successful fashion item:" not the usual businessman who knows nothing about the product but everything about strategy. Optimistic, amusing, alert.

But it was not Eddie or Arthur or Slip who I went to meet that day in the London offices of Anglo-Transvaal. It was a company lawyer, dispatched by Anglo-Transvaal at my cousin Clive's behest (his father Slip long dead) to look into the business of the Estonian minefield to which, it seemed, we might have some claim. Estonia had, for the second time in seven hundred years, gained its independence and it was putting its affairs in order. It was my brother who had heard a news item on the wireless referring to the restitution of requisitioned properties, farmlands and businesses. The consulate was issuing claim forms. It was a long shot but it seemed worth a try.

The form duly arrived. It was in Estonian. I rang the School of Slavonic Studies and found someone to translate the mercifully brief questionnaire, printed inkily – sometimes too heavy, sometimes unreadably light – on flabby Soviet-style paper. The transformation of commodities – there is nothing you can now not get in Tallinn – was yet to come.

Skeletal though it was, the form presented difficulties. I knew nothing about the mines except a name – Vanamöisa. But I did know that what was now Estonia's major industry had been dreamed up by my tailor grandfather and made to happen by my mining-engineer father who had lived and worked there from the twenties until the outbreak of war.

But memories and family hearsay were not going to help complete the form. I needed documents and now recalled a family row, unintelligible at the time, in which one of my Estonian-born uncles was berating my father for not having kept or perhaps not being able to find some crucial papers relating to these years.

There was no point in my looking now. After my parents' death I had burnt all the papers I could find, mostly letters, many of them love letters which I felt were no business of mine. But now I needed documents and thinking about documents made me think about ownership and ownership made me think about money and money made me think about Slip. It was inconceivable that my happy-go-lucky father would ever have been solvent enough to set up such a project. It must have been to South Africa that my grandfather had turned with his hare-brained scheme[n] to extract oil from shale and create an industry which would help to put the newly independent country on its feet. Whether my uncle was humouring his father or whether his technical advisers thought it just might work – and the latter seems more likely as I have been told that before too long Anglo-Transvaal had set up a similar operation in Mozambique – the money came. And, some fifty or sixty years in its wake, and bearing the necessary documents, came my cousin's emissary, the corporate lawyer, David Lazarus, en route to talks with the Estonian government to see what there was to be had.

We were used to emissaries. Seldom, if ever, did Slip, richest of the three rich uncles, deal with the family, *his* side of the family, himself. In the past it had been Arthur from whom the 'poor' relations heard: who set up the trust fund for my schizophrenic cousin, who refused help for my disabled brother, who averted my father's bankruptcy . . . And I imagine it was Arthur who organised the payment to St Hilda's when, almost overnight, my father was no longer able to pay the fees.

Of Slip himself I had perhaps a dozen sightings.[n] The first was very soon after the end of the war. The venue: the Ritz Hotel. For Slip, South Africa had not been safe enough" and at the outbreak of war he had transported his family to the States from where we were to receive occasional parcels. I remember with pleasure the dried bananas, less happily a mustard-yellow cardigan and chequered frock picked out for me by Auntie Rae.

My father who never had a mean or envious thought in his life was genuinely pleased at these modest offerings as he was to be each year at the arrival of a slim crate of avocados when his younger brother, back in South Africa, branched into farming. But the transaction at my first encounter with my uncle – on his way home now the war was safely over – was a money transaction. The whole family – that is to say, my father and us and my father's two sisters and their families, the 'English Menells' – were summoned to his hotel where I, my brother and my three English cousins were presented with £50 cheques. Our reward for seeing the war out in London . . .

I was perhaps ten at the time and it all seemed very thrilling. Less the Ritz Hotel – which was to impress me more as I got older – but my three new cousins with their American accents. There would have been a fourth but she had been left behind to 'finish at Vassar'. And fifty pounds! Unlikely as it seems, I was also given a cheque book. I remember this because it was taken away from me almost at once. I had signed all the cheques in case my signature changed.

Now Clive, the eldest of those three Americanised cousins had, in the manner of his father, dispatched a lieutenant and that evening my brother and I told David Lazarus what we knew about Estonia, which we had been visiting since the sixties, and the mines. We had this conversation over salt beef, potato latkes and lemon tea at Blooms." It seemed like the right place to be discussing Jewish family affairs and David, a solid family man, the right person to be discussing them with.

I have not seen him again since that evening but for several years, even after he and his family had moved from South Africa (and, presumably, from Anglo-Transvaal) to New Zealand, he kept in touch with my mother's relatives in Tallinn with whom I had put him in touch because he was used to going to synagogue on a Saturday and though I knew there was now a synagogue in Tallinn, I couldn't tell him where to find it."

A very decent man and, being decent, discreet. So I learned very little about the Jo'burg Menells in general and nothing about Clive in particular," but I did learn that Anglo-Transvaal employed 40,000 people. Perhaps, I thought, they could employ one more if my job should fold as it seemed that it might. But then perhaps not. When some years earlier my brother had lost his job and couldn't find work in the only business he was trained and proficient in, they had been able to supply neither a niche in their organisation nor the modest investment needed to set him up in his own business.

No. No use looking to the Menells. The family solidarity which non-Jews envy was not part of this particular family's make-up. They did not invite or welcome calls for help. Indeed they made it plain that they wanted nothing to do with us and it was a kind of miracle that for a short time I actually heard from Clive himself.

In getting up the courage to approach this cousin whom I had not seen for something like forty years, I used the same technique I had used once before when unnerved at the prospect of meeting a Very Important Person. On that earlier occasion it had been the writer V. S. Naipaul. Vidia had fallen out with his usual editor and I had been called on to look after his latest novel. It did not help to be told that no one had read the manuscript before me: for some reason he had not shown it to his wife, his usual first reader. Of course, with this writer there was no real danger that the book could turn out to be gibberish, but would I understand it as he wanted it understood? Would I appreciate it as he wanted it appreciated?

So nervous was I about reading this virgin text that I borrowed the keys to a neighbour's house where no one could interrupt me and the moment that my young son had left for school and she for work I took myself there and read the manuscript of *A Bend in the River* from beginning to end. And it *was* good, of course, and, like everything else this author handed in, pretty well word perfect, but it was also uncharacteristically stodgy and I continue to be surprised at how highly it is rated.

Anyway, I must have made a good job of concealing my disappointment because on hearing that I and my partner were going to be spending a week in Wiltshire, we were invited to supper.

How did one behave with royalty? The only way, I told myself then as I was to tell myself before writing to my cousin, was to treat them like anyone else. Which is how, in Vidia's case, I came to buy our usual cheapish bottle of wine at the Waitrose in Marlborough with the startling consequence that when he unwrapped it that evening, he declared it unfit to drink. And I had wondered whether, as a Hindu, he drank wine at all!

I would have known better had there been a next time. The table was laid with several glasses beside each place . . . Somehow, mostly thanks to his wife Pat," we survived these white waters and, surprisingly, but so it turned out, had a long and pleasant evening.

Clive might now be a Very Important Person, in South Africa at least, and must certainly have visited London from time to time without feeling the need to let us know, but he was still my cousin as was his sister Zoe who lived up the road in Hampstead and whom I would occasionally see walking on the Heath. The fact that he wouldn't have recognised me and she didn't, didn't alter the fact that we were cousins and that I could still remember how awed and respectful my father and his sisters were at my Uncle Slip's accounts of Zoe's great cleverness: at Vassar, we were told, she had gained a Fi? Beeta? Capa . . .

As for Clive, I still had the *Tatler* cutting showing him, while a student at Cambridge, dancing with a princess – a *real* princess, I was told by my aunt who also let slip in my hearing that her doctor

husband had been able to 'help Clive out', of which I didn't understand the meaning at the time. Even then I had not seen him for
several years but remember the frisson the princess caused in the
family and how dashing he looked in evening clothes.

Anyway, there it was. We shared a grandfather and that grandfather had had a dream and the dream had come true. Now it was
time for the paperwork.

I don't know if before he got my letter Clive knew of the existence
of the Estonian mines. I imagine not. I have since been told that
Slip never spoke of his origins" or, though this is harder to believe,
his Jewishness.

Anyway, though I am also told that my cousin Clive was never
a natural or even a willing businessman, it did not take him long to
understand what was at stake. He must have understood too that
if my father had any share in the ownership of the mines, I had no
papers to prove it for, after a flurry of phone calls and faxes, I never
heard from him again.

Still, it had been exciting while it lasted: the idea that thanks
to my father, hard-hatted in the Estonian forests, cheering the first
wagon-loads of ore (photographs of which I had sent copies to
Johannesburg) I might become an Oil Shale Princess and, for the first
time in my adult life, not have to worry about money.

It is possible that Anglo-Transvaal recovered something, though I
doubt it. I doubt even more that Clive, failing in this or succeed-
ing, sent the help his mining conglomerate could well afford to this
struggling, newly independent country.

I had made this suggestion in all seriousness. I knew that our
grandfather had a passionate attachment to the country he had left
as a boy – an attachment which had drawn him back, first as a fur
trader – furs from the depths of the Russian forests to complement his ladies' suits – and then, as a kind of political crusader. For

whatever reason, the independence of Estonia became a passionate cause and sustaining that independence a matter of his private concern.

I don't know when the first rumblings of independence were heard nor how my grandfather conceived the grand and quixotic plan" by which he intended to help sustain it. But I do know that a time had come when he could leave the care of the Regent Street shop to his older girl children and, more pertinently, that he had found a partner, a chemist whose motives and belief in the venture I cannot even guess at.

I knew, and by this time Clive must have known, that what our grandfather would have wanted now and what Clive's own father would almost certainly have done for his sake as all those years earlier he had invested" in the original scheme, was for us, his grandchildren, to take an active part in the re-emergence of Estonia as an independent political and economic unit – the transformation of the country from satellite and dependent into an autonomous state.

How much thought the head of Anglo-Transvaal gave to the possibility of sending aid along with claims, I will never know. Clive died a few years later and his silence on the subject is now complete.

Presumably, the mines continued to flourish, even had they been largely dependent on Soviet and Russian-speaking skills.

Be that as it may, it remains a mystery why my grandfather felt as he did. Orphaned in early childhood, apprenticed to a wigmaker . . . we did not even know where but it must have been a village big enough to have a Jewish community and not too far from Viljandi, else how would he have met my grandmother? Not an obvious seedbed for such intense and lifelong nostalgia.

And yet I should understand, for I share it. I may have left Estonia when I was not yet five years old but, almost thirty years later, when pregnant with my son and pouring out my dreams to a man in Wimpole Street, it was a dream of Estonia that told both him and me that we were reaching the end: that soon the nightmare which my marriage had become would recede and I would have my baby and be myself again.

Thinking about this later, I am surprised that it was the lake in Viljandi that surfaced in this healing dream. Viljandi was not connected with my mother or my mother's family though we had been there together once. It was 1964. I can date the visit from a footnote to one of Jean Rhys's letters" which reads: 'EW was visiting relations in Estonia.' I was already working at Deutsch. Jean was yet to become famous.

On this our first return since the war, my mother, already ill with cancer, flew to Leningrad and I followed by train, cheaper than planes then, with my husband, M. I seem to remember that we had to spend a night in Warsaw and we certainly stayed over in Leningrad because it was here, at hotel reception, that somehow security slipped, and we were issued with plane tickets to Tallinn. What we did not know until later was that foreigners were not allowed to make this journey by air as the plane flew directly over the industrial – the mining – region.

To add to the irony, my husband, though he had applied to go into something more active, had spent his national service doing air reconnaissance. To the army he had not looked like regular soldier-material. To the croupiers and managers of London's casinos, a year or two later, he had not looked like a gambler . . .

Viljandi too was out of bounds to foreigners but we had been told that the authorities would show some respect for family piety, even among Jews, and we finally got permission to visit the Hoff family graves.

My father, back in London, would not have made this a priority any more than his brothers in South Africa would have done, but it gave M and me the opportunity to see something of the country and, leaving my mother behind we set out, accompanied by an

English-speaking cousin, to visit this little provincial town where my paternal grandmother had been born.

Esther Hoff: my father's mother who had been brought to England by my grandfather and had lived to see her four sons and three daughters grow up, marry and have children of their own before, so the story goes, dropping dead in the foyer of the Marble Arch Odeon" a few months before I was born.

What caused my grandmother's death I don't know but even now, when I am older than she was when she died, I can't drive up Park Lane and see the Odeon come into view without thinking of this curious fact. And, as the first grandchild to be born after her death, I had to have her name."

Now, in my twenties, I was in the place that she and all those other Hoffs had come from and was trying, without success, to find the graveyard where still earlier generations had been buried. What the authorities in Tallinn didn't know or we would not have had their permission to come, was that the Jewish cemetery had been razed by the Germans and there was nothing left to see.

But we did see their house, or we think we did. We had to rely on my cousin, Ephraim or Fima, and he had to rely on the memories of passers-by. A big, square, wooden house, dilapidated, like every other building in this little town with its unpaved roads and few dirty-windowed shops." Maybe the geography teacher with whom I had argued had not been wrong after all when she had described the Baltic states as 'primitive'.

But, primitive or not, the Hoffs had what it took to make that quantum leap from a provincial backwater in a country few people had heard of – until a ferry bearing its name and over 800 passengers sank in the North Sea – to Paris and the 16th arrondissement . . . And what the Hoffs had and what my South African uncles inherited from their mother, was the Jewish 'business brain'.

There was evidence of it right under our feet: the rusted lines of a single track railway constructed by the Hoffs to transport

1 *The Menell family*

2 *The Gutkin family*

3 *Camborne School of Mines, 1912*
4 *(Inset) My father*

Reval. 1927.

5 *Girl guides group, Tallinn, c.1920. My mother holds the flag*
6 *(Inset) My mother as a young woman*

7 *My parents before they were free to marry*

8 *My mother in remission*

9 *My widower father*

Tallinn
1938.

10 *With my parents*

something, no one any longer seems to know what, from Viljandi, then Fellin, to Tallinn, then Reval.

I think the creator of this now defunct line whose other end could still be seen meandering through Tallinn was one of my grandmother's brothers and that it was one of *his* sons who we used to visit in Paris and who, I understood, had brought disgrace on the family with some audacious scam" which had caused the Lloyd's bell to be rung in triumph when he was eventually brought to book. But if he served a prison sentence it hadn't subdued him. Small, dark, a non-stop talker with a heavy moustache, he is indistinguishable in my mind from Groucho Marx. If sharp practice also means warmth and humour, how much preferable to the sermonising and physical coldness of that virtuous business mogul, Uncle Slip.

'Too much kissing,' he had said on a rare – mercifully rare – family outing. A boat had been hired and we were cranking our way through endless locks on the way to some riverside restaurant on the Thames. Too much kissing! Was a formal peck on the cheek really too much? What would he have made of the bear hugs that were accepted currency" on the other side of my family? That the Menells don't kiss was either said or implied and the phrase has stayed in that same back pigeonhole of memory as a teacher's devastating comment scrawled in the margin of an essay I was especially proud of: 'Who are you to criticise Dickens?'

Anyway, it wasn't true. My grandfather, by the time I knew him, was a sweet and cuddly old man with soft pink cheeks who loved to kiss and be kissed. He liked everyone to be happy and was never without a supply of barley sugars for his grandchildren with whom he would also share the sugar lumps (occasional substitute for the more usual dollop of jam) through which he sucked his lemon tea. Somewhat incongruously, though sucking his tea like a Russian peasant, he dressed like an English country gentleman and I can still see the rough gingery tweed of the plus-fours that were his favoured wear.

As a child, I didn't wonder why he lived with one of my aunts any more than I understood then or understand now why, not long before his death, he began to live on his own. Perhaps my aunt Freda, who was a doctor's wife in those days before group practices and answer machines, had finally found it too much for her but it is hard to imagine this kindly soul turning anyone out of her house. Maybe she and her older sister had meant to take turns (the glamorous Moos, of course, living in South Africa, was not part of the equation) and when it was Bertha's, she had begged off. Anyway, whatever the reason, money was provided to re-house the increasingly muddled old man and he ended his days in St John's Wood, in a flat one block down from the one in which I had been born and almost directly across from the one André Deutsch was to visit every morning to breakfast with his widowed mother.

I was away at school when my grandfather died and didn't go to the funeral, but when I visit my parents' grave – a small flat stone somewhere on the left in that desolate graveyard off Willesden Lane – I see the splendid marble hulk of his and my grandmother Esther's tomb rearing up in the middle distance. Very thirties, a bit Egyptian-looking. And, like his last temporal dwelling, paid for by his second oldest son.

Not too long ago, the man I live with now and have lived with for nearly thirty years took a small party to Kensal Green cemetery as the last destination on a whistle-stop architectural tour of Greater Kensington. A good place to end. In every sense. And conveniently non-denominational. If, when the time comes, R does not feel an urge to join his own family in the churchyard at Bakerstown, Pa we can lie together among the monuments and greenery of Kensal Green which, if it does not match the grandeur of Père Lachaise or the comforting tangle of Highgate, does at least exude a pleasant melancholy which the bleak resting place for North London's Liberal Jews completely lacks.

Liberal Jews. My grandfather belonged to the Liberal Synagogue and also to the Liberal Party and, at least in his old age but probably long before, he could not really tell the two apart. He was a visionary not a politician but he took great pleasure in his membership of the Liberal Club in Whitehall Place and even tried to go there – to the consternation of his bewildered chauffeur – when he was staying in Johannesburg, six thousand miles away. By this time, probably his last visit to South Africa, it sounds as though senility, as we called it then, had set in with a vengeance and though he continued to be happy as a sandboy, in his pyjama bottoms and outdoor shoes or plus-fours and bedroom slippers, he did not live long enough to have to be put into an institution.

Politics was not an interest of my father's either but when he did vote he voted Conservative, and when he went to a synagogue, which he did once a year on Yom Kippur, with an apple in his pocket with which to break the fast, it was one where they still used Hebrew and didn't sing hymns. And it was in this kind of synagogue – not fully orthodox for they wouldn't have us[n] – that one summer's Sunday, in 1960, I got married. Prompted from behind by a polyglot schoolfriend of M's, one in ten of whose unintelligibly highbrow jokes I managed to 'get', I spoke my few words of Hebrew and found myself married to the man I had been living with on and off for five years and who, only hours before, had been sitting at the kitchen table doing Ximenes, a crossword so perplexing that I could understand neither the questions nor the answers.

I would have felt even more of a fraud under that *huppa* if I hadn't been to see the rabbi[n] beforehand and asked what he thought about marrying someone he had never seen before and would never see again. 'It's an abomination, of course. But so what?' is more or less what he said, reassuringly unruffled behind a pillar of books. We were Jews, weren't we? And it would please our parents . . . And it did please our parents though none of them had been married this way, having been variously divorced and/or married 'out'. But it somehow seemed fitting to them and also – for they had not been insistent – to us. A minor civil servant seemed no more appropriate than a rabbi as the instrument of change and a synagogue, if only for its novelty, preferable to a government office.

But the unease I felt even then about formalising something so essentially private persisted and, though I didn't have the courage then to flout convention, and probably wouldn't have later had I not once been entitled to call myself 'Mrs', I never went through that charade again."

Divorce, like kissing, was something else the Menells – the Slip Menells – didn't do. But mine which became final exactly ten years after my marriage (though, for me, it dates to that moment, four years earlier, when I had thrown my wedding ring into the Bosphorus) didn't cause much of a family stir: which my father's, some fifty years earlier, had.

It seems – I have had to piece this together because it was never talked about openly – that when my father met and fell in love with my mother he was already married to someone else. And, to complicate things still further, so was she. But whereas my mother's first husband, a Swedish pastor's son, who must have been exceptionally sweet-natured for he not only gave her the divorce she wanted but wanted to adopt the illegitimate child she was carrying, my father's first wife was made of sterner stuff.

By all accounts, she was a bit of an ogre. But, if so, why did my father marry her and how, as an abandoned mother of two young children, did she manage to find someone else? For find someone else she did and wanting now to get re-married herself she released my father who married my mother, presumably in a registry office, and, possibly, with my three-year-old brother looking on.

As for how my father had come to marry this dragon in the first place, the story goes like this. He had only married her because he couldn't marry her younger sister with whom he was really in love because in those days in orthodox Jewish families such as hers the girls had to be married off in chronological order. How long he waited in the hope that some other suitor would remove the older sister before marrying her himself, I don't know.

Anyhow, apocryphal or not, that is how the story goes and given my father's capacity for inattention to detail it is just believable that he married the wrong sister and had two children without too much thought.

As for the two children, the boy, my half-brother, I was never to meet for he died in a raid over Germany in one of the Lancaster bombers that my father – his father too – helped to build. The girl, my half-sister, I met twice. For the first time, at our father's funeral, then, at her home in Brighton before, sadly, losing track. I still have *The Faber Book of Pebbles* which she lent or maybe gave me at that second meeting but I can no longer remember her married name.

Nor can anyone else. Or nobody I know. Of course it is possible that some of my nine surviving Menell cousins are still in touch with my half-sister, the cousin they were never to speak of in my hearing. But I doubt it. Certainly, the explosion of disapproval that occurred when my father left his wife and children to take up with my mother is long forgotten and the lifelong coolness of the Menells – the Slip Menells – towards my mother is, necessarily, a thing of the past.

For the main players, that is. But I need an explanation for that coolness or barely repressed hostility if only because of the effect it was to have on all our lives. My Auntie Freda's son Victor, the 'mentally challenged' older cousin who had inadvertently spilt the beans about my father's first family, cannot help on this one. Victor knew who those two children were whose uncaptioned pictures I always stopped on in the family album and told me one day when I was perhaps ten years old. Not much later, I worked out for myself who 'Mr Humble' must be. The slightly podgy man in a homburg hat was my mother's first husband.

But there is no picture to tell me why Slip and Rae felt the way they did about my mother and I can only think that aside from a genuine disapproval of divorce, they were annoyed that my father had left an English wife of considerable means for a foreigner of none, and a divorced foreigner at that.

I am only guessing." It could even be that the first wife's 'means' only arrived with husband number two – a kindly man, by all accounts, this manufacturer of raincoat linings who became stepfather to my father's children.

Whatever the truth may be, there was no warmth between our families and only my father was unaware of it. Even after rebuffs as cruel as the reprimand for wasting money on a telegram – he had sent Slip a greetings telegram on his birthday – he continued to see nothing but good in his younger brother and to take pride in his success.

And maybe there was more good than was apparent to me but I remember too well the barbed references to my father being the only one of the four brothers privileged to have a higher education, the homilies – directed at me – on the virtues of working from nine to five, and those crates of avocado pears which, like all his gifts, many substantial in money terms, had a mechanised feel. You knew some functionary had been given the order to send the wedding cheque" or whatever it happened to be. Which is just as well, perhaps, as the only time after that £50-for-winning-the-war episode that a gift was actually given in person – though not by Slip himself, for he was dead, but by his consort Auntie Rae – it was hardly worth having: a metal sandwich box with a picture of a footballer kicking a football on the lid. Neither new nor wrapped, it had almost certainly belonged to one of her grandchildren. Not that this made it any less desirable to my three-year-old son whom Rae had called in, most unexpectedly, to see.

The last time I had caught a glimpse of her had been at a memorial service for my uncle which had taken place at my Phi Beta Kappa cousin's house, halfway up the nearby hill. Since then, I had had a baby, been divorced, lost my father and was now living on rent from two of the rooms in my two-bedroom house. One of my lodgers was in fact sitting at the kitchen table, in full view of the front door, when my aunt arrived. Perhaps she thought he was my boyfriend – a fantasy touchingly shared by his mother who, unlike my aunt, knew only too well that Harry, the poet Harry Fainlight, now far gone in his madness" – was no longer, if he ever had been, cut out to be a married man . . .

Whether or not, Rae whose appearance never changed – iron-grey hair, a twinset with one string of pearls and a tweed skirt over a stoutening midriff – arrived, nodded in Harry's direction, put her head round the door of my son's room, handed him the sandwich box, and left. And I never saw or heard from her again.

Presumably, she's dead and her funeral, wherever it took place, was attended by mourners in bright colours such as the scarlet wool coat she had worn to my mother's years before. At the time, this had seemed like the final insult but I have learnt since that orthodox Jews don't wear black at funerals and though I still wish Rae hadn't appeared to celebrate my mother's death it wasn't, apparently, as bad as it had seemed.

What was as bad was something which had happened some years before my mother's death and in the wake of my father's last-minute rescue from the bankruptcy courts" which left him entirely dependent on his brother: that same brother who with good intent but no understanding of my father's strengths and weaknesses had stage-managed his post-war transformation from mining engineer to stockbroker: a catastrophic choice of profession for a fifty year old with no particular interest in paper transactions, careless of his own finances, and with no commercial drive. It could only be a matter of time before my father, until so recently happily employed by the Air Ministry turning planes into prefabs, came to grief.

I can't reasonably blame my uncle for trying to set his brother

– with his livelihood now cut off by the Iron Curtain – up in something else, nor for demanding that in return for paying my Oxford fees, as he was now to do, I make myself employable by learning to type. But I do think of the £30,000 a friend wired to my bank account – no questions asked and no strings attached – when he heard my ex-husband was forcing the sale of my home: money that was truly a gift and never referred to again.

The rescue package put in place by my uncle proved to be a very different kettle of fish."

Of course, he hadn't known at the time how convenient it was going to be having my parents in thrall. At the time of the 'crash' when we were living in a furnished flat in Eastbourne, ostensibly to allow my mother to convalesce after her mastectomy but also, as I soon found out, because my father could no longer pay the rent" on our London home, my poor, stuttering cousin who was to become their lifelong charge, was still living with his parents – my Estonian-born doctor uncle (it was said that the two older Menell girls had had to go back to Estonia to find husbands) and Freda, my favourite aunt – the only one of the seven siblings who had an interest in books and paintings and, it was said, in writers and painters. In her bohemian youth, it was rumoured, she had had an affair with Robert Service or was it Roy Campbell? . . . I am not even sure this *could* be true but I do know that when she died, a signed copy of *Ulysses* and a Henry Moore maquette were a part of her estate, testifying to an adventurous interest in things of the mind and, incidentally, paying off in terms the rest of the family could understand.

It is only looking back that I realise how different Auntie Freda was from the rest of the family, as different as her furniture from ours: those delicate tapestry-covered chairs which started life in an eighteenth-century French drawing-room and which my father did not consider had been made to sit on as against our three-piece suite from Harrods, upholstered in a heavy silvery-green brocade, to match the curtains, and, worst of all, though I didn't realise it then, the cream and gold Louis Quinze bedroom with its oyster-coloured quilted satin bedspread . . . My sweet-natured, untidy, bookish aunt had, from somewhere, inherited an aesthetic sense which had completely by-passed her sisters though they, like my own mother, had enviably good taste in matters of dress and were never to be seen in baggy skirts and wrinkled stockings – the unkempt look which became second nature to me as much out of laziness as from a deep-seated reluctance, whether conscious or not, to compete where I could never win.

It would be an exaggeration to say it was exposure to this more cultured household (visited more frequently after they acquired a television set) which turned me into the bookish child I became, spending most of my time reading and determined, before really knowing what it meant, to 'go to Oxford'. The reading was a substitute: I would much rather have been going to parties, as most of my out-of-London boarding-school friends did in the holidays, and meeting boys. As for the idea of university or, rather, Oxford, this came of wanting to follow in the footsteps of my two six-years-older-than-me girl cousins, one of whom, Freda's daughter Doreen, wrote me tantalising letters about her activities there and the other of whom, Vicky, the only child of my father's eldest sister Bertha, had a brief moment of fame playing Delilah in an OUDS production of *Samson Agonistes*: at that time it meant nothing to me that this production was directed by Kenneth Tynan and had I not actually met him at her parents' home I would think I was imagining the whole thing for, though my cousin Vicky was part of his entourage throughout her time at Oxford, there is no mention of her among the galaxy of other women in his Letters. Maybe in spite of his casting her as his Delilah, she was never involved with him sexually – on later evidence of his preferences, a lucky escape.

Access to books was more direct. The fact that we had very few at home, all ranged on two shelves of the glass-fronted mahogany bureau, didn't really matter because across the street (Finchley Road) was the public library where the selection though comparatively small, for it was only a branch library, did stretch beyond Churchill, T. E. Lawrence and *Quiet Flows the Don*.

And then there was the library, or what was called the library, at school – a huge room with mullioned windows and acres of parquet floor; a room which was hardly used except on the days that Miss Silvester, Victor Silvester's bony orange-haired sister, came to give us ballroom dancing lessons. Here there were hundreds if not thousands of books but it was not until a library room had been set up in a modern wing of the school that any kind of system was introduced and, for now, anyone could take anything. As far as I know, the books on the 'old library' shelves had never been catalogued and though many of them were unreadable – great tomes on land rights and eighteenth-century husbandry, the usual stuff of country houses – there was, too, all of Dickens and, even more to my thirteen-year-old taste, D. K. Broster, Mary Webb and Dornford Yates.

It was this sub-species of romantic fiction which now took over from schoolgirl stories which had, in their turn, taken over from comics (the weekly arrival of *Tiny Tots* and *Chicks Own* more intensely exciting but not so very different from that of the Sundays or the *TLS* now) and led me, with stops at Violet Needham, Georgette Heyer and Elizabeth Goudge, into the more respectable and lasting pleasures of *Jane Eyre*. But I have never completely lost my taste for romantic fiction and this was the one non-literary type I could respond to and therefore 'recognise' many years after I had set *Rupert of Hentzau* and *The Devil's Cub* aside for good.

Books, then, except at Auntie Freda's where they were held in high regard not only by her but also by her daughter, my letter-writing cousin Doreen, were not a part of family life and my reading, though not disapproved of but, like everything else, indulged, took place in the privacy of my room. Which soon had its own glass-fronted bookcase, pine not mahogany, but still a far cry from the rest of the furniture which had been hand-painted with bouquets of flowers on a watery turquoise background. There was also my reading chair: a small, winged armchair, almost certainly bought from Maples or Harrods. Covered then with blue and pink regency stripes, it is covered now in loosely woven Indian crewel and forbidden to the cat who took no interest in the firmly woven William Morris birds which covered it last.

It was in that incongruously girlish chair – my 'reading chair' still – that I first read *The Naked and the Dead*.

The book is said to have caused a stir in the world at large. It certainly caused a stir among my uncles and aunts for its author Norman Mailer was, it turned out, a kind of cousin . . . Which was going to get the upper hand, their pride in his success and excitement at their closeness to his sudden fame or their more natural Disgusted of Tunbridge Wells reaction to the book itself?

For me, in my mid or even late teens by now but still a literary and every other kind of virgin, it was a revelation: short, often one-word exchanges leaving the printed page – clogged to the margins in my rexine-bound classics – almost empty of text. And what a text. The rawness and the violence and – though perhaps I am imagining this – the *poetry* of it! I knew which side I was on and wished not only that I had met him when he had stayed with my cousin Vicky's parents in Gerrards Cross but that he was rather more of a cousin than he actually was.

The relationship was tenuous but it did exist. We shared an uncle! It went – and 'went' is the operative word, I don't think any of the English Menells ever saw him again – like this.

Norman's uncle, Louis Mailer, a South African Jew of Baltic origin who lived and made a fortune or perhaps several fortunes in South Africa, married my father's youngest sister, Moos. In photographs, nearly all of them taken in Johannesburg nightclubs, Moos, tall, thin, sharp-featured (I wonder if she ever regretted having to pencil in her eyebrows) and stunningly elegant, towers over her

husband, remarkable only for his tightly curled hair and his reputation as a gambler. A gambler in business and perhaps also at the
tables, but anyway someone who made and lost large amounts of
money.

I never knew Moos but would guess that, all appearances to the
contrary, she would have been bright and probably shrewd. Certainly
the marriage outlasted the glamour days and though my only legacy
from this aunt, who was also my godmother, is a string of seed
pearls and a name I never use, I am sorry I missed out on knowing
her and the uncle whose generosity to his less successful brother
in New York brought his nephew Norman briefly into our lives.
Though, not quite briefly enough . . .

André Deutsch, as anyone who ever worked for him knows, had
at all times to have a 'victim' – somebody in the office who could
do nothing right and was constantly in the firing line. For a small
and dapper man, not given to swearing and known as much for his
charm as for his legendary meanness, he could be very nasty indeed.
Perhaps I was lucky to get this episode over fairly early and not, like
some unlucky people, to have it happen twice. But once was enough:
the constant sniping, the irrational demands, the *power* play of the
employer untrammelled by fear of reprisal . . . It was not a pretty
sight and though others when back in the fold seemed to forgive
and forget," when it happened to me it scotched any liking I had had
for him once and for all. And the cause, in my case, though somewhat indirectly, was 'cousin Norman'.

At the time my relatives were struggling to read and to like *The
Naked and the Dead* neither they nor I would have thought to look
at the spine of the book and see who the publisher was, but had we
looked and had it been the English edition we would have seen the
name *André Deutsch*.

André's acquisition and championing of Mailer has become a
part of publishing history. What is less talked about is that Mailer

was to be the first of a long line of writers[n] who got their start with Deutsch and then moved on to older, grander, richer firms – sometimes with good cause, sometimes not.

It seems at least possible that at the time of the *American Dream* fiasco there was already danger in the air and it was this which made André combust when, given the seemingly desirable task of reading the new novel for offset[n] (he and his partner Diana Athill had already read it all or in part in a series of extracts in *Esquire*) I failed to notice that it was full of obscenities which had not appeared in the magazine version, which I hadn't read . . .

More than thirty years on, I can still remember André's fury when complaints about the book's obscenity began to come in from our agents in Australia and he realised what had happened. Whether or not the Australians had previously read the bowdlerised version, I can no longer remember. What I do remember, vividly, is the day-long session with their London-based representative considering (over sandwiches at lunchtime) the merits of every bugger, fuck, shit and arsehole as it surfaced in the text and cancelling every one of them. I imagine this exercise was to make Mailer feel we were doing our best to keep his text intact. It would have been quicker, though less memorable, if I had been left to excise the offending words on my own.

And it didn't help. Before long Mailer left anyway and it wasn't out of loyalty to all those excised motherfuckers. It was, or so we were told and it is probably true, because we couldn't come up with the kind of money he was now able to command.

All this was far in the future at the time when my mother and I used to go to the Swiss Cottage Odeon most Saturdays and to Auntie Freda's on Sundays where we invariably had roast beef and Yorkshire pudding, cooked by Mabel, my aunt's live-in maid, who seemed as much of a fixture as my poor cousin until, to everyone's surprise, she suddenly decided to leave and was never replaced.

It could have been during one of these long afternoons when I wished I had anywhere else to go and imagined my schoolfriends in Chipstead and Horsham and Angmering riding their ponies and playing tennis and meeting up for parties in the houses of their parents' friends that I first really noticed a small, grim painting of a line of miners on a hill. I think I was told that it had been given to my uncle by one of his patients and that the patient was the person who had painted it. Whether this memory is true or false, the first thing I would buy if I won the lottery today, would be any one of Josef Herman's paintings of that Welsh mining village.

There is one other type of artwork I connect with my aunt's household though not with my aunt for she had died by this time: the coloured chalk drawings on rough grey paper that her son, my cousin, brought back each day from the out-patients wing of the Halliwick Hospital: some days a vase of stiff, brightly coloured flowers, other days a boat in full sail on a flat sea. Thinking back, it was probably the drugs which produced these becalmed, unchanging images and it was mercifully seldom, for his sake and for ours, that he was in direct touch with whatever demons the drugs controlled.

These rare moments, witnessed most often by my parents, who had now become his keepers, were almost unbearable to see. This large, clumsy young man who needed to be looked after like a child and who loved and responded to kindness – liking nothing better than to be asked to do some small errand, fetch a newspaper, draw the curtains, put the kettle on – would suddenly, as it were, wake up and go into self-destruct, banging his head against the wall or, on one occasion when I happened to be there, stabbing at himself with a blunt kitchen knife. Horrifying as this was, more painful was to realise from the words that came gushing out that, Caliban-like, he knew what he was and what he should have been.

The answer was more drugs, administered now that his doctor

father was dead by the understanding psychiatrist who had arranged for him to attend those art therapy classes to give my mother some respite from his presence. Not surprisingly, he enjoyed these daily outings to the hospital – now a tract of luxury flats, the gates that used to keep the 'inmates' in now keeps them and other riff-raff out . . . Apparently, he regularly went to both tea sittings and never doubted the sincerity of the admiration with which my parents greeted that day's artwork when he got it home.

'Home' was now a spacious flat in Swiss Cottage, purchased by the trust fund set up in South Africa to take care of my cousin now that both his parents were dead. And, to kill two birds with one stone, it was decreed that my parents live there too. It must have seemed a neat solution not only to my uncle who was never, as far as I know, to see his nephew Victor again but also to Victor's sister, my cousin Doreen.

She, married now to an orthodox Jew, had, in matters of religious observance, left the rest of us behind. I remember, for instance, how startled we all were on going to a seder night with them early in their marriage and having the flowers we had brought quite roughly set aside: it was forbidden by Jewish law to put them in water on this holy day; and, more shocked than startled, by the relish with which her husband, propped up with cushions in his chair at the head of the table – another arcane practice whose significance I have forgotten – read and translated some blood-thirsty passage from the prayer book.

In a world torn apart by 'religion', it should be no surprise to find that the most ardent believers and attenders can also be the least inhibited by the most common or garden moral sense. Certainly, it was true of my cousin that religious observance and neglect of the most basic family duties went hand in hand. Not for nothing had she played Goneril[n] in yet another Tynan/OUDS production. But I reflect too that in a life which has been sustained and made worth living by friendships, the friendships which have gone wrong beyond redemption have all three been with practising Christians. The most recent and, because the shortest-lived, least painful, was with the novelist Madeleine St John whom I would go to see in her fifth-floor eyrie overlooking, or rather confronting, the spire of the church to which she made frequent visits.

Clever and delightfully eccentric, she was one of the most amusing people I have known. She was also one of the most malicious. I wish I could remember what she said when over a cup of tea at the Chelsea Flower Show, after a particularly savage remark I told her this, with something like admiration . . .

At that time her star had not yet risen. It was only a year or so later when the first of her god-laced-with-adulterous-upper-class-sex novels was short-listed for the Booker that among the flurry of excited phone calls from friends who still worked at Deutsch and thought of her as 'my author', her voice was absent."

If my cousin Doreen were to write fiction, like Madeleine, she would almost certainly display a fine understanding of moral issues. In real life, perhaps bolstered by her new religion, she behaved as though conscience were dead. It was not, of course, her doing that on the death of her mother my parents were roped in" to live with her widowed father: it must have seemed to make sense all round. A large, featureless, red-brick house was bought, in Hampstead Garden Suburb, and my parents who had been living in a series of furnished rooms were able to get their own things out of store and, setting them alongside my uncle's, make a kind of home.

There were practical difficulties. The suburb was not meant for the carless, nor was a garden meant for three adults who, even at their most prosperous, had chosen to live in flats. But, somehow the grass got cut, the shrubs survived and this ménage in which responsibility for my cousin Victor was shared continued until my uncle's sudden death.

Now the sharing stopped. Victor's sister and her husband had paid few enough visits to the house before. Now they paid fewer still. When the next move took place and the packers were due, I had a phone call asking me to 'put aside the silver'; otherwise, the transfer and disposal of my dead uncle's belongings was left to me. I did put aside the silver. As for the rest, the sad leftovers of his life – the letters, clothes, toilet things – I found ways to get rid of them. A few things, not made of silver, I kept for myself.

And so my parents moved into their final home and it was from here – the mansion flat in Swiss Cottage – that every weekday afternoon, my cousin Victor would make his way to Friern Barnet and that every Thursday evening, at precisely six o'clock, he would set out for Golders Green to have supper with his sister. By half past nine he was back and there was no change in this routine even when my mother was turned out of hospital and came home to die. In those last days and hours of her life he was a constant presence and I will never forget his poor, lumbering shape pacing up and down the hallway outside the room where my mother lay dying and then dead.

Now what? It was like a game of skittles with only my father left standing and it was only after his death, a few years later, that the family finally had to admit defeat. No one else in the large tribe of Menells[n] was prepared to spend a whole day with Victor, never mind a life. Too late now for a Steiner colony which should have been thought of many years before. A housekeeper or series of housekeepers, paid for by the trust, salved the family conscience, showing them to be one step ahead of the Queen Mother whose two mentally defective cousins were commonly known to be looked after by strangers at the public expense.

Less of a charge on the family coffer were my cousin Vicky's parents, though they too had fallen on hard times. Whatever my Estonian-born uncle's profession had been – perhaps a salesman of some kind – in his late fifties he found himself unemployed and the house in Gerrards Cross where my aunt Bertha had entertained

Kenneth Tynan and where the family had gathered to celebrate the success of *The Naked and the Dead* was a thing of the past. My uncle Harry had found work in the post office. Whether this was just over one Christmas (not that that wouldn't have been bad enough) or long-term, I don't remember and perhaps never knew. But I do remember the murmurings among the rest of the family who were aghast and their relief when he and my aunt were rescued by their daughter, now married to a wealthy Italian (his family made the blue paper that spaghetti was then wrapped in) and re-settled in Florence.

Vicky had already been there for several years and was immersed in some kind of Zionist activity which I was aware of when I visited but never really understood, not least because I spent my days in a kind of late-adolescent art-gazing frenzy and, because her husband could speak no English, could make nothing of the animated talk that accompanied our late-night suppers taken, so romantically, it seemed to me, in a small local restaurant and starting always with a steaming plate of pasta which, at home, would have been the entire meal.

Neither Vicky nor her husband Virginio – he a small, fair, slightly tubby businessman: she a Magnani look-alike with her abundant dark brown hair, strong-limbed, powerfully sexy – seemed to have a strongly spiritual take on life and certainly there was none of that orthodox flummery that my cousin Doreen now went in for, but whatever the 'cause' they were engaged in, it generated a passionate and shared excitement and, as my aunt and uncle were to find out, it did not cut out those mainstays of common morality – family piety and human kindness.

In their indigent old age, my aunt Bertha and her Estonian-born husband found a home in Florence with their Zionist daughter whose previous immersion in the world of the Hindu dancer," Ram Gopal, must surely have mystified if not alarmed them.

The Gopal interlude must have immediately followed Oxford. All of a sudden, or so it seemed to me – and I would love now to know the intervening steps but this cousin, like my half-sister, has disappeared without trace[n] – she was part of another theatrical entourage. Not, of course, as a dancer; more, I would guess, as an assistant stage manager cum assistant everything else, but certainly as a follower and in the thick of things.

I had never been backstage before but now I had only to get myself to that little street which runs down to the river beside Charing Cross station and there, in a pocket-sized theatre which may or may not still exist, I entered another world.

It seemed incredibly exciting to be among all these colourful people and though Gopal himself never took the slightest notice of me I can still remember the power he exerted – more, I would think, through the company's worship of his skill as a dancer than through his sexual presence, though I can't be sure of this. For me as a teenager reared on Heathcliff and Beau Geste there was nothing alluring about the sleek and slightly plump brown body and it was a very long time before I was to find the head-wagging and eye-rolling of classical Indian dance anything other than mildly comic.

But even I was in some way affected by his presence though not until years later, when I met R. D. Laing among *his* followers, did I again get a glimpse of what belonging to a cult must be like.

'Ronnie' Laing had become a friend of one of my oldest friends who had been one of his patients in the late fifties when we were students at Oxford. A suicide attempt, foiled by me even as I wondered whether I should be interfering, was followed by a short spell in the Warneford and then a lengthy stay in the Principal's house where, presumably, Miss Major (as she was always known) made it her business to keep an eye on this unusually bright but wayward student. I realised just the other day, reading an obituary of Miss Major who lived into her nineties, that I had never asked my friend what it had been like 'rooming' with the Principal. A less likely pair would be hard to imagine. Kathleen Major, as I find from the obituary – how incurious we are about the adults in our lives when we are young – was a scholar of some note whose field was 'diplomatic' or the study of old texts – in her case the archives of Lincoln Cathedral. Presumably even then, as she house-mothered this precocious twenty year old, her main interest, the love of her life, were the bosses and choirstalls of the cathedral in every one of whose publications that I have to hand – my partner, R, can produce books from our shelves on almost any subject – she is gratefully acknowledged.

My wayward friend, though a scholar – that is to say, entitled to wear a gown with more folds than the rest of us – was not a diplomat in any sense of the word, though it is true that she did help to negotiate me out of the psychiatric hospital to which I had fled on finding, when I was three months pregnant, that my husband was in love with my best friend.

One of my best friends. The other, the happily married mother of two small children, had been there to pick up the pieces when I arrived back from Turkey alone and half out of my mind.

Istanbul had been the scene of the débacle. Best Friend Number One, or rather Two, for she had insinuated herself when Best Friend Number One (we were all in the sixth form at a school in Harley Street) had been away sick, was Turkish. Olive-skinned, exotic, infinitely more sophisticated than the rest of us, she was irresistible and I, a bookish, pasty-faced English teenager, allowed myself to be seduced.

For the next few months, until Sevin, whose name is the imperative of the verb 'to love', went on to art school and I to Oxford, her room in Cricklewood became the centre of my world. I would sit there for hours at a time listening to her stories of past romances, all conducted behind the backs of her parents for her stepfather, Shevket Bey, a kindly giant of a man, was a traditionalist who did not believe in young women having the same freedom as young men and would never have allowed White Russian Boris or Rich Playboy Vedut, or any of the others, the kind of access (limited though it was, for Sevin, like most of us who had not been liberated by a convent education, still drew the line) that any English teenager could take for granted.

Now, sixteen years later, this passionate friendship – her letters to me would have been taken for love letters and my GP, advising an abortion, took it for granted that we were lesbians, which we were not – ended in mayhem.

It was early summer and the two of us were sitting on one of the window seats in the old wooden house overhanging the Bosphorus where Sevin, estranged from her husband though she refused to say why, was living alone. I was visiting her there on this last holiday before my baby was due when my husband arrived unannounced from London, and told me that six months previously, when she had come to London to be with me in the last days of my mother's life, he and she had 'fallen in love'. He was telling me this, he told me, because it was 'destroying' her. And it was nobody's fault, he said. And, anyway, he loved us both and we all loved each other, so what was all the fuss about? And when there was a 'fuss' – she in a frenzy of guilt and renunciation, me shell-shocked and vomiting – he retreated to another room complaining that trying to reason with us was like wading through a bog . . .

Some years later when the man I live with now described my ex-husband as an 'emotional caveman' I sprang to his defence, but thinking back, he wasn't far off the mark.

Well, unbelievable as it now seems, we did try to make it work. And for three days and nights – the nights were difficult: who was going to sleep where? – we kept it up. Then I came to my senses and got on the next plane home.

And that, or soon after, was when I first met R. D. Laing.

But Kingsley Hall wasn't my first stop. My first stop had been with Wendy, Best Friend Number One and her husband Moritz who made up a bed in their attic, put flowers in a vase on the table, and kept the meter fed. I remember that each time the gas ran out, Moritz would come up, cheerfully unlock the box and drop all the coins back again. As for Wendy, she fed me the slops which were all I could keep down alongside her puzzled three year old and his blissfully untroubled baby sister.

I could have stayed on in the little room overlooking Golders Hill Park but finding it more and more difficult to function – even walking was now hard – decided that I needed to be in the one place where I wouldn't be in anyone's way and so, against my friend and her husband's wishes, I had myself admitted to the psychiatric wing of the hospital where, had things been different, I would soon have been taking time off work to go to ante-natal classes.

Nothing could have served me better. One day in the dingy pre-fabricated building off St Pancras Way among people who were truly ill was enough to tell me that I wasn't and that I needed to get out.

Now it was my ex-Warneford friend, the only person to guess what had happened (she told me later that she had come to the house one day to find Sevin and my husband just surfacing from a 'trip' – LSD was still a pastime among slightly off-beat intellectuals – and had understood the apparent gibberish that she was uttering for the confession that it was) who now came to the rescue.

She had spoken to Laing about me so I was able to tell the mild, tired-looking person behind an untidy desk and wearing an old school tie, that I had someone to turn to. In those days you needed two psychiatric reports to get a legal abortion. But I felt it was my having been to Oxford rather than the Laing connection which made him think it safe to let me go.

By this time my husband was back. He had turned up in Golders Green with a big bag of pistachio nuts and told me that he would be glad when I came home.

But I couldn't go home. Like the duck in the little red storybook which had belonged to my friend's baby daughter and with which I had become obsessed, I couldn't go back and didn't until my son was born six months later. Even now, when I get to the last of the thick, shiny pages of *The Duck Who Ran Away** and read

> *I've seen the sun*
> *And I've seen the sea*
> *And I know that*
> *HOME IS THE PLACE TO BE*

I have to gulp back the tears.

On a Richter scale of breakdowns, I wouldn't have scored very high: I was responding to real cracks in my world, not to a riot of inner demons – a sane response, as I was told by Dr H, a friend and colleague of Laing's, when I started going to see him a few weeks later. The only thing that made me unusual was being pregnant. It was also what stopped me – one of the things that stopped me – from moving into Kingsley Hall. The other was Laing himself.

I had, of course, heard a lot about him and had read, in a half-listening kind of way, *The Divided Self*. This, like Norman O. Brown's *Love and Death*, was a book that everyone was reading or claiming to have read. More to my taste, though embarrassing now, was the in-fiction of the time, the torrid, florid *Alexandria Quartet*. But my taste for high drama in fiction didn't extend to inviting it into my life and when I finally came face to face with Laing, I almost physically recoiled.

---

* Ruth Ainsworth and Ronald Ridout, *The Duck Who Ran Away* (1964)

His dark, glittering eyes and wiry, charged body; the gloomy hall with its long refectory table, like a Shakespearean stage set; the entourage of holy fools . . . It was all too much for me. In my already heightened state what I needed was safe and quiet emptiness, not this demonic presence with its attendant artists and madmen.

Of course, they weren't all artists and they weren't all madmen. And Laing, with whom I was to have a family meal years later, was not the gothick monster he appeared to me then. But my instincts were right. This was no time for plunging into new relationships with yet more 'exotic' people. Least of all did it seem a good idea when I found that one of these was obsessed with birth and baby-hood, spent much of her time painting lurid scenes of parturition and, though I didn't actually witness this, would run around naked, free here to regress to earliest infancy, a regime which, I believe, ended in her successful re-integration. But to be growing bigger each day with a real baby while this childless woman was forging her way through the same but imagined territory was unthinkable. Kingsley Hall, it turned out, was no more the answer than St Pancras Way had been.

Of course, none of this should be in a chapter which was meant to be about the Menells, not least because the only Menell now left in my life[n] had no idea what was going on and wouldn't have known what to do if he had.

As I moved from place to place, as one friend after another came up with empty houses, flats, rooms, I would ring my father almost every evening, to pre-empt his ringing me, and it never entered his head, not even when I was using a pay phone, that these calls were made from anywhere but home . . .

The days in this time out of time in which all outside life, even the wireless, seemed an intolerable intrusion, were spent sleeping, knitting – small white vests from a very simple pattern – and lis-tening, when there was a gramophone, to one of my two records:

some Brahms songs, long overdue from the library in Kentish Town Road, and the Schubert Quintet which I had bought on a whim after someone at Deutsch told me it was her favourite piece of music. It became mine and, as I know now from *Desert Island Discs*, a lot of other people's too.

And then, in early February, some six months later, my son was born. And, with a gambler's luck, his father managed to be there. He could have been at any one of the clubs, from all of which he was eventually banned as systems players always were – the Golden Nugget, the Horseshoe, the Apron Strings – but, for once, he was at home; blackjack and the pre-Socratic philosophers, his day and night-time activities, were put on hold and he got to the hospital in time.

Five days later, all three of us went home.

And five years later, just as his grandson was beginning to show signs of being the sports-mad male child of his grandfather's dreams, my father died. Peaceful, unquestioning as ever, he slid away in the wake of a mild stroke and so the eldest of my grandfather's four sons joined him and my grandmother, Esther, and my mother, Zosia, in the Jewish cemetery off Willesden Lane. Which I barely ever visit. The cemetery where my mother should have been buried and which I visit whenever I can is in Nõmme on the outskirts of Tallinn. This is where she and my father, too, because he loved her, really belong.

✑ 2 ✑

The Sound of Russian

*In 1827 the Russian Czar Nicolas I passed a verdict according to which
Jews were recruited to serve in the Czar's Army. At that time the
military service lasted for 25 years. The Jewish recruits were named
'cantonists'. Already on the next year after the passing of the Czar's
verdict, about 500 boys in the age from 10 to 14 were forcibly torn out of
their families and brought to Reval [Tallinn] to the military disposition.
One of these boys was our great-grandfather Hirsch ben Jeddige Gutkin.*

S O BEGIN MY cousin Ephraim Zaidelson's notes for a history of
our family. Fima, as he is known in the family, continues:

*I don't know from where exactly he was brought to Tallinn where a
special Battalion of cantonist soldiers were stationed. I believe that
most of the Jewish recruits were brought from Latvia, Lithuania and
some from Poland – the regions designated for the Jewish habitation.
In Estonia at that time, Jews (as private persons) were not allowed to
reside . . .*

Here history was to repeat itself. In 1942, by which time all my
mother's family were either in Siberia or dead, Estonia was once
again *Judenfrei."*

That we were neither dead (like my grandmother) or in Siberia
(like Fima) was thanks to my father who, when war broke out,

considered it was his duty to go back to England for, like his father, George-for-St-George Grozinsky/Menell, he, while politically naive (as most of the world seems to have been) had a strong patriotic streak.

It must have seemed like madness to leave a country at peace for a country at war and Grossmama, as we called her, tried to stop us. 'At least leave the children,' was her line, I am told. But my mother wouldn't be separated from my father or from us, and my father, for once, stood firm. And so it was that haunted by pictures of children in gas masks (Grossmama had not been above a bit of blackmail) we found ourselves on a boat bound for Stockholm where we got stuck for several weeks and I had a mournful, party-less fifth birthday in a Swedish hotel. Then another boat, this time to Harwich, arriving in England just before Christmas, a Christmas that stands out for me because I noticed that Father Christmas was wearing my uncle's slippers (we had been taken in by my kindly bohemian aunt) and I was never able to believe in him again.

In fact, I have never believed in anything, and I read with some wonder of my forebear, Hirsch ben Jeddige, who resisted the temp-tation to turn Christian and – I quote Fima again – 'stayed true to his Jewish faith'. The temptation must have been strong. The boy recruits were promised special privileges if they took on the Russian Orthodox faith and harsh treatment if they did not. Of the 500 boys, 316 agreed to be baptised. My great-grandfather was not one of them and we lose sight of him for twenty-five years.

We will never know what those years as a soldier were like, though Isaac Babel may provide a clue, but we do know that by the time he left the army he had gained the right to live in Tallinn: this privilege had been granted by the Czar to all his 'Nicolas' soldiers as they were now called, and those few unbaptised boy recruits became the founding fathers of the small Jewish community – 4,000 in all – into which my mother was born.

Here things get difficult. It's one thing to write about people you don't much like or did like and like still but only in memory – schoolfriends with whom you lost touch long ago, semi-imaginary boyfriends: the bellhop in the Riviera hotel (our first holiday abroad), the Algerian kitchen boy in the Lyons Tea Shop . . . But someone you love or loved?

Andrea Ashworth managed to do it. *Once in a House on Fire*, that spell-binding story of a haplessly dysfunctional family, radiates love and when this writer describes her hopelessly feckless mother as beautiful or loving, I believe her absolutely. But how am I to convey how beautiful my mother seemed to me? Or how much I loved her?

For a very long time, I thought that everyone loved their mothers just as everyone remembers their own mother as beautiful. I thought All Mothers were Good, rather in the same way that I used to believe that the Law was Just and you could Trust a Policeman.

Then the evidence began to pile up: my friend Sally's mother wore black to her daughter's wedding and cut her out of her will. Sally wrote about it, searingly, in *Lifting the Taboo*.* My friend Carol's life was poisoned by her mother's constant disapproval. Only very near the end and after a tipple (gin was the magic potion, if only she had discovered it before) did she let up, but by then it was too late. Carol was to die soon after but not before capturing and taming the pain of that relationship in an enchanting novel.† Gwendolyn Mary had not, of course, recognised herself[n] in the baleful, life-destroying mother – now a minor character[n] – in *Half the Gladness* which had started life as one long and unpublishable howl of pain.

This was not the first time Carol had rewritten life to make it more bearable. A paranoid schizophrenic who wrote at the kitchen table, loved the constant interruptions of village life and, in a small,

* Sally Cline, *Lifting the Taboo: Women, Death and Dying* (1995)
† Carol Bruggen, *Half the Gladness* (1985)

lined notebook, kept a meticulous record of each day's medication, she had, in an earlier novel – with exquisite irony – transformed her erring real-life husband into a figment of her fictional heroine's imagination . . . He, the only husband I was to meet who read and encouraged his wife's writing – to most husbands this seems to be, at best, a threat; at worst, a joke – took this in good part. And carried on as before.

Buried now in a windswept graveyard, only yards from her kitchen door, and tended, almost daily, by her film-maker son and his family who decorate her grave as though it were a birthday cake, the creator of the lonely spinster with the imaginary husband" is now free of mothers, mistresses, and the cancer that killed her.

Cancer killed my mother too. She already had it when, in January 1964, we at last got visas allowing us into Estonia and she was dying from it when we managed to get back there two years later.

The second time my husband came with me; the first time, for whatever reason – maybe he couldn't get away from the computer firm where he was now designing systems" on washing-machine-sized machines or we couldn't get the money together for three fares – I went on my own. With my brother's help, I had bought the direct-est flights for my mother and followed her the cheapest way – a plane to Helsinki (never cheap) and then a very slow train, from which I remember seeing nothing but fields of grey boulders, to Leningrad.

Here I was put in a taxi by some official who had obviously been told to expect me though I hadn't been told to expect him, and driven to the only hotel in which foreigners were allowed to stay.

In the taxi I remember having a surreal conversation with the driver who must have been chosen for knowing some English in which I failed to persuade him that England was no longer ruled by Macbeth-like tyrants: I also failed to convince my cousin Eva that things had changed since the days of Oliver Twist and Little

Nell – that we had free schools and free medicine and that little boys were no longer sent up chimneys.

It was my mother who explained to me that Eva's mother, Nastya, a great beauty – she was descended from Pushkin and still showed traces of his Negro blood – had deliberately kept these truths from her daughter to make it easier for her to live in the world as it was. And so it was that Eva was the most thoroughly indoctrinated of all my cousins and it was many years before she could allow herself to believe that we had trade unions and state pensions, and passports which allowed us to leave the country and return whenever we liked . . .

In the years between, she and Fima (a convinced Communist since his pre-war schooldays in England) countered our 'propaganda' with propaganda of their own and we have a small library of books published by Progress Publishers, Moscow, all inscribed with love and fraternal greetings from our 'Soviet cousins'.

I'm afraid I never had the time or inclination to read *Cement*, *Time Forward!*, *Equal Among Equals* or even, when it was sent to my young son, that bracing political fable *The Screwdriver and the Lathe* . . . But my partner, R, has read every one. Those books and a scene we would prefer to forget in which my Soviet cousins laid into Solzhenitsyn, found their way into *Deliberate Regression*, one of the best and least successful of his books: so unsuccessful that Knopf, who had published it, never published him again.*

At Deutsch we dropped authors too and, in one case at least, with more drastic consequences: Knopf may have lost something by not publishing *Pharaoh's Dream* or any of the slow but steady flow of books which followed that one, but they didn't lose money. When we turned down Edmund White's *A Boy's Own Story*, however, we made

---

* Robert Harbison, *Deliberate Regression: the disastrous history of Romantic individualism in thought and art from Jean-Jacques Rousseau to twentieth-century fascism* (1980)

a disastrous mistake. The book took off like a rocket and this author, who had previously sold so miserably that I had to nerve myself to announce that his new manuscript had arrived, became and was to remain a very valuable property indeed.

I heard recently, I don't know how reliably, that it still rankles with Ed, whom I had met in New York when delivering the *Gay News* 'Oscar' he had won for the dazzling *States of Desire*, that he was dropped at that point. If he knew the resistance there had been to his first two books or had heard the groans that greeted the advent of the third, he might be more forgiving, though it wouldn't improve things to know that when I eventually got the *Boy's Own* manuscript home – it had fallen off the back of my bicycle in Camden High Street – and sat down to read it, it fell far short of expectations. It was certainly good enough to publish but compared with the earlier books this was dull stuff: I had been White's most vociferous and only champion (indulged by André because the earlier books had been cheap to buy in) but I couldn't fight his corner on this one and we let it go.

Anyone who has worked in publishing will have stories like this though not, perhaps, quite like the next one in which a manuscript so lack-lustre, it seemed to me, that I advised the author not to submit it while I was trying to get an earlier book through, turned up on the Secker & Warburg list.

Not without warning. Barley Alison, that *grande dame* of the publishing world, had rung André in a state of high excitement wanting to know what he knew about this 'young genius' and before long the novel which I had feared would spoil the author's chances had not only thrilled them all at Secker but had also won the Betty Trask . . .

The young genius whose name was Gary (or G. E.) Armitage, had behaved entirely properly. I had not been able to promise we would make an offer for the book we were considering and without this commitment he remained free to submit anything else to whoever he pleased.

So it was that this pleasant young man from Hornsea with his ponytail and flat Yorkshire vowels who had begun to think he would never get published found himself with two publishers, two names and two literary prizes. For, before the end of the year, Robert Edric as he now chose to call himself, had caught up with G. E. Armitage, by winning the less valuable but more prestigious James Tait Black prize with the novel we had published."

When a writer as sharp as Edmund White goes soft at the edges" it should serve as a warning: I don't remember any more whether an adored young mother (beautiful, of course) was a feature of his boyhood memoir but the answer is probably Yes, for nothing is more likely to have produced that sentimental haze which proved so much more popular than the baroque brilliance of his other books.

Maybe then the safest way to approach mothers on paper – Good Mothers – is with things they weren't especially good at. On paper, Bad Mothers, like the fallen angels, have a head start . . .

Well, my mother, unbeatable at unconditional love, which is what the word 'mother' has always meant to me, didn't read a lot, had no interest in the countryside, and wasn't much of a cook.

Of course, she had never had to cook until the war began and, for those first few months in England, was still getting tips from her own mother in Estonia who wouldn't have had to cook either but must have taken a bit more interest in what went on in the kitchen. Among these recipes which my mother translated for me when I left home to get married were Brown Cabbage (sauerkraut cooked with caraway seeds, paprika and tomato purée), Piroshki (little pastry envelopes filled with white cabbage and hard-boiled egg) and Kissell (the juice of redcurrants thickened with cornflour). Kissell I still make every year when, for a few weeks – fewer and fewer weeks, it seems – there are currants on the market stalls. Though not an act of contrition – we love it when I get it right, not too thick and not too runny – it has more to do with recovering a memory than

putting a dessert on the table. And I suppose Lesley Chamberlain,"
who had given me a copy of her Russian cook book, was right when
she said that in talking about Russian food I was really talking about
nursery food . . .

Already in English, or a kind of English, so it must have been dictated to her by one of her sisters-in-law, is this, in my mother's handwriting: 'BOILER. Wash all in cold water. Put in sausepan & cover
with water. Boil up, take of scum. Add one onion & one carrot cut
up halfe also parsleyrooth if available. Simmer all about 3–3 ½ hours.'

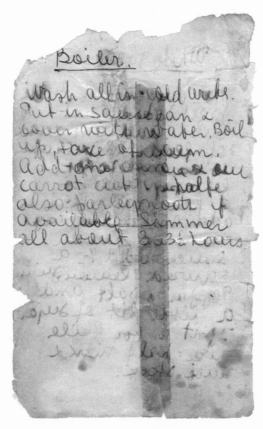

My mother's recipe

Nothing too exotic about this though chickens, of course, were not easy to come by and it does bring back vivid memories, though not taste memories, of trips to the East End with my doctor uncle, the only member of our family who could drive a car, hunting for kosher chickens. If we were lucky, we would find one and watch its neck being wrung and its feathers plucked by the brawny woman in a rubber apron who sat out on the pavement in Petticoat Lane. I suppose that the kosher chicken was also a black-market chicken even though it was sold so openly, but even if it was, we were not part of the black economy in a very big way and the only extra rations I had were my parents'.

Looking back, I doubt that my mother or father tasted butter or ate a single egg once these were rationed for, though by no means kosher – any chicken would have done and we had always eaten bacon – they did live strictly by those unwritten laws of Jewish family life which give children the best of everything. I still find it hard to believe that in my partner's regular, churchgoing family this was not the case. At mealtimes in Carlisle, Pa it was Father who came first, who had the biggest helpings and the choicest bits and, thirty years later, in our irregular little household, there were some uneasy moments as I piled my son's plate higher than his stepfather liked to see.

But habits die hard and one habit my mother couldn't break (apart from the smoking which helped to kill her) was the coffee habit. We would travel miles for a tin of Nescafé, more often to be found in Leeds or Bradford or even Otley than in Ilkley where we lived, and I remember that she always kept a few sugar lumps in a little drawstring purse for those times when we might get a cup of something-like-coffee in Ilkley's own Bluebird Tea Room or the corrugated shed which was the British Restaurant.

Our informant was my father's lady chauffeur who came to fetch him every day to take him to the factory (hidden inside a hill as I have always believed but perhaps I extrapolated" this fantasy from being told it was very, *very* secret) in Yeadon where they were building the Lancaster bombers. My father was not a VIP but he couldn't drive – one eye was slightly askew – and the only way to get there was by road.

There were informants in Tallinn too. By the time we got there in the early sixties rationing in England was a thing of the past and though it would still be a few years until you could buy almost anything at almost any time of the year we had forgotten what it was like to be seriously short of anything. But in Tallinn that winter the shops were empty. There was nothing in the market but a few root vegetables and lots of pussy willow. And there was no rationing. If you were lucky, you knew somebody who knew something. We were lucky. My aunt Nastya, Eva's mother, worked for the Fish Board. She knew when – as rarely happened for everything was bottled or canned and distributed across the whole union – there would be fresh fish in the local shops. And sometimes she would even get her hands on a fish and it would reach us in a damp newspaper parcel, slipped under the door in much the same way that you used to see marijuana changing hands in Ladbroke Grove.

Some other family, with a son or husband working at the docks or the railway depot, would presumably have known about the consignment of oranges which my aunt Leida noticed on a passing truck to which we gave chase, arriving in time to be among the first in the unruly queue when it stopped to unload. For that was how it worked. First come, first served. And it didn't take us long to realise what weeks of preparation must have gone into assembling the food for the meals that were put in front of us.

Only two things were easy to get: Havana cigars – every kiosk was piled high with these – and, from the back of cafés so bare and unkempt that they looked out of business, the richest and creamiest of 'party' cakes. The cigars, of course, signalled a moment of particular closeness with Cuba and by the time I came back two years later, they had disappeared. But the cakes, in their round cardboard boxes, are harder to account for. Were they allowed as a memory of the Viennese-type café life for which Tallinn was once known? Whatever prompted their survival during Soviet times, they continue to this day, but now they are displayed behind glass you can see through and can be bought 'off the peg'.

Not that they would be bought off the peg for a special occasion and I take it for granted that even though we didn't then know just how special the occasion was, the confection on the table, a few days into the new millennium, was made to order. What we didn't know then was that the French citizenship for which my young cousins had applied – almost eighty years earlier, Fima's wife, Lena, had happened to be born in Paris – was about to come through and, by the beginning of the new school year, Sasha and his family would be living in France.

That spectacular concoction with its slices of kiwi bobbing about on waves of sugary cream was destined to be the last of the line. Urged to join them by their children, Fima and Lena will soon leave Tallinn too and only Eva, her adopted daughter, Julia, and Bobik will remain.

Bobik had been my dog – my Hamley's dog, my dog on wheels – before the war. There are pictures of me as a two year old in the garden at our holiday house in Middleton-on-Sea where we spent those pre-war English summers, sitting on him, waiting to be pushed; then, a few months later, on the deck of the ship that took us back to Tallinn. But when we left next, he didn't come with us. I probably had to choose between him and the life-sized baby doll, dressed still in my first-birthday party dress and my first schoolfriend, Delphine's, flowery knickers, who lies sleeping in our loft. Doll-makers understood the need for a resting mode, for eyes that opened and shut, long before the computer technocrats came along with their pulsating lights."

Be that as it may, my mother must have given Bobik (not called Bobik then) to Nastya for her baby daughter Eva and, not being Jewish, they and he survived the war.

Only technically was Eva not Jewish and I think Nastya, who had been married to a cousin of my mother's, may have fled Tallinn too, but whether or not, Bobik spent his war in their little wooden house in Nömme, close to the Jewish cemetery, and it was there that I met him again.

Most like a wire-haired terrier in his prime but now, in his knitted wig, not much like any known breed, Bobik was made to last, and every time I see him (I keep his photo on my table in Kentish Town) I have a pang of regret and have to stifle the thought that he really belongs to me. Like Estonia itself, he could be fought over. Does he belong to me, his first owner, or to Eva who had him through most of her childhood, or to Julia who has grown up with him thinking of him as hers? And who does Estonia 'belong' to: the Estonian Estonians, the hundreds of thousands of Estonian-born Russians – children and grandchildren of the Russians brought in to swamp the local population – or the small but growing number of Estonian Jews?

Certainly not the last for whom most native Estonians have little liking. Like Poland and the Ukraine, Estonia has a long history of anti-Semitism and was one of the only places, perhaps the only place," where the Germans did not need to transport the Jews to a different location – out of the way of non-Jewish friends and neighbours – to kill them. In Tallinn they could be killed on the spot."

Which is what happened to my grandmother and to so many of our older aunts and cousins. On the family tree, drawn up and pasted together by Fima, their names appear on one long and terrible line. More frightened of the 'Bolsheviks' than the Germans, they had not gone to the station and boarded the trains provided by the Russians,

so recently their invaders, to get them out of the way of the oncom-
ing German army. They had chosen to stay. And who is to say they
would have survived the hardships of the journey and the years of
near-starvation, but it would have been a less brutal death and one
shared by many millions of non-Jewish Russians.

Sara
1869 – 1941

Helena (my grandmother)
1870 – 1941

Genoch
1879 – 1941

Esther
1883 – 1941

Rosa (Fima's mother)
1889 – 1941

Rahil
1894 – 1941

Garri (Eva's father)
b.? – 1941

Serri
b.? – 1941

For whatever reason – I wish that I knew it – the younger generation *did* decide to leave and certainly it is easier to imagine Nancy
and Paula, my mother's schoolfriends, packing a single suitcase and
herding their children onto these unmarked trains, than my stout
grandmother, already in her fifties, and set in her ways.

Nancy and Paula were among the crowd on the station, that same station, who were there with my mother, to meet me, when, after that one night in Leningrad, I finally reached Tallinn.

It must have been winter – it was winter, I remember the unexpected warmth from the floor-to-ceiling stove in the corner of my uncle's room in which we were to live for the next three weeks. It was one of the two rooms in the small, one-bedroom flat he had lived in before the war and, by remaining unmarried, he and my aunt Leida remained entitled to a room each and so had a whole flat to themselves. Unheard-of luxury. Sleeping on the floor among the legs of the Biedermeier furniture my uncle had salvaged from my grandmother's flat, I couldn't have guessed this, but by the time we had visited every one of the loving crowd of friends and relatives who had surged up the platform to greet me, I realised how lucky they were.

Of course, the difference between my Uncle Hermann and Aunt Leida and my mother's schoolfriends was that Hermann and Leida didn't have children or didn't appear to have children. It was some time before I fully understood how they came to have all this space for themselves when Fima, for instance, lived in two rooms of a communal flat with his wife and two young children, his own father (that erstwhile Anglophile who had sent him to school in England) and his wife's mother, now in and out of mental hospitals but an art student in Paris when her daughter, Lena, was born. Two rooms for the six of them. But was this a worse ratio than the one room in which Paula lived with her husband and two grown-up sons?

We had never experienced conditions like these before, though they must have existed in the slums of London and Glasgow, but we soon came to realise that until recently things had been so much worse that overcrowding and shortages of just about everything were of secondary importance: what we were actually experiencing was something they had not dared to dream of until now, a life comparatively free of fear.

However wretched life may have been in the Gorbals or Canning Town, no one lived in fear of death or deportation: the knock on the door could be the bailiffs but it couldn't be the secret police. And it was the secret police who some twenty years earlier had told my aunt Leida not to expect to see her fourteen-year-old daughter again. For Aili and her schoolfriends had been caught throwing paint at a newly erected monument[n] celebrating the liberation of Estonia by the Red Army and the sentence for this act of political defiance was fifteen years in a Soviet labour camp.

It was because her daughter (my uncle's stepdaughter) was still in Siberia that my uncle and aunt had the whole flat to themselves.

What had happened was something like this. Aili, in her thirties and still in Siberia when I visited Tallinn in the early 1960s, had married another political prisoner, Ülo, the son of a minister in the pre-war Estonian government. Though both of them had completed their sentences they were still not allowed to return to Estonia but my aunt was able to visit them from time to time. Now, all these years later, all three lived together[n] in a small provincial town, the prescribed distance from Tallinn. Here, in Keila, they built a comfortable little house with their own hands, very trim and Barry Bucknell – what could daunt a couple who had worked down a Siberian coal mine? – where they grow their own vegetables and make their own wine from the fruit of their own trees. And, when asked persistently enough, they will talk of those years in Siberia, when working down the mines was preferable to the surface duties for the cold was more dangerous than anything that could happen underground and where Ülo, who worked as an electrician, had taught himself English with the help of two English prisoners, English Communists, caught out by the tide of war.

It was only on my third and last visit to this remarkable couple, the realest of real Estonians, that I heard Ülo had been awarded the Estonian Order of the Cross of the Eagle for his fight against

11 *My grandfather on the site of what was to become the Vanamöisa mining complex*

12 *My father (centre) down the mine*

13 *My third birthday party, Tallinn, 1937*

14 *My grandmother with my brother*

15 *Ruti, who was raped and murdered*

16 *Soviet Estonia, early '60s: street parade, synagogue, radio factory, conservatoire, market*

17 *My uncle Hermann, back from the war*

18 *Hermann and Leida getting married*

19 *Gulag survivors Aili and Ülo Jõgi: Leida's daughter and son-in-law*

Soviet occupation: a ceremony that took place some years after Estonia had at last regained its independence in 1991.

My aunt Leida, now in her late nineties, does not have a medal from the Estonian government but at least once and probably more than once she had been singled out by the previous regime who posted pictures of that month's Best Workers on a glass-fronted notice-board that you had to pass every time you entered the old town. It was not that Leida, who worked in the local stocking factory, wanted to help the Soviets who had stolen her country and abducted her child but she was temperamentally unable to dawdle or sulk and whatever it was that she did in that factory, she did it with gusto, was liked by her workmates and adored, at first from afar, by my slow-moving, melancholic uncle, now back from the wars.

Like all Estonian males who had volunteered to fight with the Russians Hermann had been assigned to a labour unit, much as Koestler and other 'aliens' had been here. But, unlike Koestler, my uncle had spent the entire war felling trees, digging trenches, and – here the parallel fails completely – learning to live on grass, berries and wood bark when rations, meagre enough for soldiers at the front, dried up completely for those behind the lines. Just as in the Siberian labour camp it had been safer to work down the mines than on the frozen surface, so in these units death by gunfire came to seem an exhilarating alternative to death by starvation.

It was only because Hermann had been unusually fit when war began that he had survived. More of an athlete than a scholar – there are pictures of him tall and bronzed on the beach at Pirita – he must have set many hearts a-flutter among the younger sisters of my mother's friends; then, before he was out of his twenties, he and they were either dead or adrift in the vast Russian hinterland, fighting to stay alive.

Among those who were dead was Ruti, the daughter of my mother's close friends, Genya and Solly, at whose jewellery shop my father would have bought the narrow band of diamonds which was my mother's wedding ring: the one piece of her jewellery that has not been to those other jewellers' shops in Hatton Garden, hardly any of which is open on a Friday afternoon, to be valued or sold.

Ruti is special to me because I remember her or think I remember her as I look at the little girl (big girl in my memory) with her round face and frizzy hair standing in the middle of the back row at my third-birthday birthday party. She stands next to my brother who was four years older than those other little friends whose names and faces I have completely forgotten. Perhaps Ruti was as much as six years older – the same age difference as between me and those admired older cousins who preceded me to Oxford – which would make her ten years old when she was raped and murdered.

My copy of the book in which her death and the manner of her death is recorded is now in New Zealand with the nephew of a friend whose teaching of Jewish studies now includes 'holocaust studies'. For him, this crudely printed little catalogue of the dead is an interesting curiosity and something he may, from time to time, use with his students. For me, this work which it took someone more than forty years to compile is a thing of both wonder and horror: that the Germans should have applied the methods of accountancy in recording the atrocities they committed and that, years later, someone should devote themselves to the resurrection of these accounts . . .

But I am glad the book exists, acknowledging those forgotten lives and deaths, and unlike so many monuments to the holocaust so entirely free of any taint of commerce. But I don't need either it or them. For me, the small fall of rock, inscribed in Hebrew, that you could pass without noticing in the cemetery at Nömme is the only memorial that really counts; that and a handful of books.

We weren't lucky enough at Deutsch to publish Primo Levi but there were others like Bernard Gotfryd whom Levi had encouraged to write down his memories and whose Tales of the Holocaust* are as remarkable for the power of their storytelling as for the writer's capacity to understand and forgive. Forgive but not forget. The copy he signed for me in the lounge of a New York hotel is inscribed *Remember Shoa . . .*

And then there was *Maus.*

If André had still been in the driving seat we wouldn't have taken it on. He had a real aversion to books of 'Jewish interest', claimed that English Jews didn't read or at least didn't *buy* books, and considered me a bleeding heart whose ideal author would be a one-eyed Jewish poet.

But André was no longer in charge. He had sold the company to Tom Rosenthal: who has been heard to refer to himself, without a trace of irony, as a historian (he had read History at Cambridge), as a military man (he had done national service) or, when I was arguing against the way Robert Fisk opened *Pity the Nation,*† his book on the Lebanon, with what seemed to me an inappropriate emphasis on the holocaust – 'As a prominent Jew . . .' And it was in this last role, some years later, that he took Art Spiegelman's *Maus* home to read. For which he must be given credit. The loose pages of this as yet unpublished book-length cartoon – the pages had not even been in order when they reached me from the agent – did not look inviting and it had taken me longer than it should have done to get round to looking at them properly. But when I had, and with the backing of my non-Jewish partner and my 'don't-want-to-know-about-all-this-Jewish-stuff' teenage son, I got up the nerve to put this unpromising heap in front of Tom and say that he needed to read it. Which he did. Overnight. Speed was one of his great virtues. And he said that Yes, it was wonderful, very moving but, and here I quote, 'Of course, the man is no draughtsman.'

---

* *Anton the Dove Fancier and Other Tales of the Holocaust* (1991)
† *Pity the Nation: Lebanon at War* (1990)

Before too long (it seemed a good move to knock on Peter Mayer's Jewish funny-bone next) the book came out as a joint Deutsch and Penguin production and a Spiegelman original appeared in Tom's office among the Yeatses and Nolans.

But to get back to Tallinn and the stocking factory. I don't think I ever heard exactly how Hermann and Leida got together and it's a little hard to see what, except need, attracted her to him, mentally and physically ravaged by the war as he was; but whatever it was, Leida loved him: chivvied him along, looked after him, made him laugh. For the short time that he still had to live, it was her strength and buoyancy that kept him going and it isn't hard to understand how he, back in Tallinn to find his mother dead, her flat full of strangers, and nothing and no one as they had been before, had fallen for her.

As for what they did in that factory: she was on the production line turning out heroic numbers of lisle stockings with bumpy seams and he was a mechanic, there to get the machines working again when they broke down.

There were worse jobs. Much worse. And there must be people in this country today who would be glad of either one but the embarrassing truth is that my mother's family and their friends had been brought up with different expectations and when my uncle Hermann met Leida they didn't even speak the same language.

Estonian which, since independence, has at last become the first language of the country and which the Soviet settlers now have to become proficient in before they are entitled to certain basic civil rights was, before the war, the language (predominantly) of the lower classes – of the peasants, the factory workers, the servants – the 'real' Estonians, if you like.

Leida was one of these real Estonians and Estonian was her only language. My uncle, like my mother, spoke only Russian and German, the latter a hangover from the centuries-old presence of the 'Baltic barons' who, it is told, rallied as a man to Hitler's blood call and have not been seen in their old haunts since."

As it was, my uncle learned to speak Estonian as did all my relatives, long before it became compulsory, for no one wanted to be mistaken for Russian during those years of Soviet occupation. But during the three weeks of my mother's visit and always – indeed still – in the privacy of their own homes, they reverted to Russian and Leida and I, who could neither talk to each other nor understand the endless flow as my mother and her friends traced and re-traced the twenty years of exile – for me the sound of Russian is the sound of my mother and no music is as sweet or consoling – would serve up cups of lemonless tea to each newcomer or, as when we caught sight of that cargo of oranges, go out foraging, joining a queue here for a loaf of bread, there for a toothbrush or, more purposefully, tramp through the snow from one chemist's shop to another, searching for the hard-to-come-by drug which was keeping my uncle alive.

Hermann and Leida weren't the only factory workers in the family: Paris-born Lena, who is now getting ready for the move to Strasbourg, worked for more than thirty years at a bench in the radio factory" across from which, at an angle, you can see the fanciful Gothic hulk of the Conservatoire. Every day as she walked up the Narva Maantee with her friend, Renata, who worked in the factory too," they would pass the Conservatoire which, in a former life, had been built by Lena's grandfather as a family home and which has finally found its way back to her – though she and Fima have left it in the hands of the state for the rest of their lives – in the general restitution of requisitioned land and properties which followed independence.

It is not the Conservatoire but the chunk of central Tallinn inherited by Fima from his mother which has enabled this move to France.

A lifelong Communist, still remembered by his English schoolfriends as Comrade Zaidelson, Fima was living contentedly, with

Lena and their cat Dina, in a grubby high-rise on the outskirts of
Tallinn when he found himself owner, or one-third owner, of the
dilapidated block of flats in which he had lived as a child, a derelict
cinema and the department store, still called Gutkin's, which had
been the family business for three generations.

Deeply uncomfortable about his new-found wealth, but dis-
suaded from disinheriting his children and grandchildren, he handed
everything over to his son Sasha to manage and somehow this lovely
young man, of luminous goodness, who had been trained to work as
a sewing-machine mechanic, learned to be a businessman and, in an
astonishingly short space of time, the buildings had been renovated
and let. There is now a branch of the Deutsche Bundesbank in the
shop space beside Gutkin's itself and my great-uncle's store is once
again full of the merchandise, bales of cotton, silk and wool, for
which it had always been known.

I can't talk directly to Sasha[n] and will never know how he came
through this boom-town jungle intact but it must have helped that
there were stringent laws about the rights of sitting tenants and
also that he wasn't interested in making money make more money.
In fact, he got out as soon as he could and I heard only yesterday
that he has found a job in Strasbourg and will start work next week,
doing shift work in a box factory.

Of course, it was different for Sasha's generation, now in their forties. They didn't, like their parents, remember a time when it would
have been unthinkable for anyone they knew to work at a factory
bench, to serve in a shoe shop, to repair sewing machines. Their parents had been brought up to become doctors and lawyers, engineers
and businessmen, and the country might have profited from allowing them to continue doing what they knew how to do and were
often good at. But that isn't how revolutions work. The first priority
of the 'Bolsheviks', as my grandmother would have called them,
who 'liberated' Estonia in 1941 under cover of the Ribbentrop

pact, was to cleanse the country of its bourgeois element. And the way to do this – and, it must be said, a better way than death and deportation, though these were not unknown – was by confiscating all private property and excluding the property-owning class from their traditional jobs unless, of course, like my cousin, Fima, they were long-standing Party members or, like my mother's cousin, Harry Dreyer, a doctor who specialised in venereal diseases, they couldn't do without them . . .

It surprised me that there was any work for my uncle. Where did people do it? Four, five, six to a room – cold and wet outdoors for six months of the year . . . ? Again, we didn't have a common language but with my mother's help and a lot of nods and winks, I understood that Uncle Harry had never been short of business. Where there is a port there are sailors and where there are sailors . . . As for *where* – no civilian was allowed anywhere near the sea so neither the beaches of Pirita, closed off with barbed wire, nor the warehouses by the harbour, patrolled by armed police, could serve as trysting places for these young Russians and the flaxen-haired local girls: it was probably a seasonal activity and, like everyone else, they took to the woods at mushrooming time.

As for Party members, I only ever met one, for Fima had been expelled from the Party years before, in the purges of 1949, accused of concealing his bourgeois origins. Even this and the loss of his job – he had been a journalist – did not wake him up and just as Nastya had protected her daughter Eva from the truths that might have made her life more difficult, so did Lena and Renata who lived in the real world and not in their heads, allow Fima not to lose faith in something in which he had so much need to believe. It took another thirty years and the collapse of the Soviet Union for him to face the truth. The dream had failed.

But in the sixties, when we first met, Fima was still an ardent believer and, after ten years in the wilderness, was now allowed to work again, no longer as a journalist but as a librarian and archivist which gradually led to his becoming a historian and writing free-lance articles, mainly about the war. In fact, he had just completed a full-scale history of this when the whole system collapsed and the manuscript was returned from the commissioning publisher unread.

There was no room now for a book about the war from the Soviet perspective, not even a war in which Fima had proved so inept a soldier that after twice being wounded he had been assigned to writing patriotic poems and at this, because his heart was in it and it required no physical skills, he had excelled. Mothers, the mother-land, what could mean more to Fima in the wake of receiving a photograph of his own beloved mother, sent to him in the care of a Russian officer who had been shot, but not killed, while carrying it in his pocket? So it reached Fima at last, along with news of his mother's death, stained with blood and with a bullet-hole through her heart.

I have seen the photograph, in its frame, on a bookshelf in the little flat, decorated with family pictures and souvenirs of Bedford – a printed tea towel of Bedford landmarks is pinned to the wall beside a Union Jack – where Fima and Lena would happily have lived out their days, she feeding the stray cats in the tenement base-ment, he sorting and re-sorting a lifetime's papers, and both enjoy-ing their little concrete balcony and nice big television set. Radios and televisions had, of course, been among the first commodities to appear in people's homes but they had not been intended for watching CNN News or stop-whatever-you-are-doing-for Mexican soap operas.

Far more important to Fima than the new television or even the dramatic turn in his fortunes has been reconnecting with his old school and the seeds of this reunion had been planted a surpris-ingly long time ago. It seems that while still a journalist, before he had been expelled from the Party, he had been sent to Moscow to report on a trade fair and was wearing his old school tie when this was recognised by an English businessman who, returning home, wrote and told the school that Ephraim Zaidelson, whom they had presumed to be dead, was still alive.

From this chance encounter at a time when the Iron Curtain was still firmly in place was established a correspondence with one of his old teachers and through him, with one of his schoolfriends, the only other Jew in his class, the German-born Walter Stimson. But letters at this time were still censored and could take months to arrive: it was only years later, when things were beginning to loosen up, that Fima found a reference to the Old Bedfordians association in a handful of publications I had picked up in the Bedford museum. Before long he was getting letters not only from England but from all over the world. He also got a visit from another old boy of the school, the writer Frank Branston who, by a strange coincidence, we had published at Deutsch and whose piece in the local Bedford paper provides a masterful summary of his older schoolfellow's 'political' life:

> . . . Poor Jefim. On the wrong side of the twentieth century at every turn: despised by the Nazis for being a Jew, by the Russians for being Estonian, by the Communists for being bourgeois, by the Estonian nationalists for having fought in the Red Army . . .

And so, at a time when even in safe and well-ordered lives things are beginning to close in, Fima's horizons were opening out. In retirement, he was busier than he had ever been writing letters, full of apologies for his English for which no apology was needed, to Bedford and Beverley and Frome, to Seattle and Tahiti, wherever it was that the class of '34 had washed up. And in return came not only letters but packages of books and photographs and Christmas puddings: a wonderful, non-computerised network of old men remembering the past and, at that time, with no thought of ever meeting again for visas were still hard to get and the prices demanded of foreigners at the only hotel they were allowed to stay in, astronomical. As for Fima and all the other Estonians, they were still not allowed out of the country or even into the hotel in which the foreigners stayed.

Then, as if overnight, everything changed. But, like any prisoner, he was at first frightened of the new freedom and it was only the irresistible pull of a special celebration at his old school which at last brought him back to Bedford and his beloved Ouse, to Piccadilly Circus and the Strand Palace Hotel, to the England of his boyhood memories.

My mother had never shared Fima's love affair with England and when it was time for us to come home it was only the thought of being able to visit again which made the leaving bearable. But the next year she was too ill to travel. The cancer we had thought she was free of had returned and I was told by the doctor that she had six months to live.

He was wrong. She was to live for another four years and in one of the longer periods of remission, we did get back and it was almost as good as the time before, even though my mother was now taking aspirin every few hours – aspirin for cancer! – to dull the constant pain in her back (every time I get backache, I think I am dying) and was beginning to lose the sight of one eye. What made this visit not quite as good as the last was not my mother's condition but the death, while we had been away, of two of her dearest friends.[n]

Paula too had had cancer but to her death had come quickly. Now only three of the four schoolfriends – Nancy, Paula,[n] Assia and Zippa – their names are inscribed on the tooled-leather notebook they had given me as a parting gift two years before – remained. For Nancy who had never let us visit her home, things had improved. With her Russian son-in-law, daughter Dany and newly-born grandchild, she now lived in one of the new tower blocks on the edge of town. We had visited one of these with Fima to prove to him – by looking at the names on the doorbells – that the flats were being given only to Russians. Similarly, we had had to visit every bookshop in Tallinn before – still a Believer – he would concede that you could not buy a Bible . . .

Not having close Russian connections, Assia was still living and arguing with her much loved daughter, Sima, in the single room, jammed with antique furniture, that we had visited before. The surprising change in Assia's life was that now she owned a car. She could not drive or afford to run it but it had been the only form in which she had been allowed to accept a gift of money from some distant relative, possibly in Australia for that is where she and Sima finally went to live.

As for Zippa, she continued to live with her actor husband in the spacious flat we remembered from last time. Successful actors, like all 'artists', had special privileges. Zippa, though no more a practising Communist than her schoolfriends, was, like her husband, a Party member. None of her old friends resented her good luck. If anything, they pitied her for having no children, as they did my mother for living so far from home.

This lack of resentment or envy among people whose lives had been overturned was a source of constant wonder to me, so often enmeshed at home in petty wrangling about money or status or possessions. The consternation when my out-of-work uncle had found a job with the post office . . . What would they have thought if he had found work as a porter?

For it was as a porter, loading and unloading lorries at the railway station, that Katz – the other of my mother's friends who had died in our absence – had worked. I had only met Katz once, in the street: a shabby, elderly man with huge shoulders – ten or maybe twenty years older than my mother – but he had such a powerful presence and his love for her was so fierce and protective that I will never forget him even though I have no pictures of him from then or from before the war when he was among the dearest of my parents' friends.

I never knew his first name, he was always just 'Katz', but I did know that he had once owned the chocolate factory, or maybe it was chocolate factories, which supplied the cafés and cake shops of prewar Tallinn, Tartu and beyond. And I knew from my mother that he joked ruefully about the dusty white chocolates, rattling in their cardboard boxes, which changed hands at the celebration of every family event and with which we had been overwhelmed at parting. I heard too that he wished the Soviet authorities would make use of what he knew about the making of chocolate but he understood that this could never happen and like that other K, Kamuscher – dear friend to both my parents – he just got on with things and derived his sustenance from the BBC World Service[n] and from books.

Books were the safer option and Katz and Kamuscher were the only people we met who risked listening to foreign stations on the radio. They were also the only people we met who had any idea of what was going on in the outside world. But they didn't waste precious time with my mother talking about politics. Like everyone else, they wanted to reminisce about those years – the twenties and thirties – when they had been young and life had been good . . .

For Kamuscher it was not so bad even now. He had an office job, perhaps thanks to the success of his economist son, now working in Moscow. He also, unlike Katz who was entirely alone and whose living conditions we could not begin to imagine, had a wife to whom he was devoted and a quite decent little flat lined with books from floor to ceiling: uniform editions of all the classics along with whatever else the authorities considered fit reading.

Shakespeare, Dickens, Zola, Jack London – Kamuscher had read and re-read them all. And it showed. Just as listening to the World Service kept these two men in touch with the real world so did reading these politically safe books, in their rexine bindings, keep them in touch with a world of thought and feeling untouched by the universal horrors and personal misfortunes of the present.

YOU ARE WHAT YOU READ
EAT GOOD BOOKS

For a long time I had this poster on the wall of my office for though just a hand-out from some book-promoting agency and printed – the cake with a slice being lifted out of it – in rather sickly pinks and yellows, I knew it was true.

Less sickly than virulent were the pinks and yellows, the oranges and reds of the roses in the painting, the oil painting – you could see its rough and shiny surface – which my mother bought, in its gold 'rococo' frame, from the Art Department in Harrods. I know now that this, like the Louis Quinze bedroom and the Chippendale dining room, was in the worst possible taste but it took a lot of expensive schools and a still more expensive university to teach me this.

Thinking back, I realise that I know almost nothing about my mother's schooldays. Was she good at 'English'? Could she do Maths? Did she like Geography? Did she even know where Sweden was when she left home, at seventeen, to marry her Swedish pastor's son?

Like most early marriages this was, I imagine, more of a running from than a running to, but what was she running from? It can't surely have been from the prospect – the threat – of 'higher education'. My grandfather Boris Gutkin had ideas about girls advanced for his time and her older sister was already a student – of dentistry – in Vienna. But whatever tales Stefa brought back to Tallinn, they would not have been about teeth. A flamboyant character – sun to my mother's moon – she was soon to embark on the first of her several stormy marriages, this one to a feline Hungarian Count, establishing once and for all her taste for sexy, unsuitable, non-Jewish men. I have lost track of the others but her last husband, an Italian, was blown up by the British, to her great satisfaction, for he had proved to be one of those rare Italians with an enthusiasm for the war. He had also become an anti-Semite: according to her, that is. He could simply have had enough of my oftentimes trying aunt just as, I suspect, some of the people my ex-employer complains of in a piece relating his experience of anti-Semitism, may simply have had enough of him.

Whatever the truth of these speculations, by the time I first met Stefa, a year or two after the war – it had taken the Red Cross, still re-uniting families, this long to find her – she was a widow and so she remained, using the fluent German which along with her quick wits and non-Aryan good looks had helped her survive the war in an occupied country to get a job in the local Tourist Office. Here, on the sea front in Trieste, she was able to exercise her French and her English – the last a fearless hybrid – 'Nice boys don't siffle in the street', 'conditional air', 'I am exhausting . . .'

And she was. Already in her eighties when she came to London for a visit, she out-talked us, out-ate us, out-shopped us. I still shrink with embarrassment at the memory of the day when she demanded a pair of culottes be taken out of the window of a Bond Street boutique, or of seeing her being led away to the staff lavatories in the Oxford Street Marks & Spencer so that she could get at her money, stuffed beneath her skirt. Then home, after a nightmarish journey for she wouldn't hear of wasting money on a taxi, didn't like our buses and was frightened of escalators: it generally took a man, attracted as she thought by her coquettish glances, to get her onto these. Back at last, she would flop her great weight into an armchair, reach out with one hand for a cigarette and the other for whatever delicacy was on offer – the soused herrings we had just bought at

Selfridges, a handful of Belgian chocolates, a thickly buttered roll – and regale us with stories about the war before falling into bed, fully dressed, and waking revived and ready for next day's adventures.

She broke all the rules but she lived to be older than either of my parents and lies now in a corner of the lovely old cemetery in Trieste where I mean one day to return and set up a stone on her unmarked grave:

STEPHANIE MESSA (née Gutkin)
beloved sister of Zosia and Hermann
b. Tallinn 1902 d. Trieste 1988

'Beloved' might be overdoing it, but I think both my mother and my uncle would prefer the word to be there than not and I feel pretty certain – as certain as it is possible to feel about something for which one has no evidence – that it wasn't the presence (or absence) of her older sister that propelled my mother to leave home.

Nor could it have been anything to do with her father of whom all memories were fond. But, thinking back, there was surprisingly little my mother wanted to tell me about her mother. I know only that she – Helene Banker – was brought from Łodz, little more than a child bride, to become my widowed grandfather's second wife. And I can see for myself that the look of sullen discontent so striking in those earliest studio portraits, was never to be absent for long. But maybe like me, who most resembles her, she just naturally tended to look a bit glum. I can walk down the street thinking about a new climbing rose for the garden or the next instalment of *The Sopranos*, when I hear a workman calling out – 'Cheer up! It can't be as bad as that . . .'

It's possible, too, that the way her mother died" shut down all memory so that later, when I was old enough to want to know, she could talk about her father who had died long before the war but not about the stout lady in the flowered frocks reaching down to her ankles who had shown us those pictures of children in gas masks and had loved to eat and see us eat. It was chocolate, Katz's chocolate I suppose, that she would indulge in while we sat at the dining table eating our lavish nursery teas.

I can only guess, then, and my guess is that the wasp-waisted teenager with the sulky expression had not wanted to leave home and that though adored by her much older husband and getting some pleasure from the three children she presented him with, she missed her family and friends and was soon disappointed in her husband's comparative lack of success. Every time she passed Gutkin's she must have wished that she and not her sister-in-law was married to the owner of that thriving establishment. Like my own father, my grandfather was the unsuccessful brother.

But even if my grandmother was dissatisfied enough to be, whether consciously or not, envious of her daughters, she was not a monster and the Swedish interlude was perhaps, after all, more a response to a suitor's supplications and the excitement of something new than a rejection of home.

Whatever it was, it didn't last long. The sepia photos of my mother alone in that unfamiliar front parlour or breakfasting with her husband, the pastor's son, in what seems to be a Swedish hunting lodge, or standing beside him in the snow in her ankle-length fur coat, suddenly give way to pictures of my father beside a mine shaft in the Estonian woods, and then of my father together with my mother in Tallinn which is where, on one of her many visits home, they had met.

Balls, beach parties, picnics – it was to this Tallinn of the twenties and thirties – both hers and the century's – that my mother for ever longed to return. In love with her Englishman, in love, I imagine for the first time, and allowed her freedom by the man to whom she was still married and who, ten years later, was still there and ready to adopt her illegitimate son, life had never been and was never again to be so good.

20 *My uncle and aunt, Slip and Rae Menell*

21 *My aunt, Moos Mailer*

22 *My uncle Eddie and his wife*

23 *Fima and his parents*

24 *With Fima, beside the lake in Viljandi*

25 *My husband with Fima and Lena in Strasbourg*

26 *Birth announcement*

27 *With my mother, her mother in the background*

That, from time to time, my father needed to return to England and that more often than not my mother would come with him, only added to the pleasure of each joyous return. There was no thought then that one day she would find herself living in England and among those Menell relatives who crowd the one picture in which I can see my mother pregnant with me. Taken outdoors, probably in Middleton, it shows my mother sitting in a canvas chair and the bulge in the dress of printed cotton heralds both my arrival and the death, in that Marble Arch Odeon, of her mother-in-law whose commanding figure towers over the grandchildren – the Prenskys, Zimblers, Mailers and Menells – playing at her feet.

To be born in England, as I was a few weeks later, in a block of flats on the Finchley Road, proved to be providential. When I needed my own passport there was no question about my entitlement. But it took years for my brother, born in Tallinn, to be accepted as a British citizen, not least because he could not produce a birth certificate. Looking for this was our one piece of serious business on that first visit to Tallinn: trudging from one government office to another in the upper town – little changed since medieval times and now a mecca for tourists – till eventually directed to a synagogue we had not known to exist.

It was in two small, upstairs rooms in a dilapidated house near the railway station that we found the rabbi and his wife. Their holy objects had been removed to the museum in Tartu and they had there only a Bible, a pair of candlesticks and their own few possessions for this was also where they lived.

They had no congregation because no one dared to come but at least they were no longer being harassed by the authorities who had granted them permission to leave (old people – useless people – I was to learn were encouraged to leave) but they would not consider going until their middle-aged scientist daughter was allowed to go too.

I doubt that any of the three ever made it to the States where, if I remember rightly, they had relatives. What I know for certain is that they were not able to find any record of my brother's birth, for though we had left them with our London address we never heard from them again.

Roots Schmoots. It happens to us all. Only yesterday, I saw that John Gross has done it too: another English Jew writing about being an English Jew. But John Gross's book – *A Double Thread* – has a title you could ask for without flinching. It took seeing Howard Jacobson on the telly to get me into our local bookshop to order a copy of *Roots Schmoots*." I can hardly get the words out now. But it is a wonderful book – funny, caustic, unsentimental – and if anyone wonders" what it is like to go on feeling Jewish when you also feel English, this is how to find out.

   You don't have to speak Yiddish or know what it means to sit shivvah. You can even eat bacon and keep marrying 'out'. Just as you can love opera without ever going to the opera. Not long ago, R was a guest on Michael Berkeley's *Private Passions*. Almost every one of his choices – the exception a track from the Platters – was operatic but we have hardly ever been inside an opera house. Passion, commitment, an indissoluble connectedness, have nothing to do with actual attendance.

During the wartime years in Ilkley, attendance would have been difficult but not impossible; there must have been synagogues in those nearby towns where we would go looking for coffee, but not only for coffee, for one of my earliest memories is of getting separated from my mother in Brown & Muff's, the big Bradford department store where you could buy crockery or spend your clothing coupons but couldn't buy food. And it would have been easier still when we moved to Kingsbury, a London suburb within easy reach of the synagogue in St John's Wood where I had, apparently, been 'christened' soon after my birth.

I never thought to ask exactly what this ceremony was but every time I pass the red-brick building, no match for even the most modest church, I remember this and think it must have been there I got stuck with those two surplus names which it took me so long to dare to discard and which appear even now on passport and birth certificate as they will, no doubt, on the certificate of my death.

Sheila. Denise. What possessed my parents to tag me with these? How many different people can one person be? The first, which I misspelt for years – 'i before e except after c' – a misspelling first remarked on when I went for my Oxford interview, seems to have been thought up by my Mailer aunt who was visiting London at the time and became my godmother. Glamorous, amusing and unreservedly friendly to both my parents, Moos, my father's favourite sister, must have enlivened that little gathering and I still have the string of seed pearls in their silk-lined leather box which was to be her first and last godmotherly gift.

And the name she chose, if she did choose it, at least appealed to me as a child. The other, at whose origins I can't even guess, was nothing but an embarrassment and I was determined that when I had a child (I didn't then think 'if') he or she would have only one name. But, as it turned out, my only child's father felt deprived at having only one name himself and wanted his son to have more. So we compromised. Two names. The first culled from the Glaxo baby book and the second from *Ulysses* – M's copy a prize for translating English verse into Greek. It will one day be my son's, a reminder of his father-before-he-knew-him who at a very early age already preferred James Joyce to Biggles.

As for me, it could have been worse. If my grandmother hadn't died and left me with her name I would have been called Marina after that discreetly elegant foreign princess . . .

I imagine it was her being foreign that drew my mother to her. Though as a child I had the usual complement of picture books about the princesses Elizabeth and Margaret Rose, neither she nor my father had any great interest in the royal family. My father was a patriot in Churchillian mode: for him, England, whose fortunes in battle he followed minutely, every move registered with pins on the map of Europe that hung in the hall, was the Land of the Free, the land of Churchill (whose portrait loomed on the dining-room wall) and Disraeli, of Orde Wingate and the Camborne School of Mines, of roast beef and Yorkshire pudding and, perhaps closest to his heart of all, the land of football, cricket and rugby union.

For my mother, England was and remained a foreign country. Even after the war when the rambling stone house on the edge of Ilkley Moor, where the kitchen always smelled of the rich sludge on which our landlady fed her chickens, was just a memory and we were back in St John's Wood living the kind of life she had been used to, it didn't help. The sense of exile, of not being where she really belonged and wanted to be, was perhaps stronger than ever now that the days weren't filled with listening to news bulletins, putting up blackout curtains, bottling eggs (while eggs were still to be had), mending clothes, cooking, sweeping, dusting – all new activities that were soon to become familiar and about which I never once heard her complain. And then there were the nights spent under the stairs (the kitchen table was no longer protection enough once the buzz bombs started) while my father slept on undisturbed. No Jerry, he said, was going to get him out of bed . . .

What is it that makes some people slide in and fit, fit so well, in some cases, that only a few years on they can be taken for English or French or whatever it may be? I think of our surprise on finding that Robert Rubens, a novelist whose school-of-Coward 'entertainments' were steeped in Englishness – the Englishness of country houses, cut-glass decanters, stuccoed London squares – was American. Thick-set, somewhat ponderous, this Philadelphian exile of unclear ethnic origins (was it 'old money', was it native American, was it Jewish, or perhaps all three?) had expunged all trace of his American accent and presented himself to the world he wished to inhabit as one of their own. How much easier to understand our next-door neighbours who left their village in Cyprus more than thirty years ago but behave as though they were living there still. Whilst our back gardens are places in which we play at gardening – re-arranging the shrubs, slipping in some irresistible bedding plant – when not reclining in deckchairs on our little patches of lawn, theirs is a vegetable plot extending out from under a luxuriant and wine-producing vine, and their sitting out takes place on kitchen chairs in the little *front* garden, in full view of the street. Of course, the outdoor cooking which goes on almost every summer evening does take place at the back, on a strip of ground beyond the last row of tomatoes or sweet-corn and here, on a warm summer's night, you could imagine yourself on the Mediterranean – the smells, the tastes, the *language*. No longer unbroken Greek, for there are the English daughters-in-law and grandchildren, but mostly, and late into the night in this Kentish Town garden, we hear the sounds and smell the smells of the country our neighbours left behind.

My mother wasn't so lucky. There was no extended family, no colony of Russian speakers in Kingsbury where we were when the war ended and where, on the forecourt of the Green Man, we celebrated Victory among a crowd, indistinguishable in memory from every other heaving happy crowd singing English songs in English voices which I see on newsreels of the time. 'Roll out the barrel', 'Knees up, Mother Brown', 'Down at the Old Bull and Bush' … A lover of music hall and a singer-in-the-bath – what words could possibly have preceded that favourite refrain 'And remember that a cabbage has a heart'? – my father would have joined in them all as he and my mother drank to Victory along with everyone else.

And 'everyone else' I was to learn many years later could well have included at least one other non-English-speaking family for, down the road from our thatched cottage in Slough Lane (I found quite recently that this turn-of-the-century architectural fantasy appears in Pevsner) lived Eva Figes' family, refugees from Berlin.

A year or two older than me so that her German was more formed than mine that had been spoken only with cook and nanny, Eva was to remember her first language and has used it, not only when revisiting her birthplace, but reading and translating all her adult life. Would it, I wonder, have made my mother feel less alone" had she known Eva's mother and had they been able to talk in the German – banished in our household – that my mother had known since childhood and about a Europe which had no existence for anyone she knew now: our English neighbours, staunch allies in the common adversity but, in those pre-package tour days, as ignorant of 'abroad' as of sauerkraut or Latin. The first of which I had known all my life; the other I was about to have to learn.

ℰ 3 ℰ

Just Like Everyone Else

IN CHOOSING SCHOOLS, my parents turned to Gabbitas & Thring.
It's hard to imagine what the agency found to recommend about
Eversley, the school I was at when the war ended, but its not offering Latin didn't stop me being sent there for, at ten, the mirage of
Oxford and its entrance requirements had not yet taken hold. Two
years later, briefed by the parents of my pioneering cousins, Vicky
and Doreen, I was moved to Battle Abbey, a school where Latin
was taught and there, while all my friends learnt to make scones and
shortcrust pastry, I struggled with declensions and verb endings.

But all this was still in the future when, at five years old and
newly English, I started school halfway down the hill at the top of
which, in the last house before the moors began, we lodged with
Mrs Aspinall and her chickens. At the bottom of the hill lay the
main settlement of Ilkley and when, as was to happen very soon, so
desperate was I to 'belong', I became a boarder, I would often see
my father walking past on his way to the station (the car picked him
up in Leeds) and seeing me he would throw his hat into the air and
catch it, like a cricket ball . . .

He would also write me letters, cheerful, forward-looking notes,
full of dv's – god-willings. For my mother, writing in English was
a struggle and she wrote very seldom but every package which was
to reach me in that hell-hole by the Solent[n] to which I was sent to
be safely out of London when we moved south – my parents' sweet

rations, a pair of gym shoes, a set of jacks – was addressed in her round, careful hand.

At Oaklands, the school on the hill, I had arrived in the middle of term, so was 'behind' everyone else and with traces of the German we had spoken in Tallinn still in my speech: it was not an easy start but under the curious but benevolent stewardship of the Misses Perry and Clegg and in full view of the outside world, this little school for little girls was not a bad place to begin and very soon I had not only started to read and write but had made two friends – Franzi, the only other 'refugee', and a very small, very pretty girl, with long wavy hair, called Delphine. These friendships did not survive the move south but they and learning to read and write eased my way into becoming the just-like-everybody-else English schoolgirl I wished above all else to be.

And here, for a while, my memories would match those of many other sixty-plus year-olds from middle-class homes: morning prayers, tables by rote, custard with everything . . . Vivid, too, are the memories of sitting round Brown Owl on mushroom-shaped stools, of Nuts in May, played across a line on the floor of the gym and the excitement, the sexual excitement, of this roughish game . . .

Although I can dredge up no memories of abuse and am astounded at how common an experience this apparently was and is, I know very well that the seven year old dancing barefoot in her Greek-style tunic (a photo I cherish because for that one moment in time I looked almost skinny) already had sexual feelings and these physical sensations, to which I couldn't have given a name, preceded by several years the storms of emotion which came with falling in love.

With other girls, of course. Who else was there and how, without my consuming passion for Evelyn Sturt (could she one day read this? would she mind?) would I have survived Eversley for even as long as I did.

This school which gave me a taste of what prison must be like, useful now that I visit real prisoners in real prisons, was closed off from the world on one side by the mud banks of the Solent and on the other by a stretch of woodland beyond which there must have been a wall and gates but they were far enough away to be out of sight and stayed that way because, like so much else, they were Out of Bounds. Also Out of Bounds was the Senior Lavatory, the mystery of which took on mythic proportions as did so much else in this little kingdom ruled over by a sadistic old woman who was, or so it was rumoured, to end her days in an asylum.

The Senior Lavatory, I discovered when I had let my mother know of these bogeys, was no more than a lavatory with a sanitary bin in one corner. And a sanitary bin was something I would need when I was older – just like a waste-paper basket but for those pads which would soak up the blood when I began to have periods . . . And now she gave me a book called *How A Baby Is Born* which I read over and over with very little real understanding – my favourite page" had no text: it was black all over with just a pin-point of white in the centre – but a sense that whatever was going to happen when I grew up, it was going to be All Right.

Is that the message of sex education today, hedged in as it is with the direst of warnings, and is there any ten year old in the country – girl or boy – who doesn't know what a sanitary towel is, hasn't seen them demonstrated on the telly? And is learning from these glossed-up versions of the truth, or from a teacher in a classroom, any better than the haphazard way in which our mothers tried to prepare us?

The answer may be Yes, for it's hard to imagine how the unhealthy intensity of those schoolgirl passions and morbid interest in the mechanics of menstruation – looking over the partition walls was the chief spectator sport at my next school – could survive formal instruction or, so much more usual now than then, the presence of boys. But wouldn't there be loss as well as gain? I would still choose to hear prayers chanted and operas sung in languages I can't understand than hear them in second-rate English which delivers the meaning but destroys the magic.

Not that magic was on the menu in the Hampshire school: what we lived with was Fear (Terror would not be too strong a word), and the palpable discomforts – being teased about my Yorkshire accent, now much more pronounced than my German had ever been; being cold; being hungry – were pin-pricks compared with this.

When my son, at twelve years old, refused to go to the public school for which he had been destined, the teacher to whom I went to apologise for the trouble we were causing said, and so surprising was it that I remember his exact words: 'Well, at least we taught him something here.'

One could argue at length about the virtues of being politicised by an over-exposure to Bentleys, reports of skiing holidays in Switzerland and thousand-pound barmitzvah presents, but these early experiences provided indelible memories which were to reinforce, if they did not actually cause, a permanent rejection of the conventions of middle-class life.

Eversley taught me something too and what it taught was the power that can emanate from a single individual, like the power which makes whole nations succumb to the will of one man.

Like other and better-known tyrants, Fran was physically unprepossessing. She must have had 'day' clothes but the way I remember her is the way we saw her every night as, in a floor-length dress of maroon lace and followed by her dog, she stopped at each dormitory in turn to watch us as, last thing before the lights went out, we had to kneel by our beds and say our prayers . . .

A frail, white-haired, bird-like creature, she stood by the open door, leaning on her walking stick. The dog, a snappy little creature, sniffed at our bare feet. He, or it could have been she, was the only living thing within that compound who didn't freeze at her approach.

André Deutsch and Tom Rosenthal, those other mini-tyrants

who were to become part of my life, had nothing on Fran: they had the power and they had the trappings, Tom in particular went in for these – Mussolini-like, he affected a huge desk" which dominated the largest and emptiest room in the building – but it was pay-cheque power. We weren't frightened of them but only of what, unionless, they could do to us. No union or inspectorate could have defused Fran.

Luckily, we didn't see much of her but her cold, unnerving presence permeated the school and the only sure escape was in one's head, mine then full of thoughts of Evelyn; when I had seen her last, when I would see her next, and whether she would speak to me . . .

There were also the 'music rooms' – three unheated sheds which Fran and her dog never visited. I don't remember ever seeing either of them outdoors. It was only here, in Beethoven, Bach and Brahms, called after the plaster busts of the composers that stood beside the metronomes on the lids of the pianos, that one could be safe from Fran and entirely alone in a community where even the bathwater was shared.

It must, of course, have saved the school money to ration heat and hot water but it did also help the war effort and conditions at Eversley were probably no worse than at a lot of other schools in those closing years of the war. We were cold but we weren't very cold, hungry but not very hungry. Also, like Nastya and Eva who made the little plot of land round their house in Nõmme yield riches that town-dwellers could only dream of, we too took advantage of being in the country and spent our free time foraging in the woods; still young enough to collect conkers but more interested still in the sweet chestnuts and shiny, three-sided beech nuts that, for a short time each autumn, carpeted the ground.

I have never seen beech nuts in such profusion since and wonder if, returning, I would find them now. Fran I know couldn't be there, unless as the ghost she resembled even then, but maybe some old person living near by could tell me what happened after I left. Is it true that she was removed to an institution? Did the school continue without her? Is it there now, its post-war pupils drawn from the four corners of the globe, wherever parents, like my own, still want the best for their children, have the money to buy it, and believe what they are told . . .

I suppose there are still agencies seducing the Anglophile American, African dignitary and Japanese businessman" into thinking that a boarding school in the English countryside is the ultimate good or, perhaps nowadays, these schools go touting for business themselves, 'recruiting' in Singapore, Taiwan, Malaysia, in the footsteps of their colleagues in the lower reaches of higher education who set up their stalls wherever student-aged youngsters are not covered by 'reciprocal arrangements', and whatever the state of their English.

'Not many people die on the operating table,' I was told by a bumptious young houseman, not long since a student, when I was in hospital not long ago. The NIL BY MOUTH sign was already hanging on the end of my bed. English clearly wasn't his native language but this perfectly formed sentence, unlike his post-operative instruction to 'mobilise', was a mistake of a non-linguistic kind.

Be that as it may, R, like everyone else in the former polytechnics and probably some of the older universities too, has had to become used to being only half-understood.

Of course, the state-owned universities aren't primarily businesses even though so many of the functionaries at the management level are brought in from the business sector. But most of the little private schools were never anything else. Like the homes for the elderly, dotted about the countryside in much the same way, they were businesses, offering a service, sometimes good, sometimes bad and, as often as not, run by proprietors who had little formal education themselves.

Whether Fran had any background in teaching, I don't know. Maybe she inherited the school like Miss Sheehan-Dare who took over Battle Abbey, where I went next, when her niece went off with one of the prisoners-of-war" who had been helping on the abbey farm – or so the rumour went. Either way, neither school had a sixth form" on the principle, I suppose, that by the time a young woman is seventeen she has had enough 'book learning' and will be more likely to find the right husband by acquiring more practical and lady-like skills.

Among these skills, as I was to find out when I went on to Queen's College in Harley Street, a school which had been founded by the Misses Buss and Beale with something very different in mind, was how to change a fuse.

Science and the Modern World was the name of the lesson in which we were exposed to this kind of thing to which, I realised years afterwards, it might have paid to pay attention even though, like Drama on the Modern Stage, another dismal stab at broadening the mind, it had no relevance for those of us committed to taking A-levels, or 'Higher' as it was then called.

Queen's College in the early fifties had too much of the finishing school about it. I craved the high seriousness which Battle had not pretended to but which I had expected to find here. I also missed the moral discipline of that happy-go-lucky establishment where we all wore the same thing and, I have realised since, learnt more about how to behave from all those outdoor games than from any of the extra-curricular cultural activities offered in Harley Street.

Academically, Battle was a non-starter in those long-ago days. With its mostly untrained teachers, its lack of a sixth form and its strict quota of Jewish girls, it did not aspire to achieving academic honours and when, as seldom happened, a Battle Abbey girl found her way to Oxbridge or, indeed, to any university, it did not cause much of a stir, not least because it seldom if ever happened straight from there. Nor, in my case, straight from Queen's where the teaching was so lack-lustre that Wendy and I (our classmate Sevin, two years older, was already at a London art school) moved on to a crammer's and it was from there, a terraced house in Maida Vale, that I finally made it to Oxford.

No wonder, then, that years later when I came across Queen's College described as 'dilettante' in a book I was editing,[*] I didn't query it. But when it came out, the then present head did.

We received a surprisingly bad-tempered letter – surprising because it was the only letter of complaint this lengthy book elicited – from a Lady Goodhart, whose signature was followed by these qualifications: MA Hons. Oxon, Lady Margaret Hall. To this letter, after checking with the author who reconfirmed her sources, I was able to reply not just as the book's editor, but also as a dissatisfied ex-pupil *and* a fellow 'BA Hons. Oxon' – albeit of St Hilda's, one step down, socially, from Lady Goodhart's LMH.

Not all letters of complaint were as easy to brush off. Not long before, we had published a cookery book, *The Floris Book of Cakes*, which had proved a minefield of misinformation. Within days of publication I started to get letters and phone calls, one from a woman well into making her daughter's wedding cake when the recipe collapsed under her. Just as bad, though less urgent, was the letter from an old-age pensioner who had wasted precious money on ingredients which did not add up to the promised cake. To her and several others I sent apologies along with a copy of *The Random Egg*[†] as a kind of consolation prize.

The lesson, of course, is to avoid working on books where you know nothing about the subject, but this is easier said than done in a small publishing firm and, especially in the early days, when I had little choice, I had spent hours poring over texts on subjects about which I knew next to nothing – trout farming, the private life

---

[*] Gillian Avery, *The Best Type of Girl: a History of Girls' Independent Schools* (1991)
[†] George Bradshaw, *Soufflés, Quiches, Mousses & the Random Egg* (1973)

of rabbits (this book by Ronald Lockley was to be the inspiration for *Watership Down*), the Pitcairnese language . . . But none of these books issued instructions.

It was because the cake book did that I tried to avoid it. I had never baked a cake and I was innumerate, an additional hazard. But André would have none of it. For whatever reason – perhaps Diana Athill, the obvious choice, for she had created the cookery list, had flatly refused – he wanted me and countered my objections by insisting that all I needed to worry about was the author's English: Floris was a personal friend of his and he had a royal warranty. The recipes could look after themselves.

Well, the English did need a bit of attention for, like André, Floris had grown up in a Hungarian-speaking household but it didn't need much and it was only a lot later when the Home Economist, working from a proof, began using the recipes to make those few cakes we were illustrating, that we found how unreliable they were. By this time we were too far in to get out and the author was, tragically, by his own hand, dead.

There was nothing to do but put things right where we could, which is to say that every cake pictured, except the wedding cake which was cardboard under its icing, is 'safe'. As for the rest, we just hoped for the best. And we were lucky. After the first few months, even though the book did rather well and was reissued by a book club, which meant there had to be at least 15,000 copies in kitchens around the country, the complaints dwindled and then dried up completely.

Why, I have no idea. Years earlier, when working as a temp, I had been sent to a fireworks company who, the agency told me, needed extra help at the same time every year:

Dear Mrs Brown/Smith/Jones,
*   We are very sorry to hear about little Tommy's/Harry's/Emily's accident . . . Please give him/her the enclosed, with our good wishes . . .*

By the end of November, the flood of complaints had slowed to a trickle. I was given my own box of Dairy Milk and sent on my way. This made sense. But what stopped the readers of the Floris book writing in I will never know.

It was at Astra Fireworks that I first got the idea of trying a marriage agency. The lively young woman who I had been employed to help out came back from her lunch hour one day with the news that she had signed on with Heather Jenner, so, she either implied or said, her boyfriend had better look out . . . I had heard a lot about the boyfriend and was to hear more, but by the time this interesting manoeuvre had pushed him into proposing marriage, if it ever did, I was long gone and so never heard the story's end but I have sometimes wondered if, not really meaning to, she had in fact found someone else . . .

A reversal of this kind overtook the husband of a friend of mine who had pushed his wife into going with him to group sex parties – advertised, apparently, in some respectable weeklies – where she had discovered a side of herself neither of them had known to exist and which the marriage could not contain. Before long, they were divorced and the erstwhile charity worker had become a committed sexual adventurer . . .

The etiquette of group sex was not on the curriculum at any of the hundred or more schools Gillian Avery had written about in *The Best Type of Girl*, the book which had prompted Lady Goodhart's letter. More surprising and a continuing source of astonished recognition was how much my two boarding schools, which I had thought unique, were like so many others. Eversley was not the only school where the headmistress's constant companion was a snappy little dog and Battle far from being the only school without a sixth form and where hospital corners, losing gamely and behaving nicely predominated over books and exams.

It was not group sex we were being prepared for but marriage and what made middle-class parents send their daughters to these woefully inadequate schools was to mix with other girls from 'nice' homes – girls whose brothers and whose brothers' friends would make the Best Type of Husband.

My own son would not have passed muster. 'Nice boys don't siffle in the street.' The street was in Trieste. My son was eight years old. His great-aunt was mixing two of her five languages. Nor do nice boys (or girls) talk with a cockney accent, as he does to this day.

So did our only 'scholarship girl'." I remember nothing but her single plait, her glasses and her eager grin; no attempt to befriend her, though it would have been fitting. But I was already far too busy playing my part in the little gang which had formed around the golden-haired Dierdre. Together with Jennifer – a cheerful and down-to-earth presence, then as now – we came to form a happy threesome within that little gang of six of whom two, alas, died long ago.

For the next four years we were inseparable but even the friendship with Dierdre, though it never soured, didn't outlast our schooldays: that summer in Sweden, where her father was military attaché, was its last fling. Not long after, while the rest of us were variously preparing to be secretaries or nurses or nursery nurses (I, now at Queen's, was the exception), she fell in love with a handsome young soldier, as her own mother had done, married, and disappeared out of our lives.

From time to time, Jennifer – the only one of the group I am still in touch with – and I talk about trying to find Dierdre whose husband, plausibly rumoured to be a Brigadier, shouldn't be hard to track down, even in retirement. But we always stop short. I don't know what stops Jennifer, a lively home-counties doer of good works and granny of five, but I fear we may have drifted too far apart to regain the past."

'A happy school,' is what Gill heard said of Battle but the school had not found its way into her book. Like the five hundred or more country churches which R had visited but couldn't include in the guide to parish churches which he was compiling at much the same time, it wasn't quite remarkable enough.

But for me, after Eversley, 'happy' was remarkable enough in itself. And, at Battle I had found a Best Friend on the very first day. It was in the library where I had gone to practise plaiting my hair that I came across Dierdre practising the splits. We had all read *Ballet Shoes* but only she could reasonably aspire to becoming a ballerina . . . Happy is what it was: an Angela Brazil world (I still have my treasured copy of *Jean's Golden Term*) of sturdy friendships, school-girl crushes and honour on the sports field . . .

Like most girls' public-private schools, Battle was modelled on boys' public schools and games were taken very seriously indeed. Every weekday afternoon, whatever the weather, we would be out on the tennis courts, used for tennis in summer and netball in winter, or down on the playing fields for athletics or lacrosse.

The playing fields lay just outside the school boundary and only prefects were allowed to go there at other times, a prohibition which became a nuisance when all my friends could go and I could not. Although I had always been good at lessons, had even managed to make myself useful at games, and was far from unruly, there was something – I think now it would be called 'attitude' – which didn't go down. André and Tom would recognise this. So would the doctor at the breast clinic which I had been going to for more than thirty years who told me that I didn't need to come again.

Unable to jump a queue or demand special treatment – a power-ful residue of the schoolgirl ethic – I am just as unable to accept behaviour which flies in the face of common sense: why at school did we have to change our shoes on bone dry days to run to the end of the drive to collect our piece of bread and dripping? why, at Deutsch, were books consistently scheduled unrealistically so that,

28 *On Bobik, with my cousin Vicky*

29 *At school in Ilkley (kneeling right)*

30 *Battle Abbey: with Dierdre (left) and Jennifer (centre)*

31 *Ballroom dancing (centre front) with Miss Silvester*

32 '50s teenager

33 With Sevin by the Black Sea

34 Wedding day

36 *With my son and Patch on the beach at Worthing*

35 *Expecting*

37 *My son and my lodger on Primrose Hill*

time and time again, we editors would be left to tell our authors that their books had been delayed and would have to make out a case – seldom convincing – for August being better than June, or January than September . . . And why was this young doctor who I had never seen before telling me that I didn't need to come back to the clinic? Statistically, I was no less at risk in my sixties than I had been in my thirties, forties and fifties.

The answer, of course, is obvious but I didn't realise then that by the time we collect our first bus pass we have become expendable. Not understanding this and in spite of or because of his bullying, I persisted with the Whys: I was not going to leave quietly until I had a reasonable answer and because there wasn't one he finally gave up in exasperation, handing me over to a colleague who suggested transferring my file to the nearby women's hospital which is where, four years later, the routine examination I had been denied, revealed a malignant tumour young enough to be removed and leave no trace.

Breasts in those boarding-school days were a different issue: well ahead in the menstrual stakes and an object of admiring curiosity among my friends and contemporaries, I was nowhere in the race for tits and was just as admiring, and envious, of the Argentinian girl who slept for one term in the bed across from mine and not only had bumps you could see through her clothes but was allowed to wear a brassiere which we all, of course, took turns at trying on.

It was in this same bedroom and bed – a large airy room (my American partner would say cold not airy) overlooking the drive and the gateway, beyond which lay the outside world – that I was visited by Bridget[n] on that night towards the very end of term when these particular visits traditionally took place. It was the one time that if you were prepared to brave the prowling matron and declare yourself – which I never did – you could invite yourself into the bed of whoever it was that preoccupied your daytime thoughts – in my case (and many others') a strapping fourteen year old with a large bosom, wiry hair and shapely legs: not at all the type – the kind of boy-girl – I would have fallen for in adult life had there been no men around. Nor would Bridget have been my choice – a short, powerfully built, ruddy-faced girl who dominated the sports field: ran faster, jumped higher, threw further than anyone else – and it is hard to understand why I was hers. Still harder to know what to do with her when she climbed into my bed. As I remember it, we both just lay there, flat on our backs.

The awkwardness of this encounter was never repeated. Bridget, whom I realised much later was probably a Lesbian, wasn't making do like the rest of us, and someone noticed. The next term she didn't come back.

Another bed game which caused me trouble had to do with boys. On a certain date – not Valentine's Day when we were far too busy sending cards to each other – it was the custom to write the names of all your boyfriends on scraps of paper and push these down to the end of the bed. Whichever name was nearest your heart when you woke in the morning was going to be the love of your life . . .

My problem was that I had no boyfriends. The only boys I had ever met were my cousins and two friends of my brother, a charming Swede called Bo, who had given me a book about Klee, my introduction to Art, and Julian Critchley.

Whether my brother met Critchley first at that crammer's in Maida Vale or canvassing with the Young Conservatives in Swiss Cottage, where he then lived, I can't be sure. What I do know is that Critchley became a part of my fantasy life, that it was his name that I wrote on every one of those scraps of paper and that it was, inevitably, his name which surfaced nearest to my heart.

He didn't stay there long when I actually met him, but that was forty years later and he was no longer the beautiful young man about town, pictured leaning nonchalantly on a furled umbrella – the photograph that was used on at least one of his books and the way I remembered him; he had grown fat with good living and, what was far more disillusioning, disgracefully lazy."

We commissioned him to write a book about the Tory politician, Michael Heseltine, then much in the news: the idea, which I came to regret, had been mine. We had been expecting more a squib than a tome, but an *amusing* squib. What we got, very late and on uncut computer printouts which hung from a bulldog clip on my office wall like a lot of dirty laundry, had none of his customary wit and charm.

It was of course supposed to be 'my' book but when at last it was all in, I willingly handed it and him over to someone else.

It had been tempting to give up on another commissioned book a few years previously: the lead author on this project was another lazy charmer – no longer lazy, his output is prodigious – called Craig Brown.

Craig and his two friends had come up with an idea for an anthology to be made up of those passages from the Bible, the Classics, Eng Lit which one would have giggled over at school" and they already had their title – *The Dirty Bits.*

It was a catchy title and Craig the most plausible of authors for such a project. Before long, there was a contract for this stocking-filler and we – he and the woman friend: I was never to meet the third member of the team – had some jolly meetings, pooling ideas about what subjects to cover, where to look for texts and sources of out of copyright illustrations.

All went well or seemed to go well until the delivery date came and went, jeopardising the planned Christmas publication. Now harried by us, their agent handed in a boxful of bits arranged in no kind of order.

We should have pulled out then but for whatever reason, probably too much money had changed hands or we had an American publisher, we didn't and, in desperation, I began to sort the bits myself, inventing categories as I went along: fellatio, buggery, rape, masturbation . . . I didn't keep a copy of the book and can't remember the punning section titles" I thought up alone or we thought up together when, all outraged innocence, Craig and Lesley re-emerged to help.

Needless to say, my friendship, such as it was, with these particular authors, ended as abruptly as it had begun and it was a long time before I came back to Craig-the-journalist, won over by his restaurant column in one of the colour supplements, a weekly treat," and his occasional appearances on the box, hair flying, unassumingly witty and always surprisingly sensible.

Television wasn't a part of boarding school life in the forties. Perhaps today the older girls are allowed to stay up for the Late Review or perhaps everyone has access to everything all day long but then, for our entertainment and contact with the outside world, we had to rely on the occasional Saturday film show – the films provided by Mr Cohen, who was in the film business, and whose two daughters made up a third of the school's Jewish population – and the newspapers, *The Times* and the *Express* if I remember correctly – which appeared each morning on a chest in the baronial hall where we assembled for prayers.

The films were, of course, tremendously popular and the punishment we all dreaded most was being made to miss one: anything was better than this, learning lines, cleaning shoes or even undoing knots – Matron kept the string from every parcel in her sitting room. As for the newspapers, they were something to thumb through as you passed through the hall on the way to somewhere else or waited for prayers to begin. That was on every day except one: November 29, 1947 when splashed across the front page of the *Express* was a picture of two broken-necked bodies hanging from makeshift gallows – two British soldiers murdered by the Jewish Irgun.

I had no idea of the rights and wrongs of what was happening in Palestine but I knew then and have known ever since that I and the Cohen sisters and Elise Morris and Hilary Hockley who made up the quota of Jewish pupils were different and however good we became at games, however many badges we had on our girl guide uniforms, however many films Mr Cohen lent to the school, we could never be quite like everyone else.

But this didn't stop us, or at least me, from trying. For a long time I even went to church and would probably have continued had not one of the Jewish parents complained about this and then complained again when they found that instead of going to church we had been detailed to clean the baths. This second time, a more acceptable alternative was found: we were assigned a classroom, given a heap of leaflets about UNESCO and left to our own devices. Which meant two uninterrupted daylight hours in which to read *Precious Bane* or whatever else I had found in the ramshackle library and was reading by torchlight each night under the bedcovers.

It's possible, too, that I used the time to sort and admire my growing collection of film stars. Other people traded in these but I remained constant. Richard Conte (a particular favourite of both my mother's and mine), Richard Widmark, Robert Mitchum, Gary Cooper . . . I had glossy photos of them all in the standard format that the studios then supplied.

It's hard to imagine that today's twelve year olds are still writing off for pictures of men old enough to be their fathers but I doubt that, for boarding school girls at least, the pop stars not much older than they are have wholly replaced those nearer equivalents of the real thing – the all-consuming crushes on each other, the shared dreams about choirboys, or the Lawrentian stirrings evoked by the rare male presence: in our case, the two German prisoners-of-war who worked on the abbey farm and, more particularly – for we got to see him closer up, even to touch him – one of the instructors in the local riding school.

For as long as I knew I would be seeing this jodhpured godling every week, I kept up the riding lessons which I secretly detested:

this activity which had seemed so appealing in all those horsey books was not for me: I was too heavy to rise easily in the saddle, too scared of falling off to enjoy cantering and too self-conscious for mounting and dismounting to be anything but an ordeal. Once the instructor with the thrilling presence was no longer reliably there, I gave the whole thing up.

Much harder to give up when, thanks to him, I eventually made it to Oxford, was Mr Wood – I can still think of him no other way – who, though not the first male teacher I had met in the context of a classroom, was the first with a passion for learning, a passion which set my world alight.

The room in which we met was at the top of several flights of stairs in a narrow terraced house in Maida Vale. The house didn't look like a school and the room itself was under-furnished and dingy. But Queen's College with its imposing façade had proved barren of the intellectual excitement which I was to find here, for the first and last time.

It's impossible to know whether had this teacher been more Mr Casaubon than Ted Hughes he would have had the same effect. As it was, the combination of sexual attraction and intellectual passion proved the headiest mixture and those three months during which I and Wendy – my best friend then and my best friend still – spent several hours a day alone with this ill-paid, unqualified teacher, remain the high point of my student life.

It was from him that I first heard of *The Waste Land* which, he told us in passing, he had carried with him throughout the war: like my 'one-legged Jewish poet' (but this is another story) he had been on the beaches at Anzio. It was here that we were taught to look up from books: one day, in exasperation at the narrowness of our vision, he had sent us off to see Box Hill – I suppose we had been reading Jane Austen – for ourselves.

It was here, at Eaton and Wallis (both Mr Eaton and Mr Wallis could be encountered on the stairs) that I learned how to read. But not well enough to impress them at Oxford. I took the entrance exam and failed. So did Wendy, later to get one of the few firsts in her year at UCL. But, unlike her, having given up maths long before and thus failed to matriculate, I had no option but to try again. Oxford and Cambridge, with their patrician scorn for the standard requirements, were the only English universities to which I could apply.

And this time I got closer. I was called for an interview about which I remember nothing but the way in which Helen Gardner, who received us one by one in her sunny, chintz-filled room overlooking the river, had pinned down my paper on the floor with her foot. I remember, too, the tone of her voice as she asked – 'Eton and WHO . . . ?'

It wasn't, of course, unusual for girls to go to crammers but there was a hierarchy even among these and mine didn't rate very high. In fact, it didn't rate at all, and the College probably prided itself on its decision to let me in in spite of this. To let me in, that is, on condition that I re-sat the Latin paper for in my despairing attempt to translate the unseen I had mistaken the subject of the passage – either it was a banquet and I had thought it was a battle, or the other way round – and, like someone who has their fingers on the wrong keys of the typewriter, I got everything wrong from beginning to end.

That passage of Horace cost me and my parents dear. Back at the wrong Eton, I spent the next six months doing nothing but Latin unseens knowing the offer of a place could still be withdrawn. But next time round, instead of the fiendish Horace, it was Caesar. All the words were familiar and recognisable for what they were: verbs behaving like verbs and nouns like nouns. Primed, as I had been, for something more difficult it was the plainest of plain sailing and nothing now stood between me and the culmination of my dream. Nothing, that is, but the Day of Atonement.

By some quirk of fate in that year, and perhaps in others since, the first day of the autumn term was also the Day of Atonement, the one day in the year that can make even the most lapsed of Jews uneasy.

The dream of which the first seeds had been planted by my cousins, one now an Italian Zionist, the other in wifely thrall to an orthodox husband, got off to a shaky start.

There were three possibilities: I could arrive after nightfall, set out the next day, or be rational – how observant was I, after all? – and tough it out. Which is what I did, arriving in Oxford for this second time with God looking disapprovingly over my shoulder.

I have wondered since whether anyone in the administration had been aware of this unhappy conjunction: presumably, the seriously orthodox did stay at home but, for the rest of us, whether we had fasted or not, the day of our arrival was shadowed by guilt.

A different kind of shadow was cast by the first sight of my 'digs'. The ugly Victorian house stood on a corner, half a mile or more up the Iffley Road, and my view for the next year was to be of that nondescript side street, up which I looked from my attic window. Where were the Dreaming Spires? I was ready to weep.

I am still surprised that so many of us were lodged out in our first year. Wouldn't it have been kinder to have all the fledglings under one roof? But, of course, we made out, and in due course we Iffley-roaders did better than that. Those of us who didn't already know how (I was one of them: bicycles and dogs among the deprivations of my flat-dwelling childhood) learnt to ride bikes; and most of us learned how to drink.

The drinking took me completely by surprise. At home we had a glossy walnut cocktail cabinet that lit up inside when you opened the doors, but it was opened very seldom: my parents were social drinkers only and social life – the night clubs, the balls, the evenings with friends – had ended with the war. This was something else.

On my very first day which is, I suppose, why I remember it so

well, I was hi-jacked at some college gathering – willingly hi-jacked
– by another first-year student, but one who seemed completely at
home, and taken to a house still further up the Iffley Road than mine
where her large, untidy room – it looked as though she had lived
there for years – was full of cigarette smoke, beer cans and empty
bottles.

Apparently, a party had been going on but with one exception, a
startlingly attractive stick-thin blonde who, I learnt, lived in the same
house, the guests had left. But not for good. I had hardly begun on
my first mug of beer when the door opened and in came the stick-
thin girl's boyfriend, an amiable rugby-playing hunk, whose capacity
for drink more than matched that of the two St Hilda-ites of whom
one turned out to be one of that year's scholars. Which meant she
was entitled to wear a longish gown with folds. The rest of us had
little backward-looking tabards. Both appeared to be made out of
blackout curtains.

It was, of course, part and parcel of my lack of experience – or
sophistication – that I was surprised that this excitingly dissolute
household should harbour two of the year's brightest students. And
it was this liveliness which kept me with one foot in their camp even
after everyone realised I was never going to rate as a drinker.

Luckily I wasn't the only first-year student at St Hilda's who was relatively green. Most of us – the Arts students, anyway, I never knew
the Scientists – had come straight from fairly conventional schools
and homes, the one post boarding-school adventure likely to have
been au pairing in France or Switzerland with families much like our
own. But there were a few grammar-school girls, for the most part
better educated than the rest of us, and it was with one of these I
came nearest to finding the kind of excitement I had expected to be
a part of everyday student life.

Christine, who lived in the same house as me, was ready to talk
about poetry or any other of the subjects which were generally

avoided as being embarrassingly serious. It wasn't 'cool' – not a fifties word but the word that best fits – to show an interest in, much less enthusiasm for, 'things of the mind', and my other lasting friendships from that time were built not on shared intellectual excitement but on the no less precious stream of confidences about parents, boys, the whole gamut of our late-adolescent emotional lives.

Those talks with Christine, most often in front of the gas fire in my attic room, under the eaves which the landlady had allowed me to paint black, were a kind of last fling and I was to miss her when, pregnant by the boy back home – they are together still – she left to have the baby and with her went the only person who could talk unselfconsciously about real subjects and had experienced what most of the rest of us could still only dream of, which was real and enduring love.

Another gas fire that should have witnessed scenes of intellectual excitement belonged to the young woman who had been appointed my tutor. She lived in a room in a boarding house much like ours and so colourless were our meetings that I can remember nothing of what took place. There must have been an Eng Lit content of those first year exams for which we mugged up (no other word for it) one play of Sophocles, in translation, one book of Virgil, in Latin, one play of Racine's, in French, and a fair bit of Anglo-Saxon, but I can't remember what it was. We must have talked about something but so desultory was the exchange that it left no mark.

This, then, was my first taste of those one-to-one sessions on which Oxford then prided itself and it was only years later when I had friends who had themselves been employed as graduate student teachers that I understood that for her I had probably been no more than an ill-paid interruption, her bicycle at the ready for her return to the library, her mind still focused on the footnote destined to throw light on whatever murky by-way she was trawling for her PhD. And so unengaged was she as a teacher that I never even learnt who or what it was that interested her.

It was unimaginable that however heavy the syllabus or however close the coming exams, our Mr Wood would not have found time to talk about whatever had newly engaged his interest. As often as not, it would be a re-reading of a familiar classic or a contemporary poet, newly discovered, but it could also be that he had found a way to get his two-year-old son to drink his milk or had discovered a faster way of completing some household chore . . . That he was a widower and rumoured to have been a Jesuit priest in some earlier life did nothing to dampen our ardour.

We were intoxicated by the inclusiveness of his vision, and now here I was, in Oxford, being taught by someone entirely without passion. Passionless to better effect was someone else I would find myself alone with for an hour a week some fifteen years later: so discreet was Dr Heaton, so unimposing, that I did not even know what 'school' he belonged to – a triumph of discretion when most psychiatrists' patients would reveal within seconds what banner they were marching under. It was only much later, when I read a book of his, as cool and cerebral as its author, that I found he was what is called a phenomenologist. More Jung than Freud but not exactly either.

It was also much later that I saw him for the first time outside the small, windowless room in Wimpole Street and fully realised that this person who had seemed to exist just for me had a life of his own. He was walking on the Heath, in bright sunshine, with a woman who was, perhaps, his wife. I had never met or spoken to her; at the time, I resented even the shadowy figure of the previous patient I would see just minutes before Dr Heaton would appear or half-appear – he would, appropriately enough, stick just his head round the door – to summon me. The other people in that spacious waiting room, summoned by a uniformed nurse, didn't bother me: we weren't in competition . . .

On the few occasions I had rung him at his home – he had given me the number so I could call him, if I needed to, when I went into labour – it had always been he who had answered; as he did when, at his suggestion," I had taken LSD and rang to say Help! It isn't working . . . But, of course, it did, and soon I had no need of him or anyone else.

Like my husband whose LSD trips I had baby-sat in the past – sugar lumps and blotting paper had begun to circulate in the fifties – Dr Heaton neither looked nor behaved like a tearaway and though, from time to time, I would have been glad of a more comforting presence, less devoid of human warmth, I knew that this reserve was a strength and would serve, as emotional bluster and psycho-babble would not, to combat the rationality of my philosopher husband who could argue with unanswerable logic that black was white.

But my husband, that 'emotional caveman' whom I could live neither with nor without, was still then to come. It was well into that first term that we met, by which time my disappointment with the teaching at this centre of learning had been altogether eclipsed by my despair about boys. Where were they all? How were we supposed to meet them when we spent so much of our time between St Hilda's, on the edge of Oxford proper, and the Iffley Road beyond it? The answer then, as now, was Join Something.

In later life I would try and persuade middle-aged friends left on their own to do what I would do: join the Ramblers, lick envelopes for the Labour Party, sign up for the U3A . . . Then, I joined the poetry society and it was at one of their meetings that I first met M and, joy of joys, he walked me back across the bridge which linked his college with mine and which became as familiar as the Iffley Road which took me back, each night, to my room.

With that out of the way – we remained together, on and off, for the next fifteen years – other things fell into place. Prelims came and went and with them French, Latin and 'Greek' disappeared out of our lives, leaving two years and a bit in which we had nothing to do but read. There were no interruptions beyond the weekly essay, read aloud to one's tutor, no longer now the young woman with nothing to say but Anne Elliott, a long-time member of St Hilda's who, though unduly mild in her responses," never made you feel she wished she was somewhere else.

And so, in a backwards kind of way, the system began to work. Miss Elliott didn't inspire but neither did she dampen and, with minimal hurry or direction, we were let loose on 'the canon'. While Wendy, a year ahead of me in London, was attending obligatory lectures and reading the whole of *Beowulf* (curiously, we read only half) as well as Dickens, Joyce and James, we, with a syllabus that ended" in 1823, had time to give a whole term to a single writer, a luxury I appreciate even more in retrospect than I did at the time.

Of course, this traditional cut-off point did have its 'downside'. It was easy enough to catch up on the novels we had missed but I have never felt comfortable with 'modern' poetry, and the rest of *Beowulf*, as well, remains un-read. Which it shouldn't have because the Anglo-Saxon poets, unlike today's, talked a language I could understand.

Perhaps this liking I still have for *The Seafarer* and *The Dream of the Rood* had at least something to do with the way they were taught. I had never been good at languages and here was yet another but I was no more aware of having to learn it than of having learnt to speak. Dorothy Whitelock, who had lived with these poets and chroniclers all her life – like Anne Elliott and Helen Gardner, she was unmarried – could no longer see that these familiar and much loved texts might present difficulties and somehow, in memory at least, they didn't.

A frail, white-haired old lady whose scholarship was unsurpassed and was to take her on to a professorship at Cambridge (suggesting she couldn't have been quite as old as we thought), her reputation as a scholar was much enhanced, for us, by the tantalising rumour that the ring she always wore on her left hand had been given her by Rupert Brooke . . .

If Helen Gardner had any rings, she would surely have had to buy them for herself; though, perhaps not, for it was said she behaved quite differently with the men students from the way she did with us. By far the most forceful of the St Hilda's trio and the most widely known, for only she of the three had associated with a living poet, her classes on the metaphysicals (T. S. Eliot, of course, was still out of bounds) were a weekly war zone. Sarcasm was her weapon and pleasure in humiliation her strength.

If she ever fixed on me, I have managed to forget it. What I do remember and what perhaps gave me strength, was the view – for she would sit with her legs wide apart – of her knicker-covered thighs. Years later, I worked on a little book called *How to Do Well in Music Exams* whose author, Rudolph Sabor, an examiner himself as well as a Wagner fanatic whose uncommissioned translation" of *Götterdämmerung* was to be published to great acclaim, advised children to banish their nerves by imagining their examiner in his underwear . . .

Of course, being taught by Helen Gardner was considered a privilege. So was being at Oxford. But the nature of the privilege became clear only later, when looking for jobs.

✍ 4 ✍

Business Girl

F OR ALL THE TIME I worked at Deutsch, a job I had found
through someone I had known at Oxford, the two pillars of
the firm were Diana Athill (Lady Margaret Hall) and Pamela Royds
(St Hugh's) and, for more than thirty years, the three of us, for I
(St Hilda's) became Queen of the Slush Pile, were responsible for a
lot of what we published.

The other editors who came and went had also, with a few exceptions, been to Oxford or Cambridge. So had many of the secretaries of whom one of the last produced her own Oxford novel
while still working with us.

Uncertain Terms still pleases me but Clare – Clare Chambers –
three children and four novels later, has disowned her firstborn
book and it remains the only one that her present publisher has no
plans to re-issue. But, at the time, apart from an 'outside reader' who
didn't think that the writer had the makings of a novelist – a report
I withheld – everyone took its side and, after much agonising –
would she do better to try and find another publisher or should we
publish her ourselves – it was decided to go ahead.

And, so it was that, a year or two later, I found myself in Oxford
with a couple of hours to spare before the reading Penguin had
organised for Clare in one of the newer bookshops.

It was the first time for years that I had been back to Oxford,
and, as luck would have it, a perfect summer's day. I wandered down

the High Street and over Magdalen Bridge. First, to walk round the new buildings in the grounds of St Hilda's, reports of whose progress had monopolised the alumni news for a very long time. Then, to dip into Magdalen where I had once been free to come and go but now, Closed to Visitors, dared venture no further than the near end of the perfectly rolled grass which stretched down from the building where thirty years before I had spent the occasional illicit night . . .

The sight of a group of students drinking on the lawn in the sunshine seemed unreal. Could such privilege really exist? Had it always been like this? What I found nauseating now, whether because forever excluded or, as I would prefer to think, because more politically aware in late middle age than I had been as a student, had not then worried me a jot.

Even if the teaching had been disappointing much else was not. And even among the teachers there were those who could be recalled with pleasure: the few classes with Mrs Ing in her pretty little house in Holywell; the fewer sessions still – if only we had been farmed out more – with a Mrs Bednarowska on the other side of town. Years later, who from I can't imagine, I heard that Mrs Bed had characterised a young colleague of mine – yet another Oxford graduate – as having 'a clear but simple mind', an apt description of this otherwise dependable young woman who had no time for American fiction because it wasn't written in 'proper English'."

Mrs Bednarowska also stays in mind because it was just as I had settled to an essay on Malory for her class the next day that I was interrupted by the second-year student in the room next to mine – being third year myself I hardly knew her – who announced that she had taken an overdose. For the next hour or however long it took me to decide it was more important to get help than to respect her wishes, the *Morte d'Arthur* receded beyond vanishing point. But, later that evening, armed though I was with a letter from my 'moral tutor', I came back to my desk in that low-ceilinged room with its one picture – a Matisse of a faceless woman" which is still one of my favourite paintings – and got the essay written.

Had it been summer then and earlier in the evening, I might have abandoned Malory and crossed the bridge to look for M and had he not been there (do students now use mobile phones instead of their feet?) taken a turn in the Botanical Gardens that lay on the river between his college and mine. There is no place more consoling and it was to these gardens I now repaired to spend the time that remained before the reading at Waterstones began. Disappointingly, and I don't imagine it is at her insistence, the biographical note re-cycled on all Clare Chambers' books describes her as having been an editor when the novel was published. It is so much more remarkable that she was still – just back from a year in New Zealand and in her first job – a secretary, thus fulfilling the dream of every Eng Lit graduate who had entered publishing by this same route, manifestly set on getting a 'proper' job but secretly hoping to go even further than that, to be published rather than to publish.

My own fantasies along these lines didn't last long. In a two-month break between jobs, supported by my husband, still then working in computers, I had all the time in the world to get on with the novel I had started while going out to work every day. But, if anything, the pace got slower. I spent much of every morning looking out of one of the three windows in our triangular living room. The view no longer exists. The little island of dilapidated shops above one of which we lived (the slum landlord was a patient of my doctor father-in-law) was pulled down long ago. Even 10 Rillington Place, just up the road, has been spruced up – the multiple murders painted over – to fit the gentrified landscape.

It is media folk, apparently, who now live round Latimer Road – 'so convenient for Lime Grove' – where the Public Baths used to be used for having baths and doing the laundry.

One of the shops included in our view sold junk and there, straight off the pavement and for five pounds, I bought our first television set. I carried it back across the street, up the stairs that smelt of rotting vegetables – detritus from the greengrocer's below – and dropped it on the nearest stretch of kitchen floor where it stayed until, and even after, we moved on.

I had already been going to the cinema most afternoons. Now there was this added distraction. The little Olivetti typewriter my mother had saved up to buy me" had very few miles on it when I put the fifty or so pages of manuscript back in their grey marbled folder and, with more relief than regret, went out to earn some money.

I half realised then that nothing I wrote would ever please me and came to know this for certain when, as a first reader, I would come across unnervingly similar efforts in that sensitive-autobiographical vein.

What made Clare's first novel different was that it wasn't sensitive or autobiographical and that it made you laugh, her cleverness (though even she had been seduced by those French invaders of the Eng Lit scene Derrida, Deleuze and Lacan") already to be seen in those laconic titles which always mean more than one thing.

Clare was not only a better novelist than me; she was also, to begin with at least, a better secretary. Of course, she had the advantage of having typed out a whole novel before she arrived in an office. I, on the other hand, graduate of a special speeded-up course for graduates, was to learn on the job. Luckily, I was quite good at the shorthand, which my employer could actually see me at, and still enjoy those ingenious squiggles though I have had no use for them for years. But learning to type was no fun at all. Had Methuen, my first employer, given me a test at the interview, I would almost certainly have failed.

But that wasn't their style. I didn't have to lie about my speeds because I wasn't asked. What I remember about the interview was the charm of the somewhat grizzled fifty year old and his concern that the job would seem a come-down and that I would soon be bored. But how much less of a come-down than the windowless factory where I could have gone to work for a company making cartoon films or the advertising agency in Park Lane where the receptionists looked as though they had stepped out of their own ads.

It wasn't hard to convince him that I really wanted the job, for the moment I found myself in that large, plain reception room, full of books, I knew I had come home.

And these weren't just any books. The man I was to work for looked after the Arden Shakespeare. Another of his charges was a book on Greek vase painting that was something like eighteen years overdue. This fazed him no more than Anne Elliott's failure to produce a book had fazed the Oxford Establishment. Here was a regard for quality and, more important still, a pace that suited me down to the ground.

Which makes the place sound fusty, which it wasn't. Not only was the first Tintin just about to come out – translated by two editors whose rooms opened off mine or, rather, ours, for it was shared with one sweet young girl who was soon to leave for a job in Buckingham Palace, and a series of temps, one of whom became a lifelong friend – but there were far from fusty goings-on in the academic wing.

My boss was having an affair. I had, inadvertently, opened a letter from his mistress. What was I to do with it? Spread it out in front of him with all his other mail? Put it back in its envelope? Throw it away? What would Mrs Hoster have advised?" Not knowing the correct etiquette, I decided on the second option, and from then on each time one of those unmistakable envelopes arrived in his post, I would put it on his desk, unopened, and there it often remained, unopened, for days at a time. Although I knew he had a wife and children and that this woman with the florid handwriting had no business interfering in their lives, I found myself annoyed on her behalf as I am now when my partner leaves his parents' letters aside as my son, no doubt, does mine, and I would move them back to the top of the pile.

Who knows how long this game would have continued had I not gone down with jaundice – caught, my mother was convinced, from the goat-hair rug I had brought back from visiting Sevin, recently married, in Turkey. So, just as, in time-honoured fashion, I was beginning to get somewhere – for one of the editors had broken a leg on a skiing trip – I had to go into hospital myself and give the job up.

But in the nine months I had been at Methuen, nine months which had begun just before Christmas for which, flatteringly, my boss had given me not a box of fancy soap but a copy of *Resurrection*, a good deal had happened.

I knew for certain that however difficult it was going to be to get a 'proper job' in publishing, that was what I wanted, and, though this hadn't been one of the jobs entrusted to me when that editor broke his leg, I had read my first manuscript.

Among the younger men in the building was a sales rep with an unusual interest in books and a passion for films. In his lunch hour he would hang around our office, and though the main attraction was the new temp whose dusty black off-the-shoulder outfits and dark-skinned boyish looks turned every head – a kind of full-sized Mowgli – it was me he asked out. And with my husband-to-be still in Oxford and David, for the time being at least, wanting nothing but company, we spent some pleasant evenings together.

But though it was to me he talked about his home life – the parents he still lived with in south London, his aunties and uncles – and to me that he gave a ticket to *My Fair Lady* when these were hard to get, it was to Mowgli that he confided his manuscript.

Unlike me, she was a fellow writer. Only twenty-two years old but with one marriage and countless affairs behind her – I listened wide-eyed" to tales of encounters with Paul Johnson who had slapped her in the face on a Paris street when she had turned him down, of Alfred Chester who had helped get her first story published, of the well-known television film director whose lover she had been for several years – she had now finished with Life – Been There, Done That could have been coined for her – and was ready to concentrate all her forces on the novel she had begun when she was fourteen years old and never abandoned.

The distance which must have provoked her many lovers was always there, her fictional world more real to her and more engaging than anything that could happen in bed or anywhere else.

To both of us, David seemed too mild a person to have produced anything very interesting but, one had to hand it to him, he had actually finished *his* novel – written, he told us, in hotel rooms on the continent – and Carol, for that was Mowgli's name, took it home to read.

Between one and two next morning, the phone rang. She had just come to the last page of the most sexually explicit novel she had ever read.

Set in Amsterdam, one of the cities that David visited most often as a rep, and picaresque in form, it described a series of homosexual encounters in such graphic detail that not till Edmund White's *States of Desire*, more than thirty years later, was I to read anything like it.

I don't remember what we said to him about his manuscript nor whether the tenor of our outings to the cinema changed. Within a short time David Shipman had disappeared out of our lives" and we out of his: Mowgli to a stone cottage on the Pembrokeshire coast where she was to live for seven years, the first few with a new husband and the rest with a herd of goats for the billiest of whom she had designed a contraceptive belt, much like a masonic apron, later simplified to a pair of child's knickers when our randy English mongrel couldn't be kept off her majestic English sheepdog. And, of course, she had her novel."

Best described as a *roman fleuve* and set, at least in its opening volumes, in pre-war Vienna, there was nothing about it – philosophical in tone, embracing all of recent history as its subject, unashamedly old-fashioned in its handling of character and attention to the land-scapes they moved in – to prepare you for its author.

But then, as I was to find out, very few writers resemble their work and first meetings were often surprising. I remember arriving in reception to fetch someone I had imagined to be a retired civil servant and finding a young lad with a crew cut and bitten nails. That was a *nice* surprise, unlike the author of a rollicking first novel who turned out to be a belligerent middle-aged soak. Least expected was to find the author of two spine-chilling novels, awash with sexual perversity, to be a happily married man of a most sociable disposition.

It was an unwritten rule, like not poaching each other's authors, and one that was for the most part scrupulously observed: first you read the work, then you met the writer. And it was the right way round for, this way, like the jury in a court of law kept ignorant of the defendant's past, the reader comes to the work free of pre-conceptions for name and address alone do not give away the writer's colour, nor his age, nor what he sounds or looks like. None of which should matter but all of which now do. Is he or she too old to be 'on-going'? Luckily, Diana Athill has pretty well spiked that one." Could he or she grab attention with their looks? Could one say to the stony-faced salesmen that here was another Candia McWilliam or Zadie Smith . . . ?

But these considerations were not part of the steady rhythm of life in Essex Street where almost every title on the academic list had been commissioned, and it was not until a year or more later, when I went to work for Anthony Blond, that I got to be the first to see whatever treasures or rubbish the postman brought.

In those months between, once the jaundice which still makes my blood unbankable had receded, determined not to take another secretarial job now that I had checked an index and read a few galleys, I would do what Mowgli had done and go out temping.

Just as you are likely to come across more colourful people teaching at the polys than at the older universities, for their number won't include the career-minded and will include the drop-outs who wake up later than most to the need for a regular income, so the temps compared favourably with the regular secretaries for they numbered among them the out-of-work actresses, the round-the-world travellers and, of course, the aspiring writers.

But the jobs, with a few exceptions, like the homely little fireworks company, were soul-destroying. To type the same letter twenty times is one thing: to have the same letter dictated twenty times is another.

In holiday jobs, which could be hard to come by, I had put up with a lot worse but with temping, in those days, you could walk out of a job you didn't like and know that, by the next morning, the agency would have found you something else.

I would have liked to walk out of Harrods and had I not got this much sought-after holiday job through the good offices of yet another Oxford friend, whose father was high in the Harrods hierarchy, they would probably have got rid of me. As it was, unable to behave as though THE CUSTOMER IS ALWAYS RIGHT (this admonition was pasted up on the walls of the surprisingly scruffy staff quarters), I was often in trouble and the permanent staff who resented every penny of commission that found its way into the pockets of the Christmas staff, did nothing to help.

At the end of the first week, I was moved off Leather Goods, where trade had been brisk, to Stationery, where it was less so, and then to Typewriters where the permanent staff made sure I never got to sell a machine. So, while my Oxford friend was selling gift-wrapped Parker pen sets to one person after another – the regular salespeople could hardly cut her out when customers were queuing up to be served – I was standing around (we were not allowed to sit) waiting for the oddball who had waited till Christmas to run out of typewriter ribbons.

But it had not always been thus: that is to say, there had been no complaints when I had worked the previous Easter in a Lyons· Tea Shop. Here, the downtrodden customers waited patiently while Gillie or I (she, another Oxford friend, alas, long dead but then – white-skinned, grey-eyed – a creature of patrician beauty) juggled the four teapots under the four rotating spouts and ordered up the baked beans and chips from the subterranean kitchen.

There, far from Knightsbridge, no one was either rude or unreasonably demanding and though the family who owned Lyons were probably as rich if not richer than whoever owned Harrods, the penny-pinching[*] common to both seemed less offensive at the tatty end of Oxford Street than in that giant edifice in the Brompton Road, a few doors away from which I was to have another and very different catering experience.

The Sombrero was a restaurant cum coffee bar, busy all day with Knightsbridge shoppers and staffed, for the few weeks I worked there, almost exclusively by good-looking, hard-working Australians and New Zealanders most of whom were whisked off several evenings a week to work in some other establishment owned by the proprietor. Too tired to chat at the end of our self-imposed double shifts – the basic catering wage was something like £4 a week so that tips, often generous and always shared, were all-important – I never found out what went on in this other place and have always slightly regretted not being picked for the night team.

But we had our excitements too. The most dramatic was the arrest of a pleasant young man who came in every morning for a coffee at the bar and then moved on to a table round the corner for lunch after which he presented the coffee chit only at the till when he left. He had been a good tipper and we were sorry to see him go. Now the system was changed but what Management couldn't control, was what went on in the kitchen. They undoubtedly ordered the re-vamping of yesterday's goods – the dusting of elderly strudels with icing sugar was one of my favourite jobs – but they wouldn't have been pleased to see the disgruntled cook spit into the chilli sauce and would probably have been as horrified as we were to realise, as he slapped the uncooked beef rissole from hand to hand, where else his hands had been. Luckily for the customers, not many of them ordered Beef Tartare but Chilli con Carne was the most popular dish on the menu . . .

The Sombrero may still have been there when I found myself back in SW1 a few months later, but now I seldom ventured north of Sloane Square.

Anthony Blond Limited – the firm had been going for about two years at the time – was housed in a 12 by 20ish extension at the back of a charming little terraced house – all white stucco and window boxes – in Chester Row. And Chester Row was three minutes' walk from Sloane Square and Sloane Square was the nearest post office which meant that I visited it at least once a day during the two years I worked for Anthony Blond as his 24-year-old Girl Friday.

I had been determined not to take another secretarial job but the agency where I was hopefully registered as Editorial Assistant sent me no other kind and something about this particular job description – it had probably been written by Anthony himself – made me decide to go for an interview. And at the interview in this room which felt not the least bit like an office, I fell in love with an oil painting, about five feet high, which hung on the wall above what would be my desk. And it was this which decided me. I took the job. But by the time I started, a week or two later, the picture had gone. Apparently it had been lent to an exhibition; certainly it never reappeared on my wall. In fact, I was never to see it again. But, there I now was and there I stayed, just as when meeting R the other day in the foyer of our local Odeon to see *The Man Who Wasn't There* and finding it wasn't, we made do with something else.

The Philip Sutton cascade of blossoms wasn't the only painting in Chester Row which was to make things happen, or not happen, in real life. Well into my time there, Anthony, newly separated from

Anthony Blond by Bryan Kneale

his wife, had advertised for a housekeeper and hadn't returned from some outing when one of the applicants arrived.

I took this sturdy-looking lady, dressed all in black, into the nearest room, and asked her to wait. But on learning that the glowering presence in the picture on the far wall was her potential employer she turned and fled. And, it's true that in that Bryan Kneale portrait" Anthony did look alarmingly pugnacious. But the thick black hair, low brow and stumpy boxer's nose were offset, in real life, not only by his small stature (she would have found she was considerably bigger than he was) but also by his behaviour.

Of my three long-term employers, all of them, now I think of it, Jewish, he is the only one I remember with affection. He was amusing and generous and, to my surprise, for I wouldn't have thought he could keep still (or be alone) long enough, he was to write a novel of his own.

Set in England, among the Anglo-Jewish gentry to which he belonged, the novel was fun even if you couldn't match the characters up with their real-life counterparts who surely existed for Anthony was a scion of the Marks & Spencer's Sieffs and knew their moneyed, fox-hunting world as well as Henry Roth had known the world of the penniless Jewish immigrant in New York to which he belonged. For power and intensity, *Call It Sleep*" wins hands down, but *Family Business* scores high as entertainment which is fitting because, in spite of the drudgery – the packing and posting of parcels, the entering and exiting of manuscripts, the typing of lists and schedules (these were required by Mr Ranns the Printer and Mr Bowles the Blockmaker, the professionals who serviced us) – those two years were in some ways the jolliest as well as the most instructive of my 'career'.

Left on my own for days at a time, I learnt to do everything or, at least, to get it done and, even when Anthony was away, there was a steady stream of visitors: not just Mr Ranns and Mr Bowles, without whom the whole enterprise would have ground to a halt, but those author-cum-friends of his who would drop in unannounced to leave a battered suitcase of erotica to be returned to the London Library, to collect a cheque (this was usually Simon Raven), to give a progress report on their books-in-production, to collect or return a set of proofs . . .

Simon Raven was the most frequent visitor. A delightfully courteous presence, whose *Feathers of Death* had come out the year before, he was now working, supported by Anthony, on his second novel. Also reliably frequent were the visits of Hugh Thomas, a loquacious, gap-toothed young man with curly hair whose monumental history of the Spanish Civil War was still to come; Anthony Heckstall-Smith of whom I remember nothing but that he seemed very English-gentleman (could have stepped straight from the pages of *The Music of Time*) and a creepy character called Gerald Hamilton whom I connect, perhaps falsely, with the Mr Norris of *Mr Norris Changes Trains*.

And then there was Mrs Blond, Anthony's mother, who I confuse in memory with Mrs Fainlight, Harry's mother – both were short, dark and motherly – who would check on the plants in the yard and do things in the kitchen. But it was to me not her, for she lived in Cheshire and her visits were relatively rare, that it was left to perform another semi-domestic chore. This was to start up Anthony's car on winter mornings: to start up but not, of course, to drive (anyway, I didn't know how) the silver-grey Bentley which stretched the full frontage of the house.

The way Mrs Blond busied herself about the house after the final departure of young Mrs Blond, another drama for which no secretarial college could have prepared you, was what I was used to at this time when I still took it for granted that all mothers were good. My own, not long before, after a similar foray in our triangular kitchen had left a warning note on the table: MOUS IN TOSTER . . . I would never have thought to clean *inside* a toaster myself and have often wondered since, Does every generation get less houseproud than the last?

It was an appliance, too, which threw me briefly together with Anthony's mostly invisible wife. Hearing shrieks from the kitchen, I had run downstairs to find Charlotte and the room spattered with whatever it was she was mixing in her new mixer when the lid flew off. Though a member of one of the great intellectual dynasties, Charlotte was no brain box. But she was pale and pretty in a wispy kind of way – just the sort of tall, classy English girl a short, dark, Jewish boy would fall for. She was also, I had been told, a wonderful cook. No doubt their marriage, like most marriages, began in a blaze of happiness but by the time I arrived on the scene, it had become, as mine would do, distinctly rocky.

One of the reasons could have been Anthony's sperm count. Certainly, there was much play with little bottles he brought back from visits to the doctor and kept in the drawer of his desk. He was no more discreet about these than about anything else and though he never actually talked to me about what they were for, he did talk to others with me in the room, and it was no great surprise when Charlotte, like the painting, disappeared for good.

Not too long ago there was a story in the paper about a cat which the CIA had spent millions of dollars on, fitting it out with some internal listening device. A secretary – the right kind of secretary – could be just as invisible and less likely to get run over in her lunch hour which was, apparently, that poor, mistreated animal's fate. Dead then, but not demeaned. Soppy as we are about animals in our household, ruled for years at a time by the needs of geriatric pets, we don't actually think them capable of human emotions and the indignities which every 'personal secretary' has to put up with are of an all too human kind; for, however well treated, she is actually a servant. Like the wife who puts a meal that has taken two hours to prepare in front of her husband to see it vanish, without comment, in four minutes flat, she is essential to his well-being but he either doesn't know it or prefers to ignore it: probably the latter, given the speed with which abandoned husbands take up with someone else or follow their wives to their graves.

In much the same way are employers blind to how much they and their staff depend on their secretaries. Thus it was that as the firm of Deutsch went into what we then took to be its final decline,″ and there were fewer and fewer secretaries in the building, the rest of us found ourselves left to do their invisible work. Wrestling with addresses, searching for jiffy bags, trying to keep on top of mountains of filing, I would look up at the old and cherished cartoon on the pinboard above my desk, showing Christ walking serenely on the waters while, underneath him, below the surface of the sea, is a woman, arms extended, holding him up.

The cartoon was one of a collection brought in, on spec, by the artist, a young woman called Rhianna Duncan. She had arrived at reception and asked if anyone had time to look at her work and, following the custom of our legendary children's book editor, Pamela Royds, who never turned anyone away, I asked her to come down. Down, because at this time I was working in the basement which, when I started at Deutsch in the early sixties, had been occupied by a firm of rat-catchers and which R, among others, did not think a fit place to work. But, unpoliticised as we were and committed to what we were doing, none of us complained and so it was that by artificial light in a low-ceilinged room with one barred window giving onto a well – good training ground for the Verminex recruits – I met Rhianna and looked at her work which included, though she would not have thought to show it, the artwork for a children's book.″ This she was taking back home with her, in its unopened package, having been turned away at the door by two well-known publishers of children's books who would not consider anything which did not reach them through an agent.

At Anthony Blond's, too, we looked at anything and everything. This was not a matter of principle, though with me it became one, but because it is the privilege of the big, high-spending publishers only, who the agents keep constantly fed, to turn up their noses at X from Croydon or Y from Newton Abbott who have, quite possibly, never heard of literary agents: a doubtful privilege which keeps these publishers from the source, as though tap water were preferable to the mountain stream.

Of course, it goes without saying that most tap water is at least drinkable and not all mountain streams are safe in these days when they share the remotest spots with stations pumping out nuclear waste: one of the saddest sights, the glow of Sellafield looking back from Wastwater, or the leaflet inviting you to visit the power station lying beside another leaflet – in the reception area of one of the most secluded inns in the Lake District – reminding you that Ruskin, too, lived not far away . . .

Neither Ruskin (of whom we were to publish an abstract at Deutsch) nor a treatise on the pros and cons of nuclear power figured on Anthony's list but they could have done, for there was nothing homogeneous about it, neither in its range of subject nor the level of its brow. In one startling instance, a history of the Royal College of Surgeons shared a spread in the catalogue with a version, I suppose a novelisation, of *Emergency Ward 10*, one of the most popular early TV soaps.

At its best, the list reflected Anthony's natural taste but it was bumped out, as was the list at Deutsch, with what was available, including the offerings of friends of whom Tessa Diamond, one of the hospital drama authors, could well have been one. A niece of Rae Menell, my sandwich-box aunt, Tessa lived near by in one of those leafy Knightsbridge squares where I found myself not long ago as I walked these unfamiliar streets, looking for Bonham's.

I was there because I had decided to sell the one piece of my mother's jewellery which would bring in enough for my brother's half share to pay for some essential repairs to his house. I knew this particular ring, because of the size of its stone, was worth more than all the others, for I had taken them to be valued soon after my mother's death. I had thought to insure them until I learnt what that would cost and so for the next twenty years they rested, in greying scraps of tissue paper, at the bottom of a jar of breadcrumbs.

They are not there now. One of them is who knows where – the auction houses give little away – the others safely in the bank. I say this to be sure that no one goes looking. Which would be the reverse of what happened, or didn't happen, when in the Preface to a new edition of his first book, R recalled having written it when he was out of work and added disarmingly, I thought, that he was out of work still. A muted plea which, fifteen years on, has still to bear a single fruit . . .

My trip to Bonham's *did* eventually bear fruit but, with hindsight, I would have done better – for the transaction would have taken minutes not months – to sell the ring in the little shop in Hatton Garden which had offered me, in cash, exactly what I was to get from Bonham's once they had deducted X for advertising, Y for their commission, etc. etc.

Of course no one at Bonham's or Christie's or Sotheby's, those other palaces of greed, had actually pretended the diamond was glass which is what one of the Hatton Garden merchants told me, but they hadn't advised me either, as another of the Hatton Garden shops did, that I would do better to sell the gold coins I had with me (legacy of my Triestian aunt) to the bullion house down the road rather than to them.

I am surprised now that I fell for the glitz of Knightsbridge and didn't go straight back to the little jeweller in Clerkenwell with the loaded canvas holster still under my arm. But, thinking back, the smooth young man at Bonham's was the only person who had recognised the ring for what it was – not only Art Deco but Russian Art Deco (shades of my parents' jeweller friends, Genya and Solly, and poor, murdered Ruti) and, then, there was something a little alarming to me, too good to be true, about a cash transaction.

But why alarming? The bedraggled young man who tried to

blow up a plane load of people with explosives he failed to ignite in one of his expensive trainers had no problem, apparently, with cash transactions." Did no one wonder what he was up to? Perhaps there are times when it makes sense to be suspicious but I was suspicious of the wrong sets of people and for the wrong reasons, as I had been at least once before, when trying to shake off a taxi that was following us down the street.

R and I had arrived in Egypt a few days earlier with medicines for every conceivable complaint except the one that had struck me, which was the opposite of the one that everyone expects. With some embarrassment, I asked the receptionist at the grand hotel where we were staying, at package rates, for directions to the nearest chemist and to write down, in Arabic, what it was I was looking for.

Armed with this bit of paper, we set off down the triumphal way built by Napoleon to link the pyramids with the centre of Cairo and might be walking still had we not finally heeded the driver of the cab which sashayed alongside us, first offering to take us to the chemist and then begging us to believe we were walking in the wrong direction. But, afraid of being cheated, we wouldn't let him take us even when we did, at last, turn around and follow his directions, finding the shop just where he had told us it would be. Thoroughly uncomfortable at having been so mistrustful, we were happy to see that same driver the next day and this time got into his taxi without even setting a price and remained with him for the rest of our stay.

How to behave as a tourist in a third-world country was not something I was going to have to worry about for another forty years as I sat behind my typewriter in Chester Row, answering the phone, sticking down envelopes and unwrapping manuscripts, almost all of which I would soon be wrapping up again. It wasn't then my job to decide what needed to be read and what didn't: I suppose Anthony must have flipped through the pile himself, and it was just good luck that on the day I unwrapped Jennifer Dawson's *The Ha Ha* he wasn't there to look at it first. And so this little novel which was to win one of the most prestigious literary prizes and which I still see, from time to time, in unfamiliar editions on other people's shelves, became my first 'find': not quite on the scale of the explorer sighting land, or even the prospector finding gold, but a find none the less.

It is hard to convey the excitement of discovery even on this modest scale and there is certainly an element of look-how-clever-I-am to find or recognise what no one has found or recognised before; but it isn't all ego any more than is the thrill of walking on untrodden snow, which is what it is most like – a thrill we experienced only last night as, by moonlight so bright it cast blue shadows, we crunched through the farmyard outside our Yorkshire cottage, past the sheds full of huddled sheep, and out into the virgin fields. For the first time in years, we have had a white Christmas: an irony that in this of all years we had also had a glorious 'fall': on the day – at the time – the Trade Towers were exploding, R and I were bowling across rural Pennsylvania, in bright autumn sunshine, planning to return one day and stop at some of the peaceful little settlements we were passing on our way to friends with a farm on the Eastern Shore . . .

By the time *The Ha Ha* came out, I had left Chester Row. I was never to meet its author and I have never re-read the book. Could it possibly be as good as I thought it then? Almost certainly not and I don't want to know. It is one thing to come across an old lover forty years on and find this Adonis now has a paunch which could seat his grandchildren, and quite another to find that a book one has loved has lost its magic. The pages may have yellowed at the edges but books aren't subject to experience, ageing, death, and *The Brothers Karamazov* is the same book that held you awestruck at twenty. So, what has gone wrong? Talking with friends the other night, seriously serious readers of about our age, we discovered that we all now found Father Zosima the most intolerable bore and that several other much loved classics of our youth had, on recent re-reading, bitten the dust. R had bogged down in *Dombey and Son*, our host had recoiled after the first few pages of *Crime and Punishment*, and I had found *Vanity Fair* less fun than I remembered.

These were the surprises. There are also, of course, the books one would never risk re-reading, not just the early favourites but much of Hemingway and most of Lawrence. Some old favourites though never fail: Shakespeare and Conan Doyle have carried us across some choppy seas and Trollope, who for years I had dismissed without reading, was the writer who, years later, was to bring me back to books.

It was Roger Sale," an old teacher of R's, rearing up at the idea that Trollope was dull who rattled my preconceptions. Just as it was Diana Athill who convinced me that *A Suitable Boy* was worth reading in spite of the hype.

Who wants to be force-fed: to see the same photograph again and again – for there are pin-ups now among writers as there are among the younger classical musicians – or to hear the same tired anecdotes repeated: that this or that publisher's reader had sat up all night, unable to sleep with excitement, or some high-profile agent had flown to Vancouver or Karachi or wherever to secure this or that work of genius . . .

In my own time as a reader only one writer tempted me to use the word 'genius', or 'kind of genius' which somehow seems more acceptable: the then young William Vollmann whose *You Bright and Risen Angels* was staggering in its brilliance. But I am tempted to use 'kind of genius' about one other writer who, contrary to most, hasn't declined with age but is blazing more fiercely than ever.

Philip Roth's first novel, *Goodbye, Columbus*, as I remember it almost fifty years on, was pure delight. Like Madeleine St John's first novel, the gem-like *Women in Black*, it didn't stretch beyond its reach. But how can a slight novel, however delightful, compare with *American Pastoral* or *Sabbath's Theater* and what other writer is capable of those dazzling verbal riffs which can lift any subject – from how to stitch gloves to thoughts about death and dying – onto a different plane?

By an odd quirk of fate, Anthony Blond had been sent a copy of *Goodbye, Columbus* to review for a little magazine called the *Jewish Quarterly* to whom it had been sent by Deutsch, then Roth's English publisher. Being too busy to do it himself he had passed it on to me so that when I arrived in Great Russell Street a year or so later, I found my one and only published book review filed on the premises.

Just as there was to be a gap of several years between my being entrusted with editorial work at Methuen and getting my first proper editorial job, so there was to be a longer gap still between that first review and the next time I was to see my name in print. This time, too, the opportunity came unsought.

A friend who had been writing the film page in the local paper rang to ask if I would like to take it over. He had told the Editor he would be leaving and the Editor had, presumably, asked him to suggest a replacement. So, with no credentials whatever, I became film critic on the *Ham & High*.

The nine months for which I kept this up are one long blur. The friend or, rather, husband of a friend from whom I inherited the job had been doing it happily for years but he did not have the calls on his time that I did with my unemployed lover, house and mortgage, dog, cat, lodger and, taking more time than all the rest put together, my six-year-old son to whom, burdened with guilt at his fatherless only-child state, I could refuse nothing.

Of course, we are not talking here about things that cost money, of which there was none to spare, and we did have our battles about bedtime and footwear but it was only when, mistakenly or not (apparently, I was wrong about trainers being bad for children's feet) I thought what he wanted was harmful, that I held out. I could never have done what a friend did who thought their uniforms and activities too silly and said No to her son's joining the Cubs. I was as enthusiastic as A about many of the nine-day wonders which flashed across the screen in those early years, all to be subsumed by a passion for football," played in the park, on the street, under arc-lights on a field of astra-turf and, for hours at a time, on a piece of green felt on the floor of his room. This obsession, for such it was, lasted for five long years, only to be edged not out but to one side, when music took over."

And I tried to join in, had my favourites among the pin-ups – all Chelsea players, of course – which we cut out of *Shoot* and, once every season, would take him to Stamford Bridge where I would embarrass him by so clearly not understanding what was going on. I never got the hang of the rules – my mind then, as now, was always on something else as I tried, and failed, to get comfortable on the floor – and the pleasure I get out of watching football has everything to do with how beautifully the players move and very little to do with who is winning.

Which doesn't mean, as we all found to our surprise, that I like losing and the board games which the three of us would sometimes play at this time usually ended in angry tears as my son and his stepfather, no concessions allowed for the difference in their ages, both played to win and I, who like neither winning nor losing, tried to shore up the weaker side . . .

These attempts at family life, however, were soon to give way before the barrage of ancillary activity that went with my glamorous new job. For it turned out that as I wasn't an accredited journalist, I would have to pay to see the films I was meant to be reviewing unless I had managed to make arrangements beforehand to be allowed in free.

Luckily, this was before hash buttons and options or I wouldn't have stuck it for as long as I did: it might be a while before anyone answered the phone but you did, at last, get through to a person;

quite often in the local cinemas, to the Manager himself who was seldom stone-cold sober, or so I concluded from how complicated this simple transaction could become.

So, quite apart from the difficulty of getting to see the films ahead of their Hampstead showing – catching them in the West End or on the other side of town or, far too seldom, at a private screening in Wardour Street – there was all the other stuff; not only the phone calls and the weekly scouring of the *Film Bulletin* for something to say about everything I hadn't managed to see but also the actual writing – the 2,000 words for which I was paid £4 plus £1 (untaxed) expenses . . .

Of course, this was the early seventies. Even so, however one looks at it, this was slave labour and, though I didn't yet know it, a good preparation for what was to come: even I find it hard to believe that when I left Deutsch, a year short of sixty, in 1993, I was earning (not taking home) just over £300 a week."

If every film had been a *Discreet Charm* or even a *Two-Lane Blacktop*, I might have carried on a bit longer but in the course of nine months those were the only films we would actually have chosen to see and the novelty of the others – the disaster movies, third-rate Westerns, Carry Ons – soon wore thin. All these years later, I still flinch at the sight of Charles Bronson – a devoted family man, I read in *Hello!* – who looks unnervingly like my ex-husband and turned up in one senselessly violent role after another.

Finally, despairing at the ratio of effort to reward – reward in money or in kind – we decided to call it a day: 'we' because by this time, my lover, not long since my lodger, quite often wrote the reviews for me – the first time he had been in print since his days as a schoolboy journalist in Carlisle, Pa and the last time until Will Allan, working for André at the time, having read *Eccentric Spaces* in manuscript, commissioned him to write a piece about Alma Tadema for the *Connoisseur* of which he – Will – was then Deputy Editor. In fact, this piece, mauled beyond recognition, never appeared; but others soon did. Not though *Industrial Diamonds*, the book-length typescript I had found in a drawer in his room (by now more friend than landlady) which had been more than enough to convince me that the *Ham & High* were not being short-changed in getting him instead of me.

Apparently it was my delight in *Diamonds* and, possibly, too, seeing those columns in the local paper, which made him think that perhaps he could write after all and decided him, back in St Louis a few months later, looking for work, to start on something new. And so it was that the manuscript of *Eccentric Spaces* was reaching me, chapter by chapter, through the post.

His own description of writing this can be found in the short Preface (which includes that bid for a job) that appears in all later editions. It tells how he wrote it sitting on the floor at a plastic coffee table which was the only working surface in the room, borrowed the pictures he was to write about from the public library and was sustained by the friendship of a few ex-colleagues in the English Department of Washington U.

What it doesn't tell is what had happened to get him banned from using the university library (long-haired and druggy, he had failed to get tenure) nor how devastated he had been by Cornell's rejection of that earlier typescript which I was to find in his room.

Diamonds hadn't been written sitting on the floor but it had been written in an unholy rush. For seven weeks R had shut himself away – no girls, no drink – until he had got his thesis written. And then, after a lot of shilly-shallying as one expert reader gasped in admiration and another in horror, Cornell (where he had been a graduate student) didn't want it.

Anyone else would have sent it somewhere else but he wasn't anyone else and that wonderfully entertaining round-up of unreadable novels – the 'proletarian novels' of the late nineteenth century, yet to become a subject – remained not only unpublished but unread.

Years later, my son, so like his stepfather that they could not live in the same house, unconsciously followed his example: A-levels were only a few weeks off when, going to see him in the room above the chemist's shop in Muswell Hill where he had been living since just before his seventeenth birthday, I found the guitar had disappeared and he was not only studying by himself but also alongside a schoolfriend who lived near by and whose family, I imagine, were as worried by this alliance as I was pleased.

But they needn't have worried. Both of them got the marks they needed, though not the straight As they were capable of, for neither of them was academically ambitious at the time, which made it the more surprising to get a phone call from A to say he had decided to try for Oxford. The next thing we knew was that he had been for an interview at his father's old college and, the next after that, that they had turned him down."

The letter expressed what I still interpret as genuine regret, but one rejection was enough for my son as it had been for R, and Oxford, which had rejected me twice, was never mentioned again.

Which does not mean that I can put up with anything and my two years in Chester Row were to end abruptly when an eager young woman joined us and, working unpaid (a rich kid's version of what we would now call 'job experience') could not be expected to haul parcels to the post office or do any of the other chores once she had learnt how and they had lost their novelty. Anyway, things had changed. Anthony now had a colleague or partner who busied himself in an extension of the extension – the Briggs of what was soon to be Blond & Briggs. He, too, was not unfriendly but, unlike Hazel," who was mortified by the havoc she and her fortune had wrought, he must have been glad to see me go.

Oddly enough, I can hardly remember Desmond Briggs and the vague picture I have of a somewhat round and shiny young man could as well be Henry Hill, someone I like without reserve – R's oldest friend (the stray dog they adopted got them thrown out" of their Amherst fraternity for its filthy doggy habits) – now 'the most feared lawyer in New Jersey' in whose anarchic company we have had more childish and expensive fun than anywhere else . . .

Be that as it may, Anthony Blond Limited was growing up fast and fun was on the wane. The London sales rep still called in most days but with Desmond we had less need of Mr Ranns and Mr Bowles whose visits became briefer and more businesslike. As for Simon Raven – now back from Greece where he had spent a cold and penurious winter – he was living in Kent, in another kind of exile, but it must have suited him for it seems that he stayed there for much of the rest of his life, safely distant from the distractions of London.

Of course, there was still more going on than in most nine to five office jobs though one event at least is more interesting in retrospect than it was at the time: this was the interviewing of Anthony for some student magazine by a bumptious Cambridge undergraduate called David Frost whose unremarkable features were soon to be seen on television every Saturday night as we, like so many others, stayed in to watch *That Was The Week That Was*.

None of the other shows that we have stayed in not to miss – *Twin Peaks*, the Watergate hearings – had an Oxbridge cast but the number of names I recognise amongst the credits of almost any English production is staggering. Of course, I seldom knew these people, I just knew about them, with a very few exceptions. One of the exceptions was Edwin Mullins, the other John McGrath.

Edwin had married Gillie, my Lyons teashop friend, and she was the first of us to have a baby which made her more special than ever, as did her early death.

I still have her letter telling me she was going into hospital 'for fibroids' and then hearing, a few days later, that they had found she was riddled with cancer. With three young children, Gillie, who had been no more anchored than the rest of us – in fact, less so for she was as much at home in the hard-drinking camp as with us – proved unbelievably sturdy. On a diet of liquefied calves' liver – the regime devised by a clinic in Mexico which, unlike the London hospital, did not give her up for dead – she managed to stay alive for another four years and at no time, whether spinning her next meal in the mixer or setting off across the common on her bike to teach a class, did I ever see her less than composed.

Not that I saw her often and not that she didn't have closer friends than me with whom she must surely have let go. But to an occasional visitor, it seemed as though life went on as usual in that pleasant south London house where the paintings Edwin had begun to collect, crowded in their Kensington flat, now hung comfortably on ample walls. He also collected plants or, anyway, took a more serious interest in gardening than anyone else we knew and, to this day, I am perpetuating what may be a false memory in keeping my collection of camellias in pots as he did his.

But this was before gardens and gardening became staple television fare and it was his interest in painters and paintings which, for a short time, brought him into our lives on a daily basis as, in five-minute slots, he presented his 100 favourite paintings. More Melvyn Bragg than Sister Wendy, he seemed entirely at ease both with his subjects and the camera and, though I began watching for the novelty of seeing someone I knew on the telly, I kept on because he did it so well and, before the series ended and to my son's delight, for football has its colours too, had bought our first colour television.

Rothko in black and white had been the breaking point. *Z-Cars* would have been unimaginable any other way. One of the first – perhaps the very first – proletarian drama series in which policemen could behave as badly as their clients and have messy private lives, it had been conceived and written[n] by John McGrath, one of a small group of Oxford poets I had got to know slightly during the short time that I knew one of them well.[n] They were a forbidding group, not least because uniformly tall, and John, though no more unbending than the others, the least alarming, being regarded, or so it seemed to me, as the least likely to succeed . . .

Seeing how differently things turn out from the way they were expected to is one of the few advantages of getting older: the hyper-fearful child who wouldn't venture alone to the end of the road and now flies round the world to one trouble spot after another in countries where dengue fever is more common than the common cold; the fat child whose mother was ashamed of him now features her, glamorous still, in one of his films; the placid baby girl, friends with all the world, now a moody and tempestuous young mother . . . Then there were the three young composers of whom the one who seemed least likely to be destined for greatness, has so far outstripped the others.

We would meet these – new friends of old friends of ours – on weekend visits to Dorset. Sandra Miller, another Oxford friend, with whom I had shared a flat in London, had moved there with her sculptor husband and both were teaching in nearby schools, as were two of the musicians – Peter Maxwell Davies and Harrison Birtwhistle. The third, Alexander Goehr, was, like us, down from London.

Sandra, a wonderful cook, would feed us all at the farmhouse table where Sandy Goehr, a non-stop talker who looked like the urban intellectual that he was, took over the conversation whilst Harry, who could have been taken for a cowherd, said almost nothing. Less voluble than Goehr but with a startling presence was Peter Maxwell Davies.

Of course, no one thinks like this any more than twenty year olds think about pensions and grandchildren but, had we been asked to lay a bet at the time, we wouldn't have put our money on Harry. Whom I know about these days only from what I see in the papers and hear on the radio, neither of which has ever brought me news of Hazel – from those Anthony Blond days – whom I remember now with some fondness, not least because in a surge of guilt at being the cause of my 'losing' my job, and also because she was naturally generous, she had bought me a very beautiful pottery dish which has sat ever since on the green marble table – a gift from Sandra and her sculptor husband who had made it in his Dorset workshop.

Both were, in fact, wedding presents for it was just about now that M and I got married; he wearing a very old suit with shapeless legs and I a cotton dress bought for £3 in the sales which was matched, in colour, by the confection on my head that Sandra had organised for me and for which, with its little veil and blowsy blue rose, I still have a lamentable fondness.

Did I ever look as young and untroubled as that? Did I really think it was going to work? Probably not, but the urge to get married was in those days, in most of us, at least as strong as the urge to have children and I had finally overcome his resistance . . .

So, married 1960. Divorced 1970. These dates are easy to remember. What I don't remember is whether I was still working for Anthony when the marriage, celebrated in the garden of that shared house in Hampstead Garden Suburb, took place. But I do remember his taking me to Peter Jones to choose a present and I have only recently stopped using the aluminium saucepans he bought us, still only half-persuaded that they have been poisoning me for the last forty years.

The pottery dish was also 'local'. It came from a small and Sloany gallery just a few doors away from the lunch bar where I had been going almost daily for their Dates and Cream Cheese sandwiches which, it never occurred to me till this moment, did not have to become a memory for I could have re-created them any time in my own kitchen during those months that followed when I was out of work and wasting my time on that thinly disguised autobiography which was my 'novel'.

Early Days at 105

T EMPING SAVED ME from the novel and a friend of a friend
saved me from temping. Peter Tegel,ⁿ another Oxford connection, was the one to hear that a job was coming up at Deutsch:
Gina Conquy,ⁿ from whom he would collect German books to
report on, was leaving to get married. It took only a couple of phone
calls to get us together, the more so as Gina and I already knew each
other – two of an Oxford foursome who in our earliest publishing
days had met for lunch from time to time in, of all places, the Strand
Palace Hotel; presumably as convenient for the others as it was for
me working at Methuen in Essex Street, a few blocks away.

I hadn't seen Gina for a couple of years but we were much of a
muchness – linked not only by having read English at Oxford but,
further back still, by her parents having been friends of friends of
my parents and, in true Jewish fashion, having attempted to get us
together. But we were at different colleges and saw little of each
other until publishing brought us together in these modest business
girlⁿ lunches.

Much of a muchness in background, maybe, but Gina was far
more decisive than me and having made sure that I wanted the job
she made sure that I got it.

Why André had so much respect for Gina – long before the
success of the agency she was to found with her husband, Murray
Pollinger – and so little for me, at any time, ever, remains a bit of

a mystery but whatever he may have thought when he saw me in my interview outfit – a neat little royal blue skirt and jacket, such as my grandfather could have run up for me in his Regent Street shop – he didn't say No and as there were no other candidates, I got the job.

So, for the first time, I had a proper job, though I still did everything that a secretary would have done, for only the men in the building had secretaries. There was also lots of space to do it in for the three editors, of whom I was now one, shared a whole half floor of the Georgian terraced house in Great Russell Street, a space that was to be divided and divided again as our numbers grew. But then there was only one division: Diana Athill, as was fitting, had her own little room – a bite out of ours, Goa to our Karnataka. She had one window, we had two. And, of course, we shared the view: across the road, down which a bus now runs, was the featureless red brick of the YWCA, Lutyens' only irredeemably ugly building. While, a little to its left, we could see on its plinth, outside the glass and steel job that was and still is the TUC, the struggling figure of the Worker attempting to throw off the coils" of the Wicked Employer.

The YWCA, in the canteen of which I would sometimes queue up for a worker's lunch – plain, cheap and filling – is now a four-star hotel. I suppose the thinking of the developers was that once past its portals, the guests could forget the red brick and enjoy the view of the eighteenth-century terrace across the street. As Leah, short and dumpy, had enjoyed the view of Johnny . . .

Alas, long dead now, Leah Hertz was one of my most amusing authors. An Israeli who had come to England to finish her law studies but got distracted by falling in love with and marrying the handsome Johnny, she had, when I first met her, just completed a doctorate in business studies and one of my toughest battles was persuading her to drop the 'doctor' on her book – so vulgar in England, but how do you explain that to a bracingly immodest foreigner?

Most remarkable about Leah was not her PhD but that after

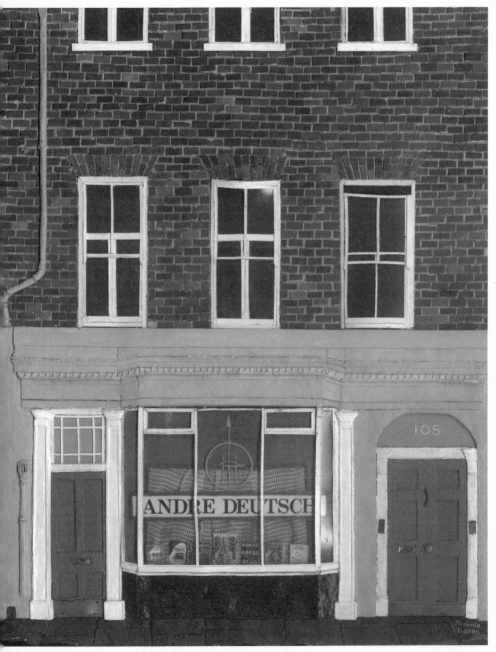

38 *105 Great Russell Street*

40 *The three arrows: Nicolas Bentley, André Deutsch, Diana Athill*

39 *André Deutsch*

41 *Tom Rosenthal*

42 *Editorial meeting, c.1965*

43 *Clarice Linden, in retirement, calling the cat*

44 *Pamela Royds at a recent Deutsch reunion*

45 *Ilsa Yardley, not long ago*

46 *Philip Tammer and Sheila Murphy*

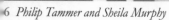

47 *. . . and Gill*

48 *Working*

49 *William T. Vollmann*

building up a successful business she had decided that she had quite enough money and had gone back to school. Also remarkable were the origins of the business for, like so many of the other women she wrote about in *The Business Amazons* – her Amazons owned more than 50 per cent of a business with a turnover of at least a million pounds – she had started at home, while looking after small children. Someone had admired the crocheted coat she was wearing and asked her to make one for them. And, so it went on till the point where Johnny gave up his job and the two of them set out for Gozo with its cheap labour and friendly climate and there they taught any of the islanders who were willing to learn how to knit how to knit – lace-making had been the cottage industry before they arrived. When they had a big enough work-force, they bought or perhaps rented a factory and Crochetta went into business on a commercial scale.

Oddly enough, I got to see the factory though I never got as far as the Crochetta shop in Beauchamp Place. It was on the last day of my two weeks in Gozo that Leah took me with her to choose, or rather to choose for me, a couple of tops which were, of course, presents, for one would have cost as much as I might spend in a year on clothes. The disparity in our incomes had come near to scuppering this Mediterranean interlude before it began. What had happened was this: Deutsch had agreed to publish Leah's manuscript but only if it was reduced to four-fifths its present length and only if she both arranged and paid for the cutting.

Realising there was no easy alternative, she agreed and, a few days later, the phone call came. I had given her the names of a few freelance editors who could be trusted with the job but she had decided she wanted me. And she made it sound like a holiday. Something I could do while R was visiting his family in the States and, at the same time, earn some money . . . Leah was persuasive and though I hadn't contemplated taking time off and doing the job myself, I was persuaded. The only thing holding me back was the thought of the dent that buying one round of drinks would make in my fee; an awkward thought to give voice to but Leah took it entirely in her stride. 'Leave your purse behind,' was her response to this worry which many millionaire entrepreneuses would have trouble comprehending, and that was exactly what I did.

So I arrived in Malta with a lot of HB pencils, a pencil sharpener, a favourite rubber, a swimsuit, sun glasses and very little else. And, as I had been told to expect, there was a car waiting at the airport to take me across the island – nothing but concrete cubes and those steel crooks which tell that a building isn't yet complete – to the public ferry to Gozo where Leah and Johnny were waiting on the pier. A short drive now through pleasant, scrubby country and we were there – there being one biggish and one smallish thick-walled house, both covered in creeping vine – magenta, orange, pink – and on either side of a swimming pool.

The smaller house was for the children and their friends. I was in the other and there had a work space such as I have never had before or since. At the top of the house, reached by a flight of outside stairs, was this room with four windowed walls – much like the top of a lighthouse – a deep sofa, low table, hanging chair and, in an annexe, a desk and typewriter. As in a fairy tale everything was laid out by invisible hands and each morning, after breakfast, when Leah went off to the factory, I would climb up to my room where the only interruptions till lunch and the lunchtime swim were the ice-cold drinks that arrived from time to time, unasked for.

The unsettling prediction of my colleagues at Deutsch that once I became an employee of Leah's her charms would wear thin turned out to be as false as I had hoped. She was an exemplary employer and watching the way she dealt with her workers and, indeed, her family, of which Johnny remained the undisputed head, was a lesson in human relations. Not once in the two weeks that I was closeted with her book did she ask to see what I was doing. For all she knew I could have been disposing of those 60,000 words by dropping complete chapters, as one of my lazier friends had suggested I should.

This would certainly have left more time for swimming but it wasn't the way I did it and, in reducing the manuscript page by page, I learnt that even a book that is not noticeably flabby can afford to lose weight.

It was in talking about weight that Leah, who was completely unfazed by her own size, made the remark about looking out at Johnny; and it is sad to think how thrilled she would have been by her outrageously good-looking older daughter, Noreena, then a sultry young teenager, now a pundit on the role of multi-nationals in the global economy . . .

All this, of course, though long ago, was aeons in the future when I started at Deutsch in the early sixties and, though as capable then as I would ever be at working on a particular text, found myself doing just about everything else which, though disappointing and at times unnerving, for I had no skills whatever for some of the jobs that were thrown at me," was probably just as well. I couldn't have done anything which needed real concentration in a room where the buzzer on my desk could go at any time and Janet Stewart, the editor who worked across from me, was constantly on the phone.

André's calls – for the buzzer was almost always his – were various: had this or that arrived? where was the artwork for X, Y or Z? when was he going to see catalogue copy? had we started on the Newsletter? Janet's were almost all about one thing.

At this time, she and a group of friends of which I remember only that Michael Sissons was one, but they were probably all recent Cambridge graduates as she was herself, had formed a company to launch a new board game which was set to take the world by storm. In fact, *Diplomacy*, whose gestation, birth and teething problems I was to hear so much about, albeit in half measure for I heard only one end of those endless conversations, was to be a nine-day wonder. Though intellectually engaging it had the disadvantage of needing not only brains but long tracts of free time; and, unless you left a country out, you needed seven players and how often can anyone assemble seven players with five or six hours to spare?

My husband who liked games and was good at them quite enjoyed the few sessions of *Diplomacy* we were roped in to play with the founders, but I who don't didn't. I had never been good at anything which required thinking fast or, indeed, moving fast which ruled out most board games and most outdoor games too. Leah and Johnny were noticeably dismayed during my time in Gozo at how bad I – the professional wordsmith – was at Scrabble just as, years before, my mother had been incredulous, if not dismayed, at coming to a school sports day and finding me hurling a discus and throwing a javelin. But, in an alien world – I could barely jump over the hurdles – I had found something I *could* do.

And I could do or learnt to do all the jobs that filled those office days in which I had imagined I would be focused only on texts, as Diana was behind the walls of her little room and Janet – in charge of the Reading Shelf – between phone calls.

The little reading I managed to do – those manuscripts that Janet passed on to me because she liked something about them – had to be done at home, above the greengrocer, or on the number 7 bus. Coming and going from Ladbroke Grove, I second-read first novels by Wole Soyinka, Earl Lovelace, Nkem Nwankwo and many others."

It may be different now but during my time at Deutsch and, from what one heard, throughout the industry, reading was regarded a bit like housework: it was taken for granted that you would do it and that it didn't need to be paid for. At least with housework there is no pretence that it is actually a privilege and most women do it because their mothers did it, because it needs to be done and because no one else is going to do it. But the reading of manuscripts, as vital to the life of publishing and as unremitting as housework and housekeeping are to daily life, had us – mostly women – in a double bind: it was, after all, '*only* reading' *and* we were lucky to be doing it. Thus, with our collusion, did our mostly male employers, for years at a time, get something for nothing.

And it is, of course, a privilege to be the first or one of the first to read *You Bright and Risen Angels*, *Good Behaviour* or *Theory of War* but it is no less a privilege to remove a tumour, pilot a plane or own a publishing company, but these and all those other preponderantly male occupations do not make you choose between job satisfaction and money in the bank.

So ingrained was the habit of taking a book or manuscript home each weekend that I feared when I stopped I might, like someone trying to give up smoking, fall back into the habit. But my reason for stopping, for putting the brake on once and for all, kept me from back-sliding. What had happened was this.

A year or so before, we had published a charming little book by a doctor's widow living in Devon. Someone, perhaps her daughter, perhaps she herself, had sent us a bundle of pieces, published with her own illustrations in the *Tatler* during the Second World War; in the First she was already producing patriotic posters. I thought the pieces enchanting and so did everyone else, but they didn't make a book. Making them into a book was not something the ninety-year-old author could now do. But, having been down to see her in Budleigh Salterton – the setting of her fictions – and having her permission to put an anthology together for her – select, cut, elide, introduce – I took this on as an outside job. A fee was agreed – this time Deutsch was to pay it – of something like £200: not a princely sum for a lot of work and a book to sell at the end of it but, in the mid-eighties, nothing to complain about.

Nor did I complain. I liked Joyce Dennys, it was fun to do – all that scissors and pasting which followed a couple of days in the newspaper library at Colindale – and it was gratifying when she and her daughter were pleased and then Penguin bought the paper-back rights." Now, everyone wanted a vol 2 and wanted it quickly. Remembering how long the first had taken, I tried to put this one out to a freelancer and, only as the deadline got uncomfortably near, fell into doing it myself. I did this without stopping to discuss a fee which I took for granted would be the same or a little more than the last time.

But it was neither the same, nor a little more: it was Nothing. I no longer remember what preposterous arguments were used to justify not paying me but I do know that they held all the cards. Like the shady developer who tears down a building in the middle of the night, they knew the job had already been done.

But the strategy misfired. The firm hung on to its £200 but, if you can be said to go on strike over not doing work for which you aren't paid, that is what I did. I was never to work unpaid again.

Not that anyone noticed or complained for, working mostly at home on a freelance basis, as I had continued to do long after my son grew up, I could still get more done than other people because, like all home workers, free of those constant interruptions you get in any office: welcome interruptions in many cases – colleagues wandering in to talk about their love life or the film they had seen the previous evening, an author popping in because he or she happened to be in the neighbourhood and, of course, those long lunches. I looked forward to my two days a week in the office as a kind of workers' playtime – nothing but letters, phone calls, meetings – but the real work, as I saw it, got done at home where, ironically, I was easier to get hold of than most of my colleagues who could be anywhere in a four-storey building.

What is more surprising is that no one noticed or complained when another editor, who had moved out of London, followed suit and would leave the office every Thursday with her small overnight bag which could not conceivably contain three full days' work. But had anyone noticed this give-away sign, she had her cover story: she was fully occupied with a translation, undertaken for the firm and hence legitimately done in their time. What the powers that be had forgotten was that a large part of the book she was translating from the German already existed in English . . .

This legendary scam which was a standing joke among the rest of us did not then unseat its author but no one's luck can last for ever, and not long after, I came back from a short holiday to find that she had disappeared. After which, for the story has a happy ending, she married a wealthy Swedish businessman and never had to pretend to work again.

A happy ending for her but a mixed blessing for me. With her demise, I lost both a constant source of irritation – Look what she's getting away with: the cry of the drudge throughout the ages – and a constant source of work. For this editor farmed out most of her books and they usually came to me. The upside of this arrangement was that I got to work on books that I already knew and liked because I had often been the first to read and recommend them.

One of these was *The Good Pit Man* by Keith Alldritt, a Lawrentian first novel which had surfaced on the slush pile and excited everyone else as much as it had excited me. Alas, or perhaps luckily, I no longer have a copy, for knowing now the strength of its author's devotion to Lawrence, Conrad, Bunting and, indeed, the whole of Eng Lit which he both taught and wrote about with passion, I think we may have been dazzled by what was no more than a lovingly crafted reproduction.

Nevertheless, when we bought the novel I would dearly have liked to meet the author but – here comes the downside – meeting the author, the forging of those personal relationships which are, on one level, what publishing and life are all about, remains the privilege of the in-house editor whether they decide to work on the book themselves or not. And it is a privilege jealously guarded. So jealously that when the barrier is removed because it is going to save the in-house editor work to have the outside-editor deal directly with the author, everyone knows their place. And it is the exception among authors, as among the upstairs characters in *Gosford Park*, to be able to see the person-with-a-life-of-their-own behind the tweenie's frilly apron.

Certainly, Keith Alldritt hadn't seen me, for years later when he and his wife" had become good friends of ours he would sometimes reminisce about the far-off days with Deutsch and recall the stupid woman who had been foisted on him as his copy-editor: a session I remember with distaste equal to his for he was stubborn, bad-tempered and had a filthy cold.

Copy-editing in those days, at least at a small firm like ours, though not at Penguin where a whole roomful of people were employed to do nothing else, was learnt as you went along. But by the time I sat down with Keith over *The Good Pit Man* I knew enough to do a reasonable job and haven't therefore been surprised by the calls for help I have had from more than one of his subsequent editors. There are many 'difficult authors', every one of whom would claim the fault was on the other side, more sinned against than sinning . . .

As it was, I had inherited from my predecessor a copy of *The Authors' and Printers' Dictionary* (Oxford: 13th impression) and had been lent a copy of *Hart's Rules for Compositors and Readers* (also Oxford: 37th edition: completely revised). Both were pocket-sized and much less alarming than Butcher's 300-page plus manifesto which I discovered much later.

Now it seems that young editors go on courses which would be a fine way of ingesting Butcher or whatever the current Dr Spock of copy-editing may be. But no course exists which can teach a person to read, of which editing is a natural extension. The relationship between the two – copy-editing and editing – not unlike the relation between philology and literature: one has a lot of rules, the other has none. And both matter but one is a lot more popular than the other.

In my time at St Hilda's only one person had opted for philology which seemed, to the rest of us, a freakish choice. How could anyone want to be studying the structure of language when they could be drifting through *The Prelude* or *The Faerie Queene*? But Vera seemed to be well satisfied and went on, I believe, to do more and more of it, whereas there wasn't an academic among the rest of us and those who didn't drop straight into marriage ('What book?' an erstwhile serious student was asked at her *viva*. 'A big blue book,' she is said to have replied, all thought on the handsome young Sikh she would be marrying as soon as term was over) aimed for those cultural institutions, the BBC and the British Council, for both of which there were entry requirements, and publishing for which there were none. Except 'knowing someone' (in Diana's case, it had been André himself, known fleetingly in the full biblical sense), and being able to type, which all three of us could do.

Not so Clarice Linden, the production manager, a stout Scottish lady whose handwritten notes on waste paper – she was as reliably frugal as André himself – were as easy to read as print and who held us all together, the bricks and mortar of the small community. Implacable in the face of André's frequent tirades she was patient with the rest of us – the 'workers' – for, like her husband, Danzig-born Stan, she had been a lifelong Communist and practised what she preached.

Someone else who couldn't type was Jean Rhys. She also had difficulty in reading her own handwriting and was, as I now know from her letters, in a despairing muddle. But what sent me down to see her, in the role of 'stenographer' – 'one of the partners, Diana Athill, suggests sending down a stenographer'" – was more André's need than hers.

One of the first things he had presented me with on my very first day in the office was a list of OUTSTANDING OPTIONS. Each of the writers listed – there were six or seven in all – had been paid somewhere between £25 and £75 and had failed to deliver. It was my job to get the books out of them, as in no case, whether the author was solvent or not (embarrassingly, the solvent ones were mostly his personal friends), did André imagine he could get the money back. But, like Fanny, a friend's Patterdale terrier, he would worry at this mound of earth until he had raised the mole, alive or dead.

So often, indeed, did he demand a progress report that though Gina had told me not to worry, that this was a very old chestnut indeed, I remained haunted by that list for years and am surprised to find I can only recall three lines:

Hans KELLER book on football
Maurice RICHARDSON Black Boxers
Jean RHYS untitled novel

Black Boxers remains the mystery now that it was then, but that untitled novel became *Wide Sargasso Sea.*

It's hard to believe that when it was decided that someone should go down to Cheriton Fitzpaine – the idea must have come from Diana who knew better than anyone else what a mess this writer was in – the only volunteer was me.

And so, equipped with a portable typewriter that I knew how to use and the sales manager's dictaphone, which I didn't but which André insisted I take, I caught the train down to Devon, to be met at Crediton station by Jean's taxi-driving neighbour, Mr Greenslade, who delivered me to the vicarage in Cheriton Fitzpaine where she had arranged for me to stay. Here I was made welcome by the vicar's wife, and from there, a short time later, the Reverend Woodward, a gentle and scholarly man who had been and remained a friend to Jean, took me along to meet her.

I have only the haziest memory of that first meeting. All I knew about Jean, whom Diana herself had not met at that time though they had been corresponding for years," was that she couldn't type, had got stuck with her novel and drank too much.

I knew nothing of Francis Wyndham who had first brought her to the attention of Deutsch for whom he had then worked, nor of the unfortunate Max (Jean's ailing husband, only recently released from prison) who would be re-installed in the cottage once my visit was over. I had not read a word of Jean's earlier novels either, because I didn't know they existed. Nor, still more to the point, had I read those pages that Frances Wyndham and Diana had seen of the one I was setting out to deliver.

What I saw was a frail old lady who had clearly fallen on hard times for the wretched little back-to-front bungalow was entirely charmless, and what I heard was heartfelt relief at my arrival, for she had high hopes of what I and my typewriter could help her achieve. I also heard repeated commiserations about the hepatitis which meant that I couldn't touch alcohol. Diana and I had concocted this story to preserve her faith in me and in the hope that my enforced abstinence might curtail her own drinking during the time I was with her."

Which it probably did, though even had I been able to sit down with her over a bottle of gin or whatever it was that kept her going on other days, she would not, I think, have let it interfere with what we were doing. This was, in the simplest terms, getting her partially typed novel into some kind of order. Untyped and often unnumbered pages lay about the room and it took most of the first day to find them, sort them out and assemble a working copy. Then it was time to type up, at her dictation, those handwritten pages which occurred at varying intervals throughout the typescript. These random encounters with the text – first heard, then read – were astonishing, but I was to have no real sense of the book as a whole for another two or three years, when she was finally persuaded to hand it over.

Unlike most writers who, wittingly or not, leave plenty for an editor to do (I have been asked to decide on the order of chapters and left to paragraph a whole novel), Jean, physically frail, practically destitute and emotionally shipwrecked though she was, remained as fastidious and self-critical as that other Deutsch author with West Indian connections, Vidia Naipaul and, like him, she would not hand a manuscript in until she was satisfied with every word and every comma.

Which is why I returned to London with encouraging news but no manuscript. But I did have a short story which I had managed to capture on that dictaphone, after many false starts in which we kept hearing the sales manager's voice dictating the same letters over and over again.

This was my first and last visit to Cheriton Fitzpaine which was to become a place of pilgrimage and I never saw Jean again, except once, in a Kensington hospital bed. So thoroughly did I disappear out of her life that Carole Angier, her biographer, had already begun her painstakingly researched *Life and Work* when she discovered that the 'stenographer' was not only alive but still working at Deutsch, a piece of intelligence she picked up from seeing a package with my name on it while she was waiting in the lobby for Diana . . .

I remember this with something more like amusement than resentment, which is not true of the Molly Keane affair. Jean was, after all, Diana's author. And, during those years between Jean's rediscovery by the public and her death – years during which Diana played a full part, not all of it easy – a lot had been going on in my life. My mother had died. My son had been born. My best friend had fallen in love with my husband. I had left Deutsch, four months pregnant, to enjoy an unsalaried breakdown.[n] I had returned nine months later on a freelance basis. I had met R.

It was my good luck that I met Jean at all: that Diana hadn't seized the opportunity herself, that the social whirl of Janet's life[n] in which, when my marriage ended, she generously tried to induct me, left no weekends free, and that we had no secretary and therefore no secretary to send. And, as it happened, at the time that it suddenly became urgent for someone to go down to Devon, I was not even living at home. A more serious blip than usual in my shaky marriage had coincided with being told that a friend with a 'pad' in Greek

Street was off to Greece and would be happy for me to use it. So, with a great sense of what would now be called 'empowerment' I moved into the flat that Michael Horowitz and Anna[n] had vacated – and substituted what my father used to call 'Shanks's pony' for the number 7 bus. And it was from there – two floors above a Soho brothel – that I went down to 'Cheriton Fitz' and had a short rest from our current marital dilemma: how was I supposed to behave when my husband's current mistress (one of several precursors to his final devastating affair[n]), whose love-sick letters I had seen all too many of, was said to be dying of leukemia, needing blood transfusions every few weeks and unable to live without him . . . ? What would Rabbi Blue or the moral mazers have recommended as Good Behaviour? Marjorie Proops – that legendary agony aunt whom we were later to publish – would, I think, have made short shrift of Bettina's agony but, as it happened, Fate stepped in: my husband, her lover, went down with glandular fever and I returned home to look after him and change his sweaty sheets.

As for Bettina, she paid a couple of bedside visits, till disappearing out of our lives but not, I think, her own, for ever.

The Molly Keane affair was different and caused a rift in my friendship with Diana which was to last a long time though, like the onset of some terminal illness, it was never spoken of.

What happened was this:[n] twenty-two years ago to the day – Gina's submission letter which I have in front of me is dated 7 March 1980 – I received a package (it could have been the one Carole Angier caught sight of) containing the manuscript of a novel called *Good Behaviour*. Gina's letter says very little for she had already rung and talked at length about this novel which she loved and believed in but in which she had, so far, failed to interest anyone else. Were we interested in Irish writers? (Anglo-Irish, of course, though I didn't know this at the time that I gave an emphatic Yes, having recently bought a couple of Irish Irish writers of whom the irrepressible

Michael Curtin[n] is still going strong.) Was there any point in her sending it? She had reached the stage we all reach when something we think wonderful has failed to impress enough people.

Anyway, the much-rejected manuscript arrived, I took it home, read it at a sitting in my childhood reading chair and was thrilled. Gina was right. It *was* exceptional. What I should have done now was wait till the next editorial meeting when, for better or worse (certainly better for me) Molly would have been established as my author. As it was, too excited to sit on the manuscript for even a day, I gave it to Diana and by the time of the meeting she had already written to the author – one of her inimitable letters – saying, albeit a little coyly, that so greatly did she love and admire the book, she was going to 'pull rank' and make it her own.

Petty stuff, but it is the little treacheries and betrayals which touch most nearly and are the hardest to forget. And I never did forget, but Diana and I still had fifteen years ahead of us and before too long our shared pleasure in books and, indeed, gossip or high-class chat re-established the friendship, but it was never quite what it had been. Thus, a few years later, when she reached out and snapped up an object I had fallen in love with but was hesitating to buy, it wasn't quite the surprise it would have been.

I should have made my mind up more quickly or, at the very least, not drawn her attention to the little Staffordshire figure she had already passed without noticing. Had it been Ilsa* who appeared first at my elbow – it was she who had organised this three-day spree to Buxton where we were spending a rainy morning at an Antiques Fair – she would have encouraged me to buy it, insisted on lending me the money or even, for this is Ilsa, bought it for me. What she wouldn't have done is taken out her purse and bought it for herself.

In Buxton, it wasn't dwelt on, nor did it spoil our enjoyment

---

* Ilsa Yardley who, after leaving Deutsch for the second time, became a much-loved literary agent

in the operas, the recitals and our snug olde worldy B & B. For no
one is better company than Diana and no one I have known a better judge of books. Her support for my slush-pile finds during all
those years was both invaluable, for André trusted her judgement,
and unstinting because she never lost her appetite for good writing," whatever its source, and would put whatever else she was doing
aside for the pleasure of tasting something new: a wholly acceptable
form of greed as, I tell myself, is the lusting after plants in a well-
stocked nursery garden, though is this really any better than lusting
after jewellery or food or clothes? Certainly it is less ostentatiously
vulgar than taking something off someone's plate: a startling scene,
with dialogue to match, which occurred when I made a better choice
than Tom at the expensive restaurant to which he had taken me with
Victor Perera, whose editor I was, for lunch. *'Droit de seigneur,'* he
muttered as he leant across and speared a forkful of aubergine or
whatever it was off my plate . . .

Of the seven deadly sins – like the seven dwarves, hard to recall
every one of them at any one time – Gluttony seems, along with
Sloth, the least repellent, as it would to someone who not only
shares the vice but, as a child, was encouraged to think it a virtue.
Over-eating, being the last to leave the table spread with party food,
was greeted with cries of admiration by my grandmother and her
friends: *'Keine horre!'"* ('Look at that!') – a Yiddish phrase that still
rings in my ears though I have no idea how to transcribe it. I had
no idea either, until two summers ago, that over-eating – 'fressing' –
was not confined to Jews. No other word could adequately describe
the activity that took place four times a day ('Tea' optional) at Capon
Springs, West Virginia.

R and I were there for a family reunion. R's ninety-year-old father,
recently widowed, was not about to break the habit of a lifetime. He
had come here for his honeymoon and, with rare exceptions, every

year since and he did not mean to stop while he could still drive a car and enjoy a game of golf.

The golf we were all in favour of. The driving we had done our best to stop. But it had not deterred him in the slightest when, R's offer to drive his car rejected, we chose to ride with R's brother and his wife. So we set off from Carlisle, tempers frayed, in two separate cars, one carrying four middle-aged drivers with all their faculties intact and the other a stubborn, partially deaf nonagenarian.

And we had a surprise in store. Not far out of town, a car swept past us and it took a minute to sink in that the figure, bolt upright in the driver's seat, was 'your father', as both his sons referred to him, who, when we met up at our destination some hours later, boasted about reaching the finishing line before us. That we had observed the speed limit and made a stop at the house Willa Cather had lived in as a child, he chose not to hear. But he did hear the bell that summoned us to meals, and so did everyone else. At the sound, these good Christian folk poured out of the cabins that edged the wide lawns and headed for the dining hall where every family – many had been coming for as long as ours – had its own allotted table already loaded with jugs and dishes. With only eight in our party we were one of the smaller groups but we, too, demolished a mountain of food at each sitting, my father-in-law who subsists for the rest of the year on portions which may well account for his longevity but leave us barely satisfied, joining in with the rest. Which he wouldn't be tempted to do at one of those hotels in the Catskills where Jewish comedians make non-stop jokes about the eating habits of the guests and where potato latkes and apple kugels – *foreign* food – displace the good, plain American fare which is the only food 'your father' considers fit to eat.

What would bother him less would be the absence of drinkable wine for at Capon Springs no alcohol can be consumed in the public areas, not even the dining room. All drinking takes place on the back decks of the cabins where, at the appropriate hour, each family collects a bucketful of ice – the source of this not far from the flag pole where the flag is raised each morning – and brings out its drinks chest, getting down to business watched only by the families on the neighbouring decks and the forest of pines that rears up on the other side of the small, cold stream.

From the absence of 'foreigners' – no black faces, no brown faces, no yellow faces – you might think they were banned too. But of course this isn't the case, they simply know not to come and we very soon stopped regretting that my son and his wife Diane had not been included in the party.

Of course, Diane's Native American ancestors had been here first. It was they who discovered the spring of pure water which was to be re-discovered by the white settlers and turned to profit first in an ill-judged scheme to sell the water on the strength of medicinal properties which it did not have and then, realising like the Indians before them that this was a magical place, marketing it with the promise, easy to fulfil, of a return to the simple life.

No television here, or none that I saw; no loud music or fruit machines. And the activities as wholesome as the food: bird-watching at dawn, camp fires at night, golf for the golfers and lawn games for the rest of us – croquet, putting, shuffleboard – plus, at any time, a dip in the dammed up water of the spring which had not, for this would not have been in keeping with the ethos of the place, been heated. But the proprietors of this little resort which takes such a pride in its old-fashioned ways know when to draw the line. The water in the swimming pool may have been cold but the taps in the cabins ran hot.

True austerity we have only experienced once and it was a long way from Capon Springs. We had found that the cheapest way for us to get to Tallinn was by sea and we had set out from Harwich on the *Baltica*, a very old Russian boat, commandeered from the Finns in the Second World War: a boat on which the only enter-tainments were deck quoits, chess and the live music – piano, fiddle, balalaika – laid on each night by members of the crew. For R and me, this genuine austerity which had nothing of Marie Antoinette about it was truly magical but my nine-year-old son preferred the thick carpets and general razzmatazz of the Swedish boat on which we returned.

What is the romance of the simple and why, if we like it so much, don't we perpetuate it in our own homes? Among our friends only Artis and Sandra (she of the Patterdale terrier) held out against mod cons and even they have finally succumbed. For more than thirty years the little house on an island in Casco Bay (pop. 300) where Artis, a poet and a teacher, spent many months of each year with her husband and their four children, had one cold water tap and, down in the bowels of the house and reached only by ladder, a septic tank. This tank had finally reached capacity on our first visit so that all nine of us had to make our way to the village hall each time the need was felt; the shier among us, which is to say the older children, carrying sheet music, as though they were off to practise, for the hall also housed the island's only piano.

And only Sandra regretted changing a house with no electricity," where she and her partner Chet had lived for ten years, for one connected to the mains. For months after the move and sometimes even now she will complain of the noise it makes . . .

Another champion of the simple life and, as it happened of electricity too was L. L. Nunn who made a fortune at the turn of the century bringing alternating current to the American West and endowed two colleges with the proceeds, one on the campus at Cornell and the other – surely the closest to his heart – in Deep Springs, a remote mountain valley not too far from California's eastern edge. Here, each year, twenty-four students, all male and hand-picked for their brains, were housed and educated free, their education comprising intensive study of the more usual kind alongside a heavy dollop of physical labour. For this was a working ranch and taking care of the stock, planting and tending the fields of alfalfa, mending fences and even slaughtering the odd cow for the meat which those on kitchen duty would cook and put on the table (huge slabs of it) was done by the students under the guidance of the Ranch Manager, the only non-academic adult for miles around.

With takers for a monastic life dwindling each year, the students were by now a mixed bunch and by the time I arrived, ten days or so from the end of R's three-month tenure, he was pretty fed up. With one or two exceptions, the young minds he was supposed to be nurturing were nothing out of the ordinary and the romance, which still gets me, of *mens sana in corpore* whatever had worn very thin. Though a lover of *Robinson Crusoe* and its literary offspring – during our film reviewing days he had even enjoyed Robert Redford ploughing through snowdrifts in his Davy Crockett hat – R nevertheless thought a lot less time should be spent with the alfalfa and a lot more with books, read in odd and often outdoor corners, for Deep Springs did not have the comforts of Telluride House, its sister-college, at Cornell. There the student body, made up of girls as well as boys – Nunn, whatever his secret desires, could not hope to replicate Mount Athos in up-state New York – were seriously clever.

At least as well appointed as an Oxbridge (men's) college, the Cornell-based Telluride was never short of applicants and the place was an intellectual hothouse to which R was lucky enough to be invited not once but twice, no duties to speak of beyond mingling with the inmates. What luxury to be provided, in perpetuity, with the means to offer free board and lodging, for a term at a time, to two guests of their own choosing, just to be around them for a while . . .

An impulse not dissimilar to Tom Rosenthal's hiring 'a male sensibility' to inspire the Deutsch harem. It took quite a while for poor Anthony Thwaite to live down this description and longer still for us to appreciate him for what he was, not only a considerable poet but also a reliable colleague and a wonderful mimic whose renderings of Japanese-style civilities became a feature of the slightly drunken tail-end of every Sales Conference dinner.

Among the Telluride students quite a few had also spent a year at the ranch and, like the alumni of the progressive schools who never quite get over them, those on whom Deep Springs worked its peculiar magic were to hanker after it for the rest of their lives. Or, as Bill Vollmann did, transform it into something else.

A natural teacher's pet, short-sighted, ungainly and painfully clever – a cleverness he took pains to hide[n] – he had found in R a mind more like his own than most, and though he kept a certain distance – persisted in addressing R as 'Professor' – they spent much time together. Thus it was to us – for I had met him too by this time – that 'Student Bill' sent us the manuscript of *You Bright and Risen Angels*.

By which time, we had been to Deep Springs and so recognised the genesis of those light bulbs and beetles. Every track had its share of these shiny-black, lumbering creatures, a lot less frightening than the rattlesnakes, of which I saw only one, and a lot less jaunty than the jackrabbits which made the desert seem to jump. For this was desert, though not the sand dunes kind: hot, dry, ankle-deep in scrub and, glimmering in the distance, the surface of the salt lake which lay just outside the ranch's eastern boundary. Peppered too with creosote bushes, now known to be the oldest living thing and, a short drive into the mountains, with bristle cone pines, then believed to be older – a tree which knows better than to grow more than a fraction of an inch each year, preserving its energy and heedless of its crude dwarfish shape.

R loved this weird landscape in which he found solace from the irritations of camp life; so, too, had Bill who (or so I imagine) had also found there the theme of his *Seven Dreams*[n] for at one time there had been people as well as jackrabbits among these mountains but of these barely a trace remains.

Like Capon Springs and just about anywhere else you could
name, Deep Springs had been home to an indigenous people before
the Europeans arrived and got rid of them by means less industrial
but just as effective as Hitler's in his attempt to rid the world of
its Jews – a cause newly taken up in the Arab world. Thus, in an
Egyptian paper recently on sale in London: 'If only thou had done
it, Brother, if only it had happened, so that the world could sigh in
relief without their evil and sin . . .' – the author of these words, the
chairman of the Arab Psychiatry Association and head of psychiatry at Cairo University . . .

Just as, in spite of a library of cookery books, I only make things
I have had at other people's houses and been told how to make,
so it took knowing Diane – my Native American daughter-in-law
– to wake me up to the history of the American Indians, and now
the Escape Narrative written by R's great-great-great-grandmother
is offset by books which banish for ever the Cowboys and Indians
version of those historical events. It was from one of these – *Black
Indians* – that I learnt that intermarriage (one of Diane's grandpar-
ents is African American) began way back when slaves, fleeing from
the plantations, took refuge in Indian villages where they were made
welcome and often stayed as, it is said, did a few white female cap-
tives who liked what they found. But not great-granny Harbison,
of sturdy Scottish descent,[n] who returned to her family and spent
the rest of her life recounting her truly hair-raising adventures to
anyone who would listen.

Bill Vollmann had not needed to have a Native American in
the family to be aware of their history. An underdog himself[n] – he
had carried since childhood the weight of guilt for a younger sibling's death – distress and injustice draw him like a magnet. But they
needn't have. Just the other day I heard Tony Curtis talking on the
box: once so radiantly handsome, now old, fat but unabashed; kept
youthful by his various enthusiasms and a wife forty years younger

than he is and several inches taller. Yet, ebullient survivor though he is, when he speaks of his childhood and the younger brother run over when they were playing together in the street, the skies darken.

The child Tony was beautiful and became a film star. The child Bill was not and would spend his adult life on a kind of self-destruct mission, which is how it came about that when I first met him he was passing through London on his way back from a war – the war against the Soviet army in Afghanistan where he had thrown in his increasingly useless lot (dysentery had got him early and he had to be helped by those he had come to help) with the Mujahideen.

He was to write about this in *The Afghan Picture Show*, the first manuscript he ever submitted and the only one, until *Whores for Gloria* (by which time I had had my fill of prostitutes and the firm was sinking under the weight of his productions") that we turned down. With hindsight, I should have read the Afghan book myself, though there's no knowing that I would have recognised how remarkable it was, but I had recently begun avoiding manuscripts by people I knew and passed it on to a colleague who worked mostly on non-fiction.

I had decided quite late in the day to pass on friends' manuscripts. It hadn't struck me forcibly until R became a Deutsch author that having as your editor someone you already know is a bit of a downer. What about those gratifying first encounters when a writer meets the person who has fallen in love with his book? What about those lunches . . . ? And so, for a while, I passed friends on to other editors but it hadn't always been so and didn't remain that way.

For, long before I left Deutsch, I had come to think it was better to miss out on lunches than on attention to the text and though no editor at Deutsch was ever as careless as publishers have since become, the kind of 'hands on' editing which came naturally to me was going out of fashion and it was common to ridicule American editors for the close attention so many of them still paid to the text.

Of course, when this amounts to changing every 'which' to 'that' and every 'that' to 'which' according to some rule of Fowler's which (or should it be 'that') Henry James, for one, did not observe, you are better without it. But I know several writers who prefer to have their books edited by their American publishers, and though one or two authors flagged during our line-by-line sessions, which could last for as long as three days, no one seemed to feel hard done by: not even R on whose church guide I worked – the only book of his I officially edited – who had to live with my second, third and fourth thoughts about how best to present the text at all times of day and night. For the first time, he realised what I had been doing for twenty years . . .

> *Now that you're outta there I want to say embarrassing things to you . . . things like . . . how much you boosted my life . . . now I have a future as well as a past . . . Editor first but also friend, comfort, mama, sister, colleague . . . This embarrassing letter is almost over so you can go and fix yourself a cup of tea . . .*

This sweet note, which reached me at home a few days after I left Great Russell Street for the last time – no formal farewell, for Tom and I had barely been on speaking terms for months – helped to justify those thirty-two years bent over other people's books.

The writer was not, of course, R but a first novelist and three-day sessionist who like so many others who hadn't struck lucky young were now desperate to be published, less to justify their irregular lives to themselves than to prove themselves to their increasingly sceptical parents.

A parental 'Where's the novel, then?' or words to that effect were, apparently, what finally spurred Howard Jacobson to get down to his first book, but the havoc that writers create in the lives of their nearest and dearest spreads in all directions: not just the worried parents but the partner who may never know the luxury of a regular income and the children whose childhood is one long admonition to keep quiet: the thud of the football against the back door, the beat of rock music, intolerable to the writing Daddy who expects to have a decent stretch of quiet every day. The writing Mummy, of course, doesn't expect to have stretches of time, let alone quiet time, when there are children at home and finds different ways around this.

One Deutsch author who began writing when her four children were not yet at school, would snatch time before anyone else in the house was up. (It was her youngest son who told everyone that his mother had written six books after helping her open the parcel of six complimentary copies . . .) Another, her third child on the way, had, in two years of Monday mornings, completed her third novel and handed it in just days before the baby's birth. Then there was the twice-divorced father who wrote four entire books (typed on the back of Council minutes) on the train to and from work, returning home to cook the supper and put his four children to bed. For this is to do with mothering, not gender. But most mothering is done by mothers and many, like Shena Mackay, put their careers on hold while their children grow up or, like one of my oldest friends," don't really get started until their children leave home, getting their first royalty statement at much the same time as their Freedom Pass.

Another category still are those women who give as good as they get. I am thinking of a photograph seen years ago of C. P. Snow and Pamela Hansford Johnson sitting across from each other at a single Tom-sized desk: precursor of the Drabble/Holroyd household as presented by the media. And then there are those couples (perhaps Snow and Johnson were one) who dispense with children altogether.

One way or another most writers – male writers, that is – make demands that are hard to meet: whether it is to keep the children quiet, field every interruption (the man from Porlock more usually now from Parcel Force or British Gas) or, most demanding of all, to weather the inevitable mood swings and admire each day's production. It's no wonder that the writer's partner is as relieved as the writer when THE END comes into view.

> I am forever reading books prefaced by writers praising the patience-and-forbearance of their wives, and frequently giving them credit for reading, correcting, and even rewriting every single word [. . .] My own wife does nothing like other people, and quarrelled with me during every day of the writing. When it was finished, she refused pointblank to read the book. But since she has been the beat of my heart for thirtyseven years I must add: 'To Renée'.

Thus Nicolas Freeling in his dedication to *Those in Peril*. But Renée, the mother of his five children, is unusual among wives. I have met a lot of women whose husbands or partners have not bothered to read their books, let alone help in their creation, and not one single male, besides the inimitable Freeling whose warm, lively, multilingual household belies any serious discord, who can say the same.

Naturally, the tensions, distortions, havoc that a writer or would-be writer can cause in the home can themselves become the stuff of fiction and one of the most graphic and amusing novels in this genre to come my way was *Chiefly About Hooke* in which, to quote the blurb, 'Tony Sullivan explores the comedy and heartbreak of one man's futile but heroic quest for publication . . .' Required reading, one would have thought, for all those would-be authors who subscribe to *Author* and, when need overcomes reluctance, join writers' groups, as I once signed up with a marriage bureau and attended soirées arranged by the local branch of the Divorced and Separated Club.

These self-help groups, like the various AAs and TVI (The Violence Initiative" which doesn't, despite its name, promote violence but helps prevent it) on whose fledgling steering committee

I sat for a while, contributing nothing more than my middle-aged respectability, are life savers. You find you are not the only thirty-five year old who has been dumped by her husband and you certainly won't be the only unpublished writer: there will even be those whose collection of rejection slips is bigger than your own.

As for the Divorced and Separated, it led, surprisingly quickly, to a couple of awkward but reassuring nights with a jazz musician (awkward because casual sex and a wakeful toddler make uneasy bedfellows) which made me realise I hadn't completely lost it, any more than my romantic novelist friend who after a long dry spell in real life announced with deep satisfaction that she no longer had to write the sex scenes from memory . . .

As if writing weren't hazardous enough when contained within the structure of a regular working life, there are the unfortunate few lured away from their 'day jobs' by a one-book contract, the momentary enthusiasm of a publisher or a publisher's influential friend, and heady predictions of future success. One such casualty was a middle-aged man with two young children who threw up a successful career in industry to write a single book the terms of which were agreed in outline, at least, at that agentless publisher's lunch at which the offer was made. How was X to resist the sirens' call when every unpublished writer and, it seems, every journalist's dream, is to have a *book* to their name. But this two-year project, so lightly undertaken at that merry lunch, was to cost the dazzled author and his wife not only his well-paid job but their mortgaged home and each time I look at that book which bled its author dry I wish that history could be re-written.

And then there was Pascoe.″ Who killed himself. The ultimate havoc. I hesitate to bring him in, unredeemed as John Kennedy Toole was to be by posthumous fame, but he would, I think, have preferred it and I hope that if his daughter, who came to collect his last unpublished manuscript and told me of his death, should ever read this, she will think the same.

Of course, I know almost nothing about this young man's death. He could have had a terminal illness. He could have fallen violently in or out of love. But I do know that he was an astonishing writer who should have been published and who knew that he should have been and for whom coming as close as he did with us was probably the worst thing that could have happened.

But it wasn't entirely our fault. André, albeit only with Arts Council backing, *was* prepared to publish this strange and difficult novel for which (for it was not Diana's cup of tea) I had solicited support from the only people I knew whose names carried any weight: one was Erik Korn, Hebrew prompter at my wedding, now writing regularly for the *TLS*. Another was R whose stock had risen sharply since Knopf had bought *Eccentric Spaces*.

Their reports accompanied the manuscript to the Arts Council offices in Upper Davies Street from where, after what must have seemed like For Ever to the author, we got an unequivocal No.

For several years after this, Pascoe or 'your genius from Plymouth' as André referred to him, kept in touch. He even submitted two more novels, neither as dazzling as the first but decent enough to follow up with had all gone well.

But it hadn't. A long silence and then news of his death.

↣ 6 ↢

Ups, Downs and Outs

I T WASN'T, OF COURSE, only writers who came to grief from their dealings with publishers and publishing; equally at risk were the publisher's staff in those pre-glomerate days which now seem an unattainable Eden. The mass sackings, clear-your-desk culture of today as global war to the civil strife of yesteryear but, given the choice, which would you opt for, death by comparative stranger or knifing on the steps? For, then, each of those revered-in-memory independent houses of which one of the last and most civilised has just been sold, was an independent fiefdom and its ruler a law unto himself.

In a book given to me the other day by its author" – she and I had met for the first time in the breast cancer clinic, waiting to be told whether, in the short term, we were more likely to live or die – she seems to be saying (the language of political discourse, even when as lucid as hers, hard for me to follow) that Capitalism wasn't the only way that mankind could have gone; that, contrary to much current thinking, there is no straight line from the earliest appropriations and barterings of our cavemen ancestors to the world ruled by Commerce in which we live today. Or, to put it another way, that Man is not *innately* the greedy, selfish exploiter of other men and of the planet itself that he appears to be.

Well, she may be right but I wouldn't have guessed it from the behaviour of those I have known in, however loosely the word is used, a political context.

Less loosely than most in the case of Tessa Jowell, that risen star of New Labour who was, for a short time, our next-door neighbour and, had such a thing been possible, would have worn our names out by that habit of ingratiating repetition, the more irritating still when asking for favours she did not mean to return. How could she have thought it OK to ask us to baby-sit her partner David's visiting children yet never offer to baby-sit my permanently on-site son in return? And how could she fail to see the irony in extolling the piece of waste ground at the end of our road as 'a lung for the neighbourhood' even as she set off for the Cotswolds in a car such as I had not seen close up since ministering to Anthony's Bentley in Chester Row: behaviour reminiscent of Tom Rosenthal sweeping out of the office in his opera cloak, in mid-afternoon, on the very same day that he had assembled the entire shrunken staff of André Deutsch Limited to announce that it was 'belt-tightening time' and, Yes (this was in answer to a question from someone in Accounts), it *was* possible that there wouldn't be enough money to pay us at the end of the month . . .

A few days ago, while tipping bags of garden rubbish into one of the 'green' skips at the local dump, which takes longer than you would think because of the way all the twiggy stuff gets embedded in the plastic, I saw, or thought I saw, a familiar face on the other side of the skip. On its third appearance over the rim, I asked this apparition, even whiter now than I am grey, if he was who I thought he was and the answer was Yes. He *was* the David who had sometimes read for us at Deutsch and who, I now discovered, had thought for all these years that we had tired of him, for the work, always sporadic, had dried up completely. Now, standing beside our leafy cars in the recycling centre, I was able to tell him what had really happened: that we had stopped using him because we could no longer afford to pay him which we couldn't, of course, tell him at the time.

In fact, he and all the other freelancers used by our department – the readers and proof readers, the copy-editors, indexers and cartographers – did eventually get their money but it was the cavalier way in which these minuscule amounts were withheld while creditors with more fat on them seemed to go to the head of the queue which led to the most virulent of several virulent encounters with my opera-going boss and to my resigning the directorship[n] that, a few years before, R, now a Deutsch author himself, had stormed in and demanded on my behalf.

By then I had been at Deutsch for more than twenty years and had seen one person's name after another's appear on the headed paper without minding a lot more than I had at school when all my friends had been made prefects and I had not. But when Anthony Thwaite (ironically, one of the few to merit the distinction) *came in* as a director, I finally snapped. And R, knowing I would never make the demand for myself, did it for me so that for the next few years I was signing letters 'Editorial Director' instead of the plain 'Editor' to which I now returned.

It had seemed so obvious to me that when there isn't enough money to go round and X is waiting for £50 and Y (a limited company) for £5,000, you pay X first, making it possible for him or her to do the week's shopping, pay the phone bill or whatever but when, desperate on a particular freelancer's behalf, I gave out a cheque of my own, all hell broke loose, which the high-powered management consultant vetting me for some function in the voluntary sector the other day said, somewhat drily, was not surprising.

It seems there are lines that can't be crossed and this was one, but who drew those lines and how can anyone think there is no longer a need for unions or be surprised that the unions often behave as badly as the forces against which they are ranged? Like those

freelancers we, too, were unrepresented and the one serious attempt
to join a union was scotched by André, whose list was known for
its left-wing leanings, and who (probably thanks to his good friend
Victor Feather*) parked his car each morning just across the road in
the underground garage at the TUC.

André is no longer around to give his side of the story. Nor is Clarice
Linden, the ex-Communist production manager, who lost her job
and never recovered from the loss. But what happened was something like this: a stringy, intense young woman – the lover or wife
of an older man of considerable political clout – turned out to have
even more flair as a political activist than as an editor and within no
time at all the place was in an uproar.

Underpaid, over-worked, badly housed, we were ripe for picking
and one union official after another came along to offer their wares
– organised by the indefatigable Jill with enthusiastic help from
Clarice, politically dormant since Hungary. In the office only one
day a week, my son still a baby at the time, I missed most of these
presentations and only heard at second-hand how, at one point,
André had answered in kind, bringing in his own man and confus-
ing the issue of which union to join even further. This, at least, had
an element of black comedy about it which his conniving with the
younger and more impressionable members of his staff did not.

And then the bubble burst. When everyone was pretty much at
the end of their tether André, incandescent with rage – how *dared*
we! – played his trump card. If we joined a union he would close the
place down.

We survived. By backing off. But the exercise, save for the corpses left
on the field, had been worthwhile for just as the Queen, when under
attack, saw fit to start paying tax on a portion of her vast unearned

* Then General Secretary of the TUC

income so did André make a few concessions. We didn't, it's true, see any immediate difference in our salaries, for he was incapable of parting with money unless someone held a loaded pistol to his head, but our holiday allowance increased dramatically from an across-the-board fortnight to three and even four weeks: it was evidently less painful handing out Time than Money. It's also possible that for a while, at least, the fright he had had made him easier to stand up to in those ghastly sessions when, pushed beyond endurance by some financial crisis, one screwed oneself up to ask for more.

The first time I did this was when I needed another ten shillings a week to get a mortgage on the house in which I still live. If my husband had still been working there would have been no problem but having inherited a few thousand pounds he had given up his job and our joint income was £11 a week. And to have told Camden Council that M, studying Edward Thorp's *Beat the Dealer* as he had once studied Plato and Wittgenstein, was expecting to make more from playing blackjack than he had from his regular job, would not have cut much ice . . .

About the confrontation itself, this old-style 'salary review', what I remember most clearly is the urgency of my need, for we were not the only people trying to buy that rose-covered cottage, but it would certainly have been interrupted by phone calls, often in Hungarian; and though I got what I had come for, so demeaning was the experience – from knocking on the door to waiting through those endless calls, often initiated by André himself, and trying, in between them, to justify one's request – that it took more nerve still to do it the next time and, like so many other Deutsch employees, I would allow my salary to stagnate for years at a time.

Little wonder that I get impatient with friends who complain about their unions – that they hold too many meetings (mostly ill-attended) and send too much bumph (mostly left unread) – and then take for granted the annual pay rise which manifests itself on their pay slips as though this had arrived by divine intervention or, less likely still, through the goodness of their employers' hearts.

They are no more aware than the baby enjoying the world from its pram that without 'mother' they would roll down the nearest hill and there would be no one there to pick them up. Which is what happened to Clarice, the gravest but not the only casualty of our attempt to join a union. In her late fifties when André got rid of her – curiously, he felt more venom towards her than towards the real ringleader – she was never to find another worthwhile job. No longer a member of the CP – Hungary the watershed – she had lost both her faith and her calling but she had many friends, a rock-solid marriage and, in her last few years, a beloved ginger cat.

How different it would have been" had we been able to refer our troubles to some outside body: the whimsical hiring and firing, the moribund pay, the smell of gas that permeated the basement where we worked alongside the ancient boiler and among an array of pipes, one as heavy as a soil stack, and none of them – as innards have since become – intended for show. But, just as after the first few minutes you stopped noticing the gas smell, so those of us who stayed got used to the conditions. It took some crisis, like that futile attempt to get unionised, both to wake us up and to show us how powerless we were and would remain.

Which is why, I suppose, I was more moved than irritated by the success of a General Strike which left us, the other day, in a small, hot, Spanish town unable to get a cup of coffee. Every bar, every café, every shop was closed and the one five-star hotel had a discreet note gummed to its palatial entrance informing us that in support of the strike they were servicing only their own guests.

We could certainly have got through the day with the water in our hotel room and the remains of our 'car food' – the fruit and cheese bought at a market in La Carlota, a 'new' town" founded to re-populate an area decimated by the expulsion of the Moors and the Jews – and the almond biscuits collected at convent turnstiles.

But we didn't have to. We were rescued by a nice lady who had thought fit to open up the Tourist Office, put up a handwritten note saying 'Back at 11' and took us home with her for breakfast.

This didn't seem like strike breaking. Whatever the fight was about, it had nothing to do with tourists and, like the feisty Irish grandmother we ran into in Cordova, doing 'classical Spain in five days', I might have joined in, waving my flag For women's rights and Against welfare cuts (or whatever the issues were) as she had, to the consternation of the rest of her group who feared she would be arrested and hold them all up. But there were no demonstrations in Baeza unless they took place in those afternoon hours that we spent in one of the smallest and loveliest of all our stops.

Like Baeza, Sabiote had charm. So did André. He was also small: the standard size of tyrants, though not all conform to the pattern. It is impossible, for instance, to imagine Robert Maxwell dwarfed by his surroundings as André was to be in the portrait commissioned to celebrate his seventieth birthday which now hangs, not far from Diana's, in the National Portrait Gallery.

This painting by Leonard Rosoman was the brainchild of a member of André's staff who was and remains a friend[n] though I could not share her devotion to our employer. But there were others who did and among those most loyal to him were his two long-serving secretaries; also, less surprisingly, a number of his authors.

One of these was Robert Fisk who was about to deliver his Lebanon book when André sold out to Tom. Nothing I could say would reconcile Fisk to the change. But no one was more professional. I had less trouble liaising with Robert on the war front than with many a home-based author and though he evaded direct contact with Tom as far as he could the book went ahead, and before very long we all found ourselves round the same table at the NCR Book Awards where Simon Schama, alas, walked off with the prize.

Since the schism in my own relations with Tom who, at that time, I was genuinely trying to promote, I have often reflected that Robert got there first: he took an instant dislike to his new publisher and no amount of flattery, at which Tom excelled, could win him over. It did not even weigh when, backed by some visiting American publisher, Tom took his side in that disagreement we were having about the way his book began. I was against the emotive opening chapter, set in Auschwitz, thinking that with all this preliminary stuff about the suffering of the Jews he was loading the dice (the 'of all people they should know better' argument) in what was, in every other way, an exemplary and moving book. So, with the magisterial weight of Tom on his side, the chapter stood but so did our relationship and each Christmas I still receive a card, almost always some lovely but little known painting from the Dublin museum.

If André had still been in the driving seat, I would not have expected him to take my side in what seemed, though I maintain it was not, a case of hyper-sensitivity for, unlike Tom, he had no Jewish funny bone: in fact, quite the opposite. All the more galling, then, when in a characteristically scabrous profile *Private Eye* described him as 'a little Hungarian Jew'." Devastated, he rushed to me – the only Jew" in the building since Clarice had been booted out – for consolation, which I found hard to give for I knew that any other week he would have been reading that same page with relish. But this momentary aberration provided the one flash of intimacy in our long relationship as André fished in his pocket and came out with an earring – a single earring – which he said had belonged to his mother . . .

Bizarre at the time and comic in retrospect, as was my fulfilling his prediction that one day I would come up with a 'one-eyed Jewish poet'. What I did come up with and what we did publish, because it came with a subsidy, was an anthology on deafness* by a partially

* *The Quiet Ear: Deafness in Literature* (1987)

deaf, one-legged, German-born Jewish circuit court judge.

An altogether remarkable man, Brian Grant, by this time retired, had lost his leg and begun to lose his hearing after stepping on a land mine on an Italian beach. Apparently it was the heroic but foolhardy custom of the Marines to collect the bodies of dead comrades . . . Be that as it may, Brian who had left Germany only a few years before the war became more English than the English, celebrating one particular anniversary of his first arrival in the country by taking his whole extensive family across to France and back again: to arrive, together, on English soil.

This love of his adopted land extended to its literature in which he was steeped and, thanks to the subsidy from one of the associations for the deaf and, more still, to Margaret Drabble who had provided him with a thoughtful Preface, this unlikely little book saw the light of day. So, too, some years earlier, thanks to the open-minded generosity of a well-known academic, did Bella Aronovitch's *Give It Time.**

Brian Abel-Smith was Professor of Social Administration at the LSE when Bella, a complete unknown, arrived on his doorstep with her manuscript. Encouraged by her sister – the two of them had drunk in Culture, as the Williams sisters tennis, at their father's knee – she had written an account of the four years she had spent in hospital, as a teenager, when the wound from an appendix operation wouldn't heal. So impressed was Brian Abel-Smith by this plain-speaking description of life in the East End of London before the NHS was even dreamt of that he 'introduced' it, and his Introduction enabled us to take it on.

Give It Time was, of course, a 'once-off' but it did more to change its author's life than publication generally does. Just as R, an out of work English teacher at the time his first book was published, found himself invited to lecture in architectural schools, so did Bella, who

* *Give It Time: An Experience of Hospital 1928–1932* (1974)

never finished school, find herself in demand as a speaker in hospitals and at nursing-related conferences, activities which filled more and more of her time after she retired and for which she had been well prepared by a lifetime's active involvement in her union.

That Bella had worked in the fur trade and as a union delegate had once visited Moscow in mid-winter, proved a boon to me for when she heard that R and I had scraped together enough money to go to Russia one late December, she offered to look at my mother's furs and shortened the too-long beaver coat, making a belt from the bottom few inches, so that it was as comfortable as a dressing gown. And it proved a lifeline. So did the woolly hat from M & S of which, luckily, I had two for R, having grown up in a country where you expected snow in winter, was dismissive of all this talk of cold. But after our first night walk – my thighs like frozen hams when we got back to the hotel – he conceded that the cold in Moscow was in a different league from the cold in Carlisle, Pa and borrowed the unflattering headgear which he wore for the rest of our stay . . .

It was December 1980 and, like any year, the domes of the Kremlin were snow-covered, the river was frozen solid and the windows of the train that took us from Moscow to Leningrad were so thick with frozen dirt that we couldn't see out. Every morning, against expectation – it was the first time we had been away in a group – we were very happy to see the others in our Thomson party at the breakfast table – reassuringly English in this alien place. After which we took ourselves off, R having mastered the alphabet so at least we knew which stops were which on the metro, coping magnificently in the realms of Art and dismally in our choice of items from restaurant menus: the boiled potato with chips we had once had in Wales put in the shade by the plate of watery cabbage served with a half-cooked egg . . .

Like Bella (though she had grown up talking Yiddish) I had failed to learn Russian from a Russian-speaking mother but I was, nevertheless, a 'Russian Jew': not a category I had ever put a name to until a friend, not known for her tact, was prompted to extol the superior virtues of the 'German Jews' as though these virtues were evident to all. Since when I have found myself putting Jews in boxes – as tiresome a habit as always noticing the makes of cars which overtook me after an afternoon spent poring over back issues of *Which?* in the local library when we needed to buy one – and finding that, in my book, with a few exceptions, the Russian (English) Jews came out on top. One of these exceptions was Brian Grant who, like Bella, was to do us a most useful service.

It had been several years since we had published his anthology and we were no longer in regular touch when, returning from Scotland with R and heading for the cluster of churches round Whitehaven, our car broke down. Today, finding ourselves stuck in the middle of nowhere, we would get out the mobile phone and call the AA but there weren't mobile phones then, which made it all the more miraculous to see *Armathwaite* on an arm of the nearest signpost and to recognise it as part of an address I knew from the past.

Towed to a phone box by a helpful driver, we looked up Brian Grant's number and within no time at all, a tow truck from the local garage – 'the judge's garage' – pulled up beside us and we were taken to his home where you would have thought he and his wife had long been expecting us, the beds made up, the welcome so complete. That night, too tired to go to a concert in Carlisle with our hosts, we made ourselves at home in the unfamiliar kitchen and went to sleep in the unfamiliar beds to wake, revived, and able to enjoy a jaunt round the countryside in Brian's car: concert-goer and driver, he was not someone to let being deaf and having only one leg interfere with his life.

I don't think André met either Brian or Bella more than once, but it was enough for them that he had published their books. He did, however, spend plenty of time with Richard Ingrams, both before and after the *Private Eye* upset. In fact, we published both a book *by* him and a book *about* him. The subject of the first was Malcolm Muggeridge; the second was a biography – commissioned by André with its subject's full approval and, perhaps, at his request. But though it was written by a writer of his own choosing, biographer and subject were soon at odds, or so the distant rumbles led us to believe. Was it possible that the editor of *Private Eye* was objecting to things being said about him . . . ?

André, so domineering in other contexts, was putty in Ingrams' hands. Not a side of him that will be easily recalled by Leo Cooper or any of those other Great White Hopes who came and went at a dizzying rate, their arrivals heralded as Second Comings, their departures shrouded in silence.

André really believed that he wanted a right-hand man and – another dream of his – a stream-lined office (he had badgered my husband M unsuccessfully to design a system on the giant peg board with coloured threads that he kept in his room) but, of course, nothing was further from the truth. He was not ready for power-sharing and never would be, nor would he have enjoyed or observed any system that man could devise. He liked things just the way they were but he didn't know it. Looking back, it can't have been fun to be wooed for an important-sounding if ill-defined job – André must have been at his most charming during those interviews – and then found wanting. Even though most of these Young Turks went on to better – much better – things, the memory could rankle. As it clearly did with Leo Cooper who, to André's surprise, didn't come to help celebrate the firm's twenty-fifth anniversary.

We didn't go in much for parties at Deutsch but this was one and, held in a hired venue (in itself a departure from the norm), it was slightly more lavish than usual. André's penny-pinching in which

I had always seen some virtue – he probably did insist on 40-watt bulbs in the loos and he certainly complained every time he found a window open when the heating was on – was to become a fond memory during the days of his successor's crippling extravagance.

More lavish still was the party – also an away affair – given to launch *The Business Amazons* and anyone used to the OK wine and plates of crisps we usually served up must have been surprised by the flow of champagne and delectable eats, but then they didn't know – and Leah Hertz had better sense than to let it be known – that she had footed the bill. Fair enough, as was André's strategy for saving money on expensive lunches by providing inexpensive food on the premises.

At some point in time, and before long we had forgotten it had ever been any different, we had colonised the top floor of the building, until now someone's flat, as the basement had been someone else's business. Now the largest room became the Deutsch dining room and was presided over by a succession of cooks just as colourful as the succession of right-hand men who were obliged, like the rest of us, to use it. Which, though convenient for those who preferred not to squander time, was seldom a pleasure, for André, abstemious himself, insisted on fare so plain that no self-respecting cook would put up with the strictures for long; among these was Camilla, the wafer-thin ballerina, once married to Constant Lambert, who could have produced meals to rival any restaurant, but whose run-ins with André proved too much for them both: this was not a marriage made to last and it didn't.

Nor did that with Ilsa Yardley though this one was given a second try. The first time round, after an interminable harangue from André about having bought one slice of ham too many for an Editorial Lunch (though the publicity director, Ilsa had been appointed to cater for these), she allowed herself to be poached by Walter Neurath at Thames & Hudson who offered her twice what she was getting from us for doing the same job. And there she stayed until poached back by André who sent Diana down to Eastbourne, where Ilsa was convalescing, with the offer of a newly-created job – Editorial Manager – and, more persuasively still, heartfelt messages of love and tales of how much she was missed.

So Ilsa came back. But the honeymoon didn't last. Less than two years had passed when, returning from a boozy lunch to find André at his most unreasonable, she was pumped up enough to answer back . . . The blazing row that followed was followed later the same day by a bookend visit by Diana, sent, this time, to give Ilsa the sack . . ."

Delegating the dirty work was one of André's most unattractive habits: one of the most likeable was how quickly he would forgive and forget. To the end of his days, he refused to acknowledge that he had been instrumental in Ilsa's departure, referred to her in the most loving terms and greeted her enthusiastically whenever their paths crossed. More curious still, to someone like myself who has never read the Old Testament but instinctively follows its old morality, that is to say *doesn't* believe in forgive and forget or think old age or the passing of time absolves criminals like Pinochet and Waldheim of their guilt, was the fact that two of the three founders of the Aurum Press which André helped fund into existence, had been Deutsch employees and all had left his employ in various degrees of disarray: the fiery Sheila Murphy, after a shouting match to equal Ilsa's."

Whether Dieter Pevsner, one of the gentlest of men, or the genial Will Allan, brought in to beef up our non-fiction list, retained any affection for André after their departure, I don't know. Will may even have chosen to leave of his own accord. Not so David Harsent who lasted a bit longer and whose assistant, Ariane,* left with him, so tarnished did she feel she had become by association, for André's

---

* Ariane Bankes, now a frequent contributor to *Slightly Foxed*

Loves turned to Hates before they settled down into those unpredictable memories, many of them fond.

For whatever reason, perhaps the confidence he exuded, it took André a surprisingly long time to realise that David had been a mistake. He was decorative – a good-looking, slightly raffish figure, as becomes a poet, who would sit at those editorial meetings with his stylishly booted feet on the table, which must surely have horrified the fastidious André, but the books that David was supposed to attract didn't materialise. For the two years that he stayed, the fiction list was, if anything, thinner than usual.

Whether Diana was enlisted to sever the Harsent relationship or André for once wielded the hatchet himself, I don't know but, like Leo Cooper who was soon to found his own successful publishing firm, David, too, went up in the world; last heard of by me, on the airwaves, as librettist for Sir Harrison Birtwistle's *Gawain*.

If André was such a monster, why did any of us stay and why did almost everyone take his side when, years later, he declared war on Tom? An unjustified war if ever there was one.

For myself, I stayed because there was no one else to pay the bills and I was frightened of launching myself on the job market. Also, who else would have let me work at home, paying me by the hour so that I was free not to work when I needed time for all those blips in routine – ear infections and tummyaches, school plays and sports days – with which every parent is familiar?

Like most single mothers I couldn't afford to pay for help, and being motherless had no ready substitute. Nor had the have-it-and-eat-it culture of the coming decades yet arrived when childless workers would have to smother their fury when colleagues rang to report that Baby X had a runny nose or a rash and it wouldn't be right to leave him, would it?

As it was, the arrangement which lasted for more than ten years suited André as well as it did me: he didn't have to pay me when I was distracted by my son's needs, at the dentist or on holiday; and I could be sure of getting as much work as I had the time to do.

But, of course, it wasn't the beauties of this arrangement which had brought Ilsa back that second time and kept Diana, Pam Royds and June Bird – that pillar of the accounts department now enjoying a retirement devoted to golf and bridge – working for André for most of their working lives.

It was that in spite of this tyrannical parent – indeed, because of him, for there would have been no André Deutsch Limited without him – the place felt like Home. Hard to imagine that today's corporate structures could ever engender the familial intimacy of that rabbit warren where every editor had his or her own private space, however ramshackle, and none of the communal offices housed more than a handful of people. And these people were generally as pleased to see us when we brought them our problems as we to see them.

Of course, there were occasional rows among the siblings and, every now and then, a really bad egg, disliked by one and all, but it was a friendly place and many of the people who matter to me most, I first met there.

But not all. R, like several of my closest friends, began as my lodger for it was by letting rooms I made out during those first years when my son needed less sleep than I did and our nights were punctuated by endless games of solitaire and desperate readings-aloud from the more soporific poets: Wordsworth's 'Michael' was a particular favourite. But though A was only four when R arrived on the scene, he had been younger still when our first lodger moved in, only hours after his father had moved out, and only days before we brought back from the local pet-shop the dog – he cost ten shillings – who was to fill, so triumphantly, the *emotional* void. Mixed as my son's feelings now are about all of us – his four parents – he remembers Patch with nothing but pleasure. A paragon among dogs, this disreputable little mongrel was also one of the household features which attracted R when he got my answer to his ad in the *Statesman.*

It was the first time I had answered an ad – the rooms usually filled up by asking around or putting up a card in the corner shop – but this time I had been left in the lurch by the sudden departure of a Dutch cartoonist who had barely moved in when he got offered a job in Paris and moved out, taking his light-board but leaving his drawing board which, supported on the arms of the Finmar chair (wedding present from one of the South African uncles), became R's writing desk.

It had seemed too good to be true: here was this 'American professor looking for congenial lodgings' who had not only read the interminable novel of Walter Scott's I was proof-reading for Penguin when we met but had almost won me over to it before we turned to the subject of the rent; and though, to my eyes, a thing of beauty with his long, cadaverous face, lean body and mane of red hair reaching halfway down his back (since going white he has been taken all too often for Andy Warhol and now for Andy Warhol's ghost) he didn't give any sign of being either married or gay . . .

But, it wasn't too good to be true and though I didn't heed the advice of friends to get out of my dressing gown and tidy myself up, and though my son had him playing the Guess How Old I Am, Guess How Old Mummy Is game sooner than I would have chosen, here we still are, no longer thirty-seven and thirty-one but sixty-six and sixty . . .

One of the first people to know that I had, so improbably, 'fallen in love' was Diana. I remember bursting into the room where she was working – a gloomy ground-floor room off that corridor which had once held our Trade Counter, long since removed to some anonymous warehouse – to tell her the news and the generous delight with which she received it. So, too, do I remember the sympathy with which, some twelve years later, Dieter Pevsner heard – I had not meant to talk about it but he was such a kind and reassuring presence as well as a parent himself – that that morning my sixteen-year-old son had left home.

Only André had no idea of what was going on in our lives. On one of those grim occasions when I went to him about my pay, reminding him that it had to support two people, he actually asked me who the second person was even though A had often been around the office in the school holidays, sticking down envelopes in Rights or running errands for Publicity, his favourite department because of all the commotion.

Of course, not even Diana – the best of confidantes, whose meaningful life (unlike André's) took place *outside* the office and whose exotic affairs I was to read about in manuscript long before those manuscripts could be published – knew everything. I didn't, for instance, tell her that I had decided to try a marriage agency . . .

If I had ever thought that lodgers could be the answer – that I would find a 'life companion' or even a lover through letting rooms, I would soon have known better. Harry, startlingly present the other day, though long dead, when a film of that legendary Albert Hall Poetry Reading was shown on TV, was unsuitable in several ways. (Will A, when he sees the video," remember him? The fragile, bony face and piercing eyes, fixated one Christmas Eve on the top I was trying to wrap which had a lotus flower in the middle which opened up, as you spun it, to reveal a fairy prince . . .)

George wasn't a possibility either: George Andrews who I knew had compiled *The Book of Grass* but didn't know was married, so was taken completely by surprise when a lady in flowing robes with glitter on her eyelids turned up one morning to visit him in his cupboard-sized garden room. The lady turned out to be his wife,

Tatiana – his lady-wife, my father would have called her – with whom,
I now learnt, he had fathered five children . . .

No more suitable than Harry or George (who made me a batch
of hash brownies[n] when he found I didn't smoke and that I preferred the rent in money) were the gay German art student, the
beached-up hippy who decorated window dummies for a living or
my son's favourite, Norman, a very Australian Australian who would
watch football with him and didn't smell of pot.

Even less suitable, alas, were the people I was to pay to meet.
Convinced by now that I was going to spend the rest of my life
on my own and fired up by the memory of that engaging girl in
the fireworks office, I got out the phone book as she had done and
rang Heather Jenner, as she had, to find that they would only put
me on their Jewish register and had very few Jewish men on their
books. Which was, indeed, the case and after meeting three of them,
I decided to go up-market. Surely this other agency which charged
almost five times as much could do better than the one very dis-
agreeable Indian Jew with whom I had met at the Cosmo Restaurant
in Swiss Cottage, where we ended up arguing about the bill, the
Manchester businessman whose only subject was money and –
though had only the chemistry been right, he would have made a
lovely husband – the woodwork teacher who took a real interest in
A and framed for me the tall, narrow oil painting, given to me as a
teenager by my friend Wendy's older sister, Edwina,* of a striped cat
in a snowy landscape, stalking past a stand of tall, straight trees. In
the years to come, her paintings – still stripes but now completely
abstract – would be bought by museums and exhibited in one of
those off-Bond Street galleries where I try to get out of them what
I know has been put in.

Also off Bond Street or, more precisely, off New Oxford Street
and housed in a single room several dingy flights above street level

---

* Edwina Leapman, two of whose paintings are now in the Tate collection

was the five-times-as-expensive agency or 'bureau' as the proprietor preferred to hear it called. She also preferred her female clients to be 'well groomed' – nothing less would do for her class of gentleman – but there were lengths I was not prepared to go to and though she would clearly have liked another Oxbridge graduate on her books ('My gentlemen are educated gentlemen') and I would have liked to see pictures of her male clientele these were to be kept under wraps until I had signed up *and* my cheque had been cleared.

So much for self-help: 10 out of 10 for effort, nil for achievement. I might have done just as well to go out into the street and 'look for another daddy', as my three year old suggested one bedtime when we were both in a gloomy frame of mind.

Finding writers was easier. There was always the slush pile and, in the early days at Deutsch, the incentive of £20 'head money' for anyone any of us brought in. Whether this would have covered published writers as well as unpublished friends I would have found out had the Asterix books been taken on.

Carol – my writer-friend met at Methuen, when they were launching *Tintin* – had already netted me £20 with an enchanting children's novel, recently re-issued in Japanese." Returning from a trip to Paris in the early sixties, she brought in one of the Asterix books – 'Better than *Tintin*,' she said – a preference in keeping with her rating the Rolling Stones above the Beatles and, about the books, I was soon to agree.

She loved them, would have liked to be their English translator and, fluent in French, not just classroom French either, would have been perfect for the job but our enthusiasm wasn't enough to overcome the difficulties the French publisher put in André's path, and the project was dropped.

So, too, was the head money scheme, long before I met Jill Cox in the gynie ward at UCH, her bed opposite mine a hive of writerly activity. A food and wine journalist, like most journalists, she dreamed of writing a book. A dream that came true a few years later when we published her cook book for children* illustrated, most delightfully, by herself.

To find that Jill really could draw was a nice surprise. Every editor will recognise the dread on being told that some writer is also an 'artist' and would like to have a go at their own jacket. Everyone, you are told when you hesitate, likes their productions – 'Everyone' being that same Auntie B (who knows about books), Nephew Jim (who has just gone up to college) or, in the case of male writers, supportive spouse who cannot understand what it is that you don't like about X, Y or Z – a second or third book, painfully turned down . . .

Another writer with real talent as an artist was Paul Lyons though his Blakean swirls would not have won many votes with the salesmen. I had met Paul for the first time when, working at home, I became aware of someone digging at the end of my neighbour's garden and, after a cloudburst, went out to bring him in. Like the frog in the lily pad who was really a prince, this soaking wet layer-of-flagstones was really a poet and, some seven years later – for a young family and long working days didn't leave much time for writing – we published his surreal comedy *The Eden Man*.[n]

Someone who *did* manage to write, although he too had a young family, was Ray Salisbury who was bringing up four children on his own. On the train to and from his job in a council office, he wrote the greater part of the four 'Simon' novels which took his central character to the age of eleven – the age the author had been when his beloved grandfather died. As a picture of childhood – a West Sussex childhood just after the war – I know nothing to equal it. And it – or they – only happened because Ray, who had left school at fourteen, went to sign up for an upholstery class, found it full and

* *Keep Out of the Kitchen, Mum* (1984)

50 *Carol Filby*

51 *Eva Figes*

52 *Madeleine St John*

53 *Leah Hertz*

Some other writers who arrived unagented . . .

54 *Nadeem Aslam*

55 *Robert Edric*

56 *Clare Chambers*

57 *Kanan Makiya*

58 *Jane Rawlinson*

59 *Bella Aronovitch*

60 *Joyce Dennys*

61 *Faith Addis*

62 *Rudolph Sabor*

63 *Michael Curtin*

64 *Paul Lyons*

65 *Carol Bruggen*

67 *Gwendolyn Mary, Carol's mother*

66 *Murray Bruggen, Carol's husband*

68 *Tom Bruggen, Carol's son*

69 *Kate*

put himself down for Creative Writing instead." Here Carol enters the story again, for it was she who taught those classes and sent him on to me . . .

So, a hospital bed, a rainstorm, an over-subscribed upholstery class . . . There is no knowing where the next writer may come from, or how he or she may be found.

As for the 'slush pile', which I had been doing for years before hearing the heap of unsolicited manuscripts called by this name, it yielded as regularly as any well-tended crop, which is to say that there were good years and bad years but there was always something. And it was all too easy to separate the wheat from the chaff. It took perhaps an hour each week to whip through the thirty or so submissions and put to one side the two or three that seemed worth looking at; and, if the truth be told, it didn't take much longer with that week's agented intake though the agents would have been less surprised that their submissions didn't get read.

Agents didn't, of course, take on authors they didn't expect to sell but we weren't their first port of call for these and we got more than our share of those titles they handled for their American 'ends', in which they had no particular stake. For every *Men Are From Mars, Women Are From Venus* or Thomas Pynchon's *V*, already hot properties before they reached these shores, there was a sub-stratum of lack-lustre fiction, biographies of people whose names we barely knew and variants of *101 Different Ways to Cook Squash*. These, like so many of the slush pile submissions, could be turned around in thirty seconds flat, for it takes no longer to know that a certain subject won't do or that a writer can't write; which doesn't mean can't spell, begins sentences with 'And' or commits any of the other crimes against literacy that we had been warned about at school. What it does mean is that however well plotted a novel, however deeply felt a work of non-fiction (holocaust memoirs, tales of bereavement) they were never meant to be read outside the family circle because words are not that person's medium. We can all sing, but how many of us would it be fun to listen to?

After an early and misguided attempt to reject every submission with a letter, I resolved to do what seemed like the next best thing which was to get the manuscripts back into circulation fast. If we *were* interested in something – particularly an unagented something – we could be as slow as anyone else while we tried to find an American publisher, waited to hear what they thought in Australia or applied for an Arts Council grant, but for the rest, no one had to wait months for a straight rejection and were thus spared those sleepless nights wondering whether their manuscript had even arrived (acknowledgement cards, like 'Esq.', a thing of the past) and afraid to ring up in case they should rock the boat.

What some writers did, though the practice was frowned on, was to send out more than one copy of their manuscript at a time: this way, with the average publisher taking three months to reply," at least the writer could get through more than four of them in a year . . .

In these circumstances, it seemed fair enough and yet I advised it with caution: like advising unagented authors that they should claim back their rights, it raised the question of whose side you were on. But when, as actually happened, a well-known publisher expressed interest in a manuscript that had been lying around their office for more than a year, to find we already had it in production, how could they reasonably complain? In that case, the author had not sent out multiple copies but had come to us despairing of ever hearing from the publisher of his first choice and probably thought it presumptuous to alert them to this possible rival. Certainly, it was this which had stopped me from telling André that my partner's *Eccentric Spaces* was also doing the rounds in the States and we were, as so often, waiting on the Arts Council when, to everyone's surprise, Knopf came through with an offer and bought world rights.

Reversion of rights was an altogether more serious matter. Very few people outside publishing know that when a book has been out of print in all editions for a certain length of time and the publisher has been asked to reprint and hasn't, the rights in that book revert to the author. Which means that if it should ever be re-issued, in whatever form, the writer does not have to share what he earns with the original publisher, the contract between them now null and void.

Any halfway competent agent has a system in place which tells him to activate the reversion procedure, for he (or she) knows that such a procedure exists and how important to the writer it can prove to be. But most authors *don't* know this, among them Faith Addis whose Herriot-like books about country life were discovered by a producer long after we had given up hope of seeing them succeed. Now, years later, they have been re-issued by the BBC to accompany *Down to Earth*, the TV adaptation, already into its third series of prime-time one-hour episodes.

What Faith gets is surprisingly little – a fraction of what the writer gets who has turned these light-hearted books into unwatchable issue-filled dramas." But it would have been less still. It seemed logical, if 'disloyal', to tell her and all our other slush pile authors that this right existed. After all, we had told them that they would be just as well looked after by us as by any agent; that we would, in fact, *be* their agent and this at no cost to themselves and, unlike 'real' agents who charge for them," with free proof copies thrown in . . .

Thinking back, I don't know why André and Tom were always so ready to deal with authors direct, nor whether those authors would have been better served by Curtis Brown or whoever. Certainly, the writers, many of whom had tried and failed to find an agent, were happy to sign up with us and, by far the biggest hurdle overcome, were in no hurry to pay 10 per cent of their thousand pound advance to someone who now appeared to have nothing much to do. The exception was Jane Rawlinson, one of the most interesting writers we were ever to publish, who, taken by surprise by our offer, panicked and, apparently, more distrustful of publishers than agents, cast round till – by good luck – she happened on Gina Pollinger (that same Gina whose job I had stepped into). Gina served her well but was honest enough to admit that she had not been as taken as we were with the raw power of this novel which had fallen into her lap.

I had been surprised" not to hear from Jane sooner: an offer to publish usually elicited a reply by return. I was less surprised by the occasional defection, as agents, trawling our catalogue for unagented authors, made a play for those same authors they had shown no interest in before. This had less serious consequences for us than the poaching, by the big publishers, with or without the help of agents, of the small and often out-of-town publishers' occasional successful authors.

Luckily, there are writers who stick with their publisher," as Updike did with Deutsch until close to the end, and there are those, too, who resist the blandishments of agents. One of these was Leah about whom I got a call one day from an agent whom I had never met, to say that she had been approached by Leah Hertz and was wondering whether to take her on. Could I tell her – this would be in the strictest confidence, of course – more about her? What had she been like to work with? What did we think of her new project?

Leah was by this time as much friend as author and I was surprised that when she decided she needed an agent she hadn't talked to me first. Whoever she went to, I would manage to get along with them. Even the worst transitions which began with a lot of huffing and puffing about the conditions to which their new clients had been subjected, soon settled down. There were even times when you wished an author *had* an agent, to act as a buffer when relations grew rocky.

But what had made Leah feel she needed one, and why hadn't she told me she was unhappy? The answer was that she hadn't and she wasn't. To prove it, she sent me a copy of the agent's letter, soliciting her as a client.

What was it with these people that they preferred stolen goods and that the greatest coup of all was the bagging of a mega-buck author who had belonged to someone else instead of finding one of these writers in the first place? Not something I was ever lucky enough to do though I may, of course, have missed them. Certainly, I had too hastily dismissed" or failed to support a number of writers who went on to do well. Every now and again, I would see a name or title I recognised in the Sunday paper and think oh-my-god, we saw that one . . . But none of these writers have yet become household names though one of them, Peter Carey, is getting close . . .

Just as André had a prejudice against books 'of Jewish interest' so, too, was he averse to short stories, so it must be thanks to Diana that we had published both Alfred Chester and Grace Paley, both of whom could have been out on both counts. But neither she nor I could salvage Peter Carey whose *The Fat Man in History and Other Stories* had reached us (me), in galleys, from the University of Queensland Press.

Provenance was not a problem with the slush pile: Solihull, Petts Wood or Leicester just as likely as each other (and anywhere in Ireland *more* likely) to produce a natural-born writer. Is it the nuns, the Christian Brothers, or something in the water which accounts for almost every Irish offering being worth a second look?

The truth was that the next best-selling author could come from anywhere: who would have predicted that great swathes of North Yorkshire and Teesside would one day be known by the names of two writers who, in some sense, never left home? With Cookson and Herriot we enter household name territory: authors so popular that they are sold in Woolworths and dominate the boxes of books at every jumble sale.

At Deutsch, we never had an author who sold on anything like that scale. The nearest was a single book, Peter Benchley's *Jaws*, bought by Piers Burnett who, for years, André failed to realise *was* his right-hand man and is now one of the executors of his estate. *Jaws* was, and thanks to the film remains, one of the few books we published that more than a handful of people have heard of.

Like every publisher, we had some wonderful writers on our list whose names were exceedingly familiar to us but not to the world at large, not even the bookish world, and they stayed that way unless, like Joan Brady, they were lifted out of obscurity by winning one of the grander prizes. But even with the Whitbread behind her, there are plenty of potential readers who haven't come across Joan's *Theory of War* and would probably mistake the book, because of its fearsome title, for non-fiction which, in some sense, it is. But it is a novel too and of such harsh power" that as I read it, in manuscript, I had to turn back more than once to remind myself that the writer was a woman.

Titles, like jackets, were a source of endless trouble, and it was not uncommon for a book to be delayed because we or the author were stuck on one or the other. At least the jackets were entirely down to us (only Updike was consulted about his) which should have made things easier but the job was never entrusted to the two or three people most concerned – whoever had commissioned the artwork, the book's editor and André who was, after all, entitled to have the final say. Instead, it became a free-for-all at those weekly meetings with Sales complaining about the size of the lettering, Rights about the shade of orange, Publicity about the choice of subject itself, not one of them realising that their responses were entirely subjective. So maddening, indeed, was the cacophony that I made it a rule when I was no longer responsible for the jackets – a job which André handed me along with policing that options list on my very first day – to stay out of the ring except when a book that I knew better than anyone else was under fire.

For we did know our books better than anyone else and we were also, and just as important, the author's only representative at those and other melées. For myself, like any other 'desk editor', I reckoned to have read any book I worked on at least three times before it went into print and though as we got bigger and began to send work out, I was glad to shed the copy-editing and could not have got through the Vollmann years without the help of Howard Davies who took those dizzying flights of post-modernism in his quiet stride, I never gave up proof-reading. To miss out on the first sight of one of your books in print is a lesser deprivation than losing the sight of a child as they grow into an adult but not dissimilar.

Titles *couldn't* be imposed on an author, though in one case at least there was a degree of coercion. I can no longer remember the long list of alternatives to *Season of the Rainbirds* which no one much liked, including its author, Nadeem Aslam, but it didn't stop this remarkable novel from getting the attention it deserved and, had we hung about longer, the book might not have been published at all. Nor, conversely, did *Half the Gladness*, culled from Shelley's 'Skylark' after a day batting ideas back and forth in Carol Bruggen's Lancashire kitchen, help sell her book though, so lovely in itself and so exactly matching the spirit of the novel, it remains my favourite title of all.

Names, too, presented problems though the odder the name the more difficult to forget. It was days before I got round to ringing Eva Figes, whose first novel we had kept for over a year, because I had no idea how to pronounce her surname. This turned out to be Fie-jeez and we soon became familiar with it for though Faber had bought her second novel while we were still sitting on her first and we were never to publish her adult fiction, we did bring out a couple of picture books, written for her children, Kate and Orlando; most memorably, *The Banger*, which had to be re-titled before being published in the States where 'to bang' has more than one meaning."

An author, not one of ours, whose improbable and unforgettable name should be as familiar as Rushdie, Amis or Drabble, is Janette Turner Hospital one of whose books I was lent by a friend on the verge of our travelling to India together: Trivandrum, the setting of *The Ivory Swing*, was to be our first stop.

It doesn't make sense that this writer should have only a modest following when others are household names: Penelope Lively, for instance, whom I had avoided reading when she became a valuable Deutsch author, because I feared I wouldn't like her, a gut feeling confirmed only yesterday as I listened to a radio adaptation of one of her novels over which Time and Memory hung like a damp cloud. Less elemental a fiction it is hard to imagine and though both it and Hospital's Trivandrum novel begin in quiet domestic fashion (like Jane Rawlinson's *Cradle Song*, so similar to *The Ivory Swing* with its colonial setting and cataclysmic ending) the one peters out, a feeble twist in its tail, while the other explodes, rocking both protagonists and reader alike.

So disturbing, in fact, was the violence in *The Ivory Swing* that it was a relief to find Trivandrum and our first night's lodging – we had lit, by chance, on a Christian household – as friendly and familiar as they were. So, too, after turning the last manuscript page of Eric Lindsay's *A Charm Against Drowning* and being forced outdoors by the dog's expectation of her nightly walk, had I been relieved to find the streets of Kentish Town no more eventful than usual . . .

My other preparatory reading for this Indian adventure was *Kim*. First read as a child, it was this book which had made me determined to get to India one day.

Of course, it wasn't set in Kerala but I had only the haziest notion of where anything was – anywhere in India was good enough for me – so when, drawn by the heady conjunction of sporadic Communist rule and a traditionally matriarchal society, my friend proposed Kerala, that is where we went, a choice neither of us would regret.

Nor had R and I, a few years earlier, regretted going out of our way to Aliano, a little hill town in Basilicata, though this expedition had been prompted not by the book, but the film of the book. Anyway, whether the town was preserved by its remoteness or the comparatively small number of people who had seen or read *Christ Stopped at Eboli*, pilgrims were thin on the ground. But the impulse which took me to India and us to Aliano is no different from that which brings busloads of tourists to Thirsk for the 'Herriot' experience, and train-loads to Goathland – once one of the loveliest spots on the North Yorkshire Moors, now the hub of Heartbeat Country. Needless to say, India is capacious enough to absorb Western pilgrims of whatever kind – the spiritual seekers among them, who, like the cluster flies that drive us out of the same room each autumn, tend to clump together in their ashrams. In spite of the poverty and dirt which stop some people coming and drive others away, India exerts an irresistible spell. The colour, the pace, the warmth of the welcome wherever (as in so many places) foreigners are still a rarity are, like the exotic temples and rites, the strange plants and dramatic landscapes, an endless pleasure.

India is also cheap. And this may have contributed to the good humour in which the novelist Laurie Devine found her publisher, André Deutsch, when both were visiting the exact same spot on that vast sub-continent at the same time.

According to Laurie, André was at his most charming and munificent. They had some kind of ride together – on an elephant? I no longer remember – but it stayed in Laurie's memory as a decidedly happy experience: which is not to suggest that there was any kind of holiday romance between André and this writer of romances for, to the best of my knowledge," he never cheated on Gwen, his twelve-year-older married mistress whom he had met in the fifties and with whom he was still sharing his life when he died.

I learnt from Piers quite recently – Piers Burnett who had bought *Jaws* – that André, who had been a semi-invalid for several years, had altered his will, not long before his death, so as to leave money for his last, devoted carer to buy himself a house. A generous move – still more surprising in its thoughtfulness than its largesse; but what, I wonder, became of Pierrot, André's factotum and our cook for so many of the preceding years? Good-natured, untidy in his person (it was said he had once tried on André's cashmere sweaters, leaving them somewhat baggy), I have a special affection for Pierrot who, when our office dining room was dismantled, put the best items aside for me – no one else, it seems, had my boot-sale mentality – whence they finally made their way to Yorkshire where the old Deutsch bread bin keeps the mice at bay.

And what about the Balzacian power play which I experienced at first hand? Not once but twice, André, embittered by his dethrone-ment – he seemed to have forgotten that he had *sold* the firm to Tom – but still at large on the premises, wandered into my room to let me know that if I didn't change sides – by this time everyone in the building was either for André or against him – he would cut me out of his will. Which – if I was ever in it, which I doubt – he did.

But not quite, for, as I understand it, there is some provision against the day – may it never come – when the £3,000 per annum ex gratia payment which the lawyers procured for me should cease. It had taken André, my friend now that Tom was my enemy, a very long time to do anything but make suggestions about ways in which to bring my pension up from the £2,500 at which it stood to the £8,000 that it should have been. At no time did he offer one penny of the £30,000 that this would have taken. (All figures have been rounded off. The precise figures are a matter of record.)

André's first suggestion, made over lunch in the Gay Hussar, was that he should meet my 'rich friend'. He had, evidently, heard from Diana that someone had given me a large amount of money to pay off my ex-husband. It was she, hopeful that his avid interest in my affairs might bear fruit, who had engineered this meeting, for he and

I had not spoken since that last visit to my office more than a year before.

So preposterous was the idea of André, who was largely responsible for the fix I was in, turning to an unknown American businessman for help in putting together a rescue package that I didn't have to think twice. I said I would be glad to take the money from him, but it was out of the question to involve this friend of R's whose name I kept to myself.

André's next suggestion was almost as surprising: he would like, he said, to meet my lawyer – my lawyer being a young man who worked in the Pensions Division of the West End firm which had taken me on as a pro bono client. It was hard to see how such a meeting could be useful and I was loath to waste Peter Ford's time but I passed the invitation on and, as healthily curious to meet André as André was to meet him, a lunch was arranged.

Nothing, of course, came of this nor of André's next suggestion, that he take me to meet Lord Goodman . . .

When he first proposed this, I was dubious. I already had a lawyer. Lord Goodman would have been useful in *finding* one, but what use could he be to me now? And wouldn't it seem an affront to young Peter in whom, by now, I had complete faith, if I went, so to speak, 'above his head'? But Peter's response was characteristically open-minded. 'Shake the tree and see what falls out,' is what he said and that is what I did.

For all the good it did, which was none beyond adding to the little store of stories which still serve to fill the occasional silence when we find ourselves among people who haven't heard them before.

The story goes like this:

I was to meet André at Lord Goodman's flat in Portland Place, a venue so familiar" to André that he did not describe the entrance procedure clearly and I arrived first at what turned out to be the tradesman's entrance of the wrong flat.

Now that I come to think of it, the flat we had lived in in St John's Wood had had a kind of servants' quarter with its own separate lift which could be – the shared bourgeois-Jewish background – what made this lord less scary to meet than most lords would have been. But perhaps because I arrived rattled at having got lost in the building and being, therefore, a few minutes late, I remember very little of what actually took place; only the Buddha-like presence of Lord Goodman, wedged in a chair at one end of a room, furnished much like my parents' sitting room had been, and André in the unfamiliar role of supplicant, rehearsing my plight and the manifold evils of Tom.

Lord Goodman listened but said almost nothing and I came away convinced that if he had chosen to speak it would not have been to say anything that either André or Tom would have wanted to hear. Which makes me think that Peter Ford was probably right when he steered me away from trying to take Tom to the rabbinical court about which I had read in the *Guardian* and a picture of whose bearded elders I had pinned up in my office. Lord Goodman was no more likely than they were to up-end a male pillar of the Jewish community.

Be that as it may, André and I who had arrived separately left together and I remember still our slow progress across Portland Place to the RIBA where he had some business and I left him, wondering how he would manage without an arm to hang on to, and caught the C2 back to Camden Town.

André had become, quite suddenly, an old man. Hard to believe that he and Diana were the same age. She, ten years and two books later, has recently taken up painting and fits this new hobby (the last was gardening, begun when most people put their feet up) in around increasingly frequent public appearances. An exceptionally entertaining speaker, and as ready to talk in the local church hall as the Edinburgh Festival, she is enjoying her renaissance and looks set to live well into her nineties as did her mother and her mother's two sisters, all three of whom were still driving along the lanes of Norfolk when most nonagenarians are lined up in armchairs against the walls of the day-room in some old people's home.

But not Kate: my father and Victor's housekeeper, paid for by that South African conscience money which also provided the flat in Swiss Cottage in which my mother had died. Kate had not meant to take this job but, as she was to tell me, when my father took it for granted she would come, she had not the heart to say No. And there she stayed until, after two or three years alone with my cousin Victor, prevailed upon to find a less consuming job.

Only last week, I met one of her grandchildren, now living with her bee-keeper husband in a Yorkshire village not far from ours, and heard how she and her brothers had enjoyed Victor's visits, for Kate had not abandoned him when she drove down to Cognac each summer to visit her daughter but took him with her, which no member of his own family would have done.

But Kate wasn't like us, the Menells, or like most other people. She had grown up in a Cotswold village, the only child of working-class Socialists whose beliefs she would carry with her for the rest of her life. In her teens, trained as a milliner, she set out for London where she married and divorced a handsome Irishman. Now followed a series of jobs – club receptionist in Curzon Street, hostess at the Arthur Murray School of Dancing in Trafalgar Square, saleslady in the Burlington Arcade – till, adrift in her sixties, with this kind of job and men friends behind her – she turned to something she could still do and signed up with a domestic agency.

She didn't need to do this. Her daughter, who had married into a French wine-growing family and lived in a moated castle, surrounded by vineyards but with few mod cons, would have made her welcome. But Kate cherished her independence and if that meant cooking (which she loved), cleaning, and turning down some old gentleman's bed (on one occasion with the old gentleman in it), so be it. Like Diana, she behaved as though life were beginning not ending. She joined and became active in the Labour Party, she learnt to drive and ferried patients to and from hospital in her old banger with no reverse gear; and when re-housed in a tower block, talked more about the view than about the stink of urine in the lifts.

It took a stroke to stop her. Disabled now, she still refused to move to France and was lucky enough to get a room in the old people's home, recommended by my friend Wendy who had been a geriatric social worker," and which Kate could actually see from the window of her council flat.

This home, run by someone who really *likes* old people – it would not surprise Eileen that I felt not sixty-seven but sixteen as I watched an Elvis video last night – and treats the place like a family home with dogs and babies the most welcome of visitors and her own teenaged children often about, this red-brick Edwardian mansion, once the home of Clara Butt, was to be Kate's final stop.

Never one to sit against the wall of a day-room or, indeed, eat communal meals as most of the residents chose to do, she stayed in her room, watching the birds outside her window and the telly at the end of her bed until one day – she had been there for nearly seven years – she decided she had had enough. No one knows how she managed to get across the room and lock the door but she did and without implicating me (I had no idea my last visit was to be my last) or anyone else, she had asserted her freedom and opted out.

Not as surprised as I would have been if she hadn't shown me her collection of cuttings about Exit, of which, like most radical causes, she greatly approved, I marvel still at her finding the courage to go through with it. Unimaginable that I could ever do what she did: Death, the thirteenth floor at which my lift never stops. I can imagine Before only too well, and like my friend Sally Cline, who when her heart played up made lists of who to invite to her funeral and what to give them to eat, I can imagine After. Though I think less about Hoop Lane and the attendant festivities and more about Death Duties or, in more melancholic and less agitated mood, about where I would like to 'rest'. Hampstead Heath or the North Yorkshire Moors? Or both . . .

For André's funeral I was, mercifully, on those moors, so I didn't have to go along and pretend to grieve though his death, of course, put a final end to the Will he? Won't he? (help out with my pension deficit) which had been keeping everyone else – friends, doctor, counsellor – on tenterhooks for several years. I don't even know if André was buried or cremated but I do know that physically frail though he was when I last saw him, several years before his death, he hadn't lost the mental habits of a lifetime and at a moment in time when it seemed the two sides in the battle over my pension would be deadlocked for ever, he came up with the most startling suggestion of all: that we break into the office and raid the files . . .

The rational basis for this outlandish plan in which André was anxious to play an active part was knowing that Tom had been asked a number of awkward questions by the Pensions Ombudsman, who was now also a player in this drama, but not knowing what they were or how they had been answered. Because though Tom had inadvertently circulated a letter[n] to the Ombudsman referring to these 'eleven points' and asking for more time to answer, he had not slipped up again and circulated his reply.

The idea of breaking into Great Russell Street and rifling the files had been as easy to dismiss as that first idea of involving R's wealthy friend but, as weeks passed in continuing stalemate, it began to seem more and more attractive. But what would we do when we were, like any burglar, stuck with the stolen goods? How could you act on something you weren't supposed to know? What would Nabarro

Nathanson, the solicitors who had taken me on as a pro bono client because, I can only suppose, I came over not only as wronged but upright, think of me in Rififi mode?

Very recently, a new friend, a lawyer friend, told me that they would have been less shocked than I supposed: that it is not un-common for desperate clients to perform desperate acts and that he himself had been rung not long before, in the middle of the night, by a client who was actually in the *act* of 'burgling' the office of his old employer and that though he had advised him to get back home, he had not refused to look at the papers he had brought out with him.

It was this same friend who on hearing that I worked for André, told me he had often met him at the Garrick in the past and had thought him a most charming fellow . . .

And so he was or could be. It depended on where you were standing. I am reminded of a series of photographs of the same man as seen by his wife, his secretary, his mother, his teenaged son, etc. (a half-page 'feature' in my father's *Daily Express*) which I had been riveted by as a child. Or how, among a roomful of Weightwatchers, I no longer felt fat. Or of that mysteriously moving inscription on a bench above the tarn on Hampstead Heath: 'On one side an angel. On the other a Gorgon.'"

End of a Working Life

❦ 7 ❦

ARLY IN THE Tom years I had a sabbatical. It was only for three months but it had been granted without hesitation. Where André would have prevaricated for weeks and taken no interest whatever in why I needed this time off, Tom was not only decisive (if you sent him a memo in the morning, you had an answer by afternoon) but sympathetic. Which makes it more of an irony that he was so soon to become my adversary in a legal wrangle over my pension that was to last for four long years.

More of an irony still, in retrospect, is the care I took with the help of the new Financial Director to protect my pension so that those three months on half pay didn't create some irreversible blip. As out of place as the care with which R and I struggled into our swimsuits on the back seat of the car (we were in France and had just taken in our *n*th Romanesque monument) only to find that the beach on the other side of the dunes was a nudist beach . . .

I don't remember just how long my personal honeymoon with Tom lasted but I certainly took his side during that increasingly desperate duoregnum when André's resentment culminated in a long and vicious piece in one of the Sunday supplements which painted Tom (pictured, most unflatteringly, from behind) as a monster and André as his victim.

To me, at least, it seemed that Tom was being amazingly tolerant, treating André – who became more and more unmanageable – as though he were an elderly relative who deserved respect but could not be left holding the reins of the kingdom he had handed on, or in this case sold, to his younger kinsman. So it was that until the day some months ahead on which it had been agreed that he vacate the building, André remained in his old office – the loveliest and most spacious room in the building – while Tom perched where he could, his first choice of temporary habitat being the box-like room into which I had been shunted for my two days a week. Commandeering this was reasonable enough but could have been done without making sure I understood that the room wasn't really suitable for someone of his importance and had he not, while we were discussing the move, got a call from somewhere lower in the building and told the caller he would send whatever it was down at once as he had 'a piece of warm flesh' (me) conveniently at hand.

I was never to forget that revolting phrase nor the time, several years later, when the entire staff was summoned to his office to stand, like serfs, round the desk at which he stayed seated as he announced that our financial troubles were over: he had sold the children's list to Scholastic, a name he was asked to repeat as none of us except our children's editor, Pam Royds, had heard of them. And in that semi-circle, standing while Tom sat, were Pam, at least ten years his senior and the person whose industry had saved our bacon, and Diana, already into her seventies.

The crudity of his everyday behaviour could be staggering but though ruling him out as someone to spend the evening with, these lapses of taste, most evident in those early days when he was marking out his territory, did not rule him out as an employer. Tom was the very antithesis of André in almost every way, and it was a nice change to work for someone who didn't shy away from making decisions, didn't complicate even the simplest transactions and showed a genuine respect for writers – part of his Germanic inheritance perhaps, like his taste in literature – which André, though he had good relationships with many of his authors, did not so obviously share.

Tom also had the good sense not to impose the bureaucratic practices he had been used to in the larger firm from which he came. For instance, he soon abandoned a typed up agenda for those editorial meetings at which I would arrive carrying all that week's agented submissions plus anything interesting off the slush pile. Primitive though this method was, it had the virtues of speed, cheapness and physicality. No list can replace the presence of the thing itself.

Mercifully, computers which shed lists like confetti became un-avoidable only after I had left. They and word processors which had already deranged so many writers were around but in Great Russell Street we were still handing the production manager typewritten pages, not plastic discs. This was so even of William T. Vollmann's *You Bright and Risen Angels* which had originally opened with a series of flow charts and been written at night in the offices of the com-puter company where Bill worked and from which, as he didn't drive, he had no easy means of getting home. Here was a writer who had to go into technological reverse when he came to us: Howard Davies, his brilliant copy-editor, to this day, uses a manual typewriter with a red and black ribbon.

Luddites though we were and I remain, R and I had advanced as far as an electric typewriter when he began work on his Shell guide to parish churches and set out armed only with a bic and a box of index cards. Returning home from these trips, he would type up entries from his notes and the typewritten pages eventually came back to us in yet another semi-obsolete form – the galley proof. It was thus that they reached the vicars. And all hell broke loose.

Thinking it both a courtesy and a safeguard to let the incum-bents see what had been written, I had sent out each entry with a letter asking to be told of factual errors or significant changes and an order form offering a substantial discount. To avert irrelevant comment, I had finished the letter by saying we hoped the recipient would be happy with the description of his or her church which had been chosen, with only 500 others, from an existing stock of 18,000 by the writer who, to make him sound more authoritative, I referred to as Dr Harbison.

Well, Dr Harbison and I, returning from a weekend in New York attending a friend's wedding, found a deluge of mail. To call it hate-mail would not be much of an exaggeration. For every letter giving useful information, there were dozens complaining about the content and style of the descriptions. One west country vicar had supplied a substitute entry, written by one of his parishioners, another had slashed out 'remarkable'" ('remarkable bench ends') and scrawled UNIQUE in the margin, still another argued about the turbulence of the stream that ran through its grounds so that R, in a footnote, had to bring Ruskin in on his side. Most alarming of all was the phone call from a worried lady saying that her vicar was 'seeking to take out an injunction': but perhaps the most shocking was from the vicar of a church in Sussex who asked to be paid. Luckily we heard no more from him nor from the litigious incumbent of one of the finest Saxon buildings in the country.

Through all this, Tom stood his ground. So, to their great credit, did Shell to whose chairman one of these letters was personally addressed and, in the end, we made only two changes: we removed 'horror comic' from the description of a recently endowed window and 'grumpy' from the description of the north country vicar who after a surly start – he had been reluctant to leave his fireside – had proved unusually helpful. As for the 'straggly plants' which roused such fury in yet another vicar who failed to understand that to the author they contributed to the decaying beauty of the building – they and everything else remained and we were thrilled, some years later, to get a letter from a young woman asking permission to have the 'straggly church' entry read at her marriage service. It seems that the appearance of this modest church in the guide had persuaded her parents it was a fit place for a wedding.

There weren't many such rewards. The book – one of my favourites, so evidently a labour of love – sank without trace. In spite of the publicity manager's efforts it got few reviews and, Shell logo in midstream," drifted into oblivion. All the more pleasing therefore to hear that it was the one book besides Betjeman and Pevsner which Simon Jenkins carried on his travels for his hugely successful guide a few years later.

A labour of love, maybe, but it was also R's most lucrative commission for he emerged from a meeting with Tom with £10,000 more than he would have settled for. It would be churlish to complain. Nor is £20,000 too much, or even, in any other context than publishing, enough for two years' work but here was an instance of that largesse which we, who worked for him, later came to see as a form of self-aggrandisement, helping to bring about the firm's demise.

But, in those early days, before we realised where it was leading, we basked in this new lavishness which brought me, for instance, my first company car. The one Diana was driving, bought for her by André, was found to be unsuitable for conveying Tom to the office each morning, as she now did, and I inherited the cast-off, marvelling both at my luck and at a car so basic it did not even have a glove compartment.

So, one way or another, we all benefited. I even came to prefer my new location: a low, dark room (I was back in the basement) such as I had chosen as a student and such as my dark brown living room, shaded by the lime tree outside, has always been. R's initial horror when he came to view it as a prospective lodger, has long since given way to affectionate habit.

The only downside of my move back into the basement was the ill-concealed irritation of the person who continued to use it on the other days of the week. A striking presence, often wrapped in shawls – more Clytemnestra than Stevie Smith though her instrument, too, was the typewriter – she made it plain that she resented my presence. But this was nothing to the battles raging upstairs.

For one thing, Clytemnestra and I hardly ever met. André was seeing Tom every day. Some moments, of course, were tenser than others. Such questions as who-is-going-to-sit-at-the-head-of-the-table at meetings (the answer was Tom, as it should have been) replicated the where-was-my-husband-going-to-sleep which had arisen that long-ago summer in Turkey. But André who had begun to fall asleep at meetings – none of us knew why he had decided to sell but his diminishing energy may have had something to do with it – found this intolerable and spent much of his time shuffling round the office complaining of his fate: there wasn't a chair for him to sit on (nonsense), Tom wouldn't pay his fare to Frankfurt (why should he?) and, most memorably, that the desk I was working on was not Tom's but his. To tell me this, he had waited in my office through a long and difficult phone call. Even so, I was surprised, when I came in next, to find the desk had disappeared.

It wouldn't have been so bad if André kept his complaints in the family. But before long it seemed as though the whole of literary London had heard how badly he was being treated and we began to get calls from agents – Gina Pollinger was one – asking what we were doing to poor André ... A more urgent question was what poor André was doing to us. I heard only recently that Christobel,[n] one of the best publicity directors we had ever had, had been encouraged by André to apply for a job at Aurum ...

The damage that André did to the firm is hard to measure but it was considerable. Not least, when he went at last, he left behind a divided camp: a kind of Oranges and Lemons in which you were either for Tom or for André, our Hungarian uprising that scurrilous piece in the colour supplement: only the most naive believed André had had nothing to do with it, and there were several defections.

But, in spite of these divisions in the office and the rumblings from the world outside where André was doing his Ancient Mariner act, life continued: books were bought: books were sold. Subjects of Jewish interest were no longer taboo and Tom recalled Victor Perera's *Rites*, the story of his Guatemalan Jewish childhood, which André had made me turn down. He brought in, too, some very non-Jewish favourites of his: Tom Sharpe, for instance, and Nicolas Freeling. Neither of these writers had those Germanic qualities which Tom so admired – exemplified in Hermann Broch whom we were also to publish – but one of them, the first, did display another of his preferences . . .

No one would have thought to arouse André's interest in a manuscript by flagging the steamiest passages but this was at least worth trying with Tom and it is not too surprising that he interpreted Bill Vollmann's obsessive interest in prostitutes as constituting a prurient interest in sex. He assumed the same of Eric Lindsay. But he was wrong about Bill and wronger still about Eric, who would never, as Bill did (but nothing prurient in this), invite a pretty youngster who was helping out in the office up to his hotel room near the BBC. Luckily, I knew nothing about this rendezvous until it was over for the girl or, rather, young woman was the star-struck niece of one of Tom's most cherished authors.

At this same time – in fact, it was she who had encouraged this adventure – we had another temporary Gill-of-all-trades, a twenty-some year old, good to look at and smart as a whippet, who could turn her hand to anything and did so with such style and good humour that we all missed her when she moved on to become manageress of a transvestite club. Rumoured to have spent one lunch hour having a ring attached to her clit, she had such an air of sexual achievement and was so attractive to men that I was surprised when a year or two later she strode into my office dressed in what looked like combat gear and accompanied by an equally handsome young woman, with brilliantined hair, who looked like her identical twin.

Gill was now, perhaps always had been, in same-sex mode; had plans to move to Cornwall[n] with her artist friend, open a gay hotel and write a book. In all three of which aspirations I hope she succeeded.

No less surprising and at about the same time, had been the attempts of a well-known novelist to grope the little-known novelist whom I had brought along to perform at a bookshop event. So drunk was the star of the show that, leaning boywards, he finally lost his balance and landed – all four contestants were seated in a row on kitchen chairs – on the floor where I can picture him still.

Seated not in a row but in an excited huddle round the television set in Tom's office[n] is how and where, returning late from lunch one day to what appeared to be an empty building, I found everyone. What they were watching, in Tom's absence, was a film recently premiered at the Edinburgh Festival which consisted of a relentless series of close-ups of penises, accompanied by a sound track of women's voices.

The film had been made, as I knew from the usual media blitz, by the youngest of my Menell cousins looking now, in his fifties, much like our Uncle Arthur who had been a highly respected president of the Johannesburg stock exchange.

To find Jo, a perky twelve year old when I saw him last at one of those clan gatherings in the Ritz Hotel, living in San Francisco and making the occasional improbable film was not too surprising, but for anyone to think it could be turned into a book was; and this idea had popped into the head of a very self-possessed young Englishman, in Henman mould, soon to leave Great Russell Street and publishing to bring order out of chaos in some distant outpost of Empire.

Just as improbable and of course it never happened either, was the project to make a film of R's *Eccentric Spaces*, a book peopled only by buildings, books and works of art. The dreamer of this dream was Peter Greenaway which did, at least, give it a flying start.

The number of false starts in publishing as in life itself are legion as were the proposals for books and outlines of books that arrived with each post and I rooted through once a week. Most of the non-fiction offerings were bad, sad, mad or all three, some barely literate like the densely typed page claiming that the writer could prove that Shakespeare was a Sephardic Jew. But there was the occasional treasure like Rudolph Sabor's *The Real Wagner* or Isolde Wigram's *Olivia* in which she dovetailed the letters her mother, an Edwardian groupie, had sent to her idol Beerbohm Tree ('I am thirteen and never loved so passionately before') with his few but kindly replies, hectic letters to her governess and confidante about the progress of the 'relationship', plus an occasional interjection from Beerbohm's half-brother Max, a sweetly quizzical onlooker:

> It was about this time that I almost met that remarkable woman Olivia Truman. Beautiful, in the strict sense of the word, she was not, but she had the remains of great prettiness, and was liable to become pretty again at any moment. She had, moreover, her 'nice nights', one of which was the one on which I did not meet her. She is said to have been the one and only authentic prigg the world has ever known, and there is little doubt that she was conspicously femine. To have almost met her is to have lived not in vain.

None of these 'treasures', alas, translated into large amounts of money but they did increase turnover and did nothing to diminish our reputation. As for why we seem to have published more unsolicited manuscripts than most people, it wasn't just a readiness to take them seriously but that our name" occurred high on that alphabetical list of publishers in *The Writers' and Artists' Yearbook* to which beginning writers with no connections in publishing turn.

A more considered approach, sending your manuscript to the

publisher of a favourite author, as Margaret Drabble is said to have done, was rare. Rare, too, though by far the most sensible way, was to choose a publisher known to have an interest in the kind of thing the novice writer is trying to do. Rarest of all is the Donna Tartt syndrome: being recognised by your college professor, himself a published writer, and then passed from one well-connected hand to another without ever needing to go to the local library and consult the *LMP*.

During Tom's early years, we did not need the slush pile to bulk out the list for he brought with him a raft of well-known writers – not just Tom Sharpe and Nicolas Freeling but Gore Vidal, George V. Higgins, Cynthia Ozick, Gail Godwin and others, the last of the most interest to me, for though I had never met her I knew the main characters in her first novel . . . The hero of *The Perfectionists* was not only the older brother of one of my closest friends but also, as we were to discover, my husband's half-brother. A large, clumsy man with a lopsided grin, he had a startling success with women: an inherited trait, maybe, for his father had not been monogamous either and he was the fruit of a long-standing affair with my friend's mother who had passed him off as her husband's child.

Thanks to Gail Godwin and the rest our list expanded. So did the number of staff. With extra hands in every department, the place was buzzing but it was also filled to bursting and one of two new appointments – a Contracts Manager – left almost as soon as she arrived. An elegant and fiercely well-organised lady, she was not prepared to share a desk in a shared office, or park herself in the bulge of the corridor that was now deemed a work space.

In the oldest of old days, there had been about a dozen of us and we had occupied the midriff of one building. Now there were more like forty and though spread across two buildings, for André had acquired all but the ground floor of 106 some time before, we were seriously short of space, a shortage compounded by Tom's palatial new office which had swallowed up the little room next to it where Nicolas Bentley – the third arrow in the firm's colophon, alongside André and Diana – had once worked.

The second of the new appointments – who was to last longer than the Contracts Manager but not long enough – was our first Financial Director, Michael House, who would have been a welcome presence in André's time to serve as a buffer between him and us, but was even more necessary now that we had a proprietor who was more spendthrift than miser.

What follows now is hard to write about because the only time that I attempted to 'go public' on the dispute between myself and Tom – with a letter to the *Bookseller* which they didn't use, so I sent it to Tom instead – I got a letter from his solicitor which ended like this:

> *Our client will not stand by and see you misrepresent his actions; neither will he submit to intimidation. In the circumstances, we must ask you to confirm by letter, within 14 days please, that you will not repeat inaccurate statements, defamatory of our client, to third parties . . .*

What had prompted my letter was a letter from Diana which the *Bookseller had* used, in which she apologised profusely for a passage in *Stet* to which Tom had taken exception. In this passage she had talked fleetingly about the change in the company's pension arrangements.

Now, as anyone who has read Diana Athill's books would know, a pension scheme is not a subject that would interest her nor would she fully understand it, for one of the several things we have in common is that we are both pretty well innumerate. Those few lines in her light-hearted history of the company weren't meant to raise a storm, but they did. Tom demanded a public retraction, and in much the same way that Ronald Reagan gave voice to the words of his advisers, Diana gave voice to Tom:

> *In my book* Stet *I implied that Tom Rosenthal had 'adjusted'*
> *the André Deutsch pension scheme to the disadvantage of myself*
> *and some of my colleagues. In fact the company had simply, in a*
> *manner increasingly prevalent . . . switched from a proportion of*
> *salary to a money purchase scheme. This did not disadvantage me*
> *in any way . . . A younger senior staff member was going to be*
> *disadvantaged and the company, under Tom, made a substantial*
> *ex gratia additional pension award to that person before she reached*
> *pensionable age . . .*

Provoked by this version of events which made it seem as though Tom had behaved generously towards me – for 'the senior staff member' was me – I decided to answer back. It had after all taken nearly three years to wrest that ex gratia payment from the company. Also, by whose standards was £3,000 a substantial sum? It would not seem so to most white-collar workers and certainly not to Tom himself.

It was now my turn to set the record straight and having heard from the Editor of the *Bookseller* – in a call that showed more decency than courage – that he wasn't going to use my reply, I typed out another copy, addressed it to Tom, put the dog on his lead and marched off to the nearest letter box.

As everyone knows who has fought any home-front battle – with their bank, the Inland Revenue, the parking authorities or any other of those mechanised bodies – it is rage which keeps one going; as empowering as the amphetamine a certain Harley Street doctor used to pump into the thighs of his overweight customers. Put off even more by the lack of decorum (this speed merchant did not even allow us time to remove our tights) than frightened by the manic energy which his needle unleashed, I never went back. Thirty years later, my rage was not chemically induced.

Was I intimidating Tom or was he intimidating me? I took his solicitor's two-page letter, which ended with that gagging order, to yet another solicitor for advice and was warmly received by *Private Eye*'s solicitors, who having read the relevant documents not only didn't charge me but were ready to go one step further before switching on the meter.

But there wasn't to be a further step for, within those '14 days' I learnt I had cancer and the need to clear the decks, to rid myself of all distractions forced me to concede. On March 25 I sent a four-line letter to Tom's solicitors in which, repeating their words back to them, I confirmed that I would not 'repeat inaccurate statements', trusting that as I never had and didn't mean to, this would not be the straitjacket it seemed. Not many days later, I checked into the cancer ward at the Middlesex Hospital.

In the past few days, I have twice been offered a seat in a crowded bus and once had a young man, who looked like police line-up fodder, hold up that rare bird – the 46 bus – until I had arrived panting at the stop. The kindness of strangers is immensely touching but a bit unnerving too. Am I beginning to look as old as I am but seldom feel?

But to the kindness of lawyers, there has been no downside" and I was to experience it again and again. This firm was not the first to waive its fee. The barrister who represented me in the battle over the house never sent in a bill for the day we spent in the corridors of the law courts waiting to be summoned, and the High Street solicitor who had engaged her and whose determination never flagged, charged me rates commensurate with my income. These two women, terrier and tiger, were the best of allies, bringing a human dimension to this sub-human wrangle: no one can help 'falling in love' – hence our peaceful no-divorce-settlement divorce – but they can control their greed. In coming back to claim his share of the house he had left, with us in it, fifteen years before, my son's father was arriving, as it were, for the dessert course only; my dispute with Tom was also about money, but whereas my ex-husband had been fighting for a share in something that had become more and more valuable (I the hen who had kept his investment warm), I was fighting to have something which had become less and less valuable restored to something like its original worth.

A less quixotic quest than it might appear, for at the very first hint that all was not well under the new pension scheme and despite the Company's efforts to dismiss my fears, I kept up the 'unnecessary fuss' until given a letter guaranteeing to make my pension good should the unimaginable (to everyone but me") occur.

I did not examine the wording of the letter then as I was later to do but I did put it in a safe place – in the secret drawer of the rosewood davenport which had so thrilled me as a twelve year old that my father had bought it for me then and there, though we had gone into that olde worlde tea-cum-antique shop, on this Sunday outing from boarding school, with only buttered toast and kunzel cakes in mind.

Too obvious a hiding place now that the *Antiques Roadshow* has become a kind of Open University for burglars, so I have had to resort to the bank for the safe-keeping of those bits of paper which will suddenly matter on my death, as that letter, signed by Tom, came to matter when my pension – last forecast, unofficially, at well over the £8,000 I would have had under the final salary scheme – was now forecast, officially, so far *under* that it came to less than £3,000.

By now the firm was in such a parlous state and Tom's reception of this news so offhand that I decided I had better get advice about the validity in law of Tom's guarantee so that I knew where I would stand in the queue of creditors should the firm go bankrupt, as it seemed that it might.

Although I had yet to learn about the three categories of law firms – High Street, City and West End – I already knew that different firms specialised in different things, and that as they tended to be cripplingly expensive it was important to choose the right one.

But how? The Law Society, based somewhere in the Midlands and not allowed to recommend one firm over another, was no use at all. There was, though, something called the Association of Pension Lawyers listed in the London phone book and it was to this august-sounding body that I sent a copy of the guarantee letter with a brief covering note asking where I should take it for the best once-off advice.

The very next day, as I was numbering the pages of a manuscript (one of the least glamorous but most essential of an editor's jobs) the phone rang and it was the chairman of the association to which I had written. He not only talked to me at length but gave me the numbers of three firms of solicitors, reassuring me about ringing them out of the blue.

Which, the next morning, I did. And, each one of these top of the range establishments went out of their way to be helpful, the last one ringing back to say they would see me on a pro bono basis and I should come in with the letter and anything else which might be relevant.

A few years later things might have been different. Pensions are now everyday news and hundreds of thousands of devout nine-to-fivers (an expression used the other day by a remarkable lady in her nineties, who is still leading the bohemian life) are – for all the care they took and all the promises made to them – facing a penurious old age. But the public demise of the Final Salary Scheme was still a long way off (it is a curious thought that Deutsch were pioneers in this) and even hard-headed lawyers, still reeling from the Maxwell affair, were affronted by this mini-version of those events – as one hopes they are now by New Labour's recent pronouncements on this subject, along the lines that if people will only learn to *save* during their working lives and take advantage of new laws which will allow them to continue working till they drop dead, all will be well: this message conveyed by a well-fed politician whose own over-generous pension has recently been made more secure than ever . . .

Here was someone who would have felt immediately at home in the offices of that law firm at whose doors, in a side street opposite the Ritz, R dropped me and my wodge of papers five minutes ahead of the appointed time. It had been pouring with rain and, nervous as I was – could I really have heard right? – it seemed important to arrive not only on time but also dry and neither of us thought my plastic pac-a-mac suitable for the occasion.

Though it would have been, for the young man who appeared on the dot of eleven and looked so impossibly young that I assumed he had been sent to fetch me, was not the kind of person to worry about what you were wearing. Recently involved, on the miners' side, in a major dispute, and soon to become a father – two baby girls while our case dragged on – he was reassuringly down to earth: sharp, fast-thinking and, despite appearances (the short hair and the suit) refreshingly unconventional. He was also, like any good lawyer, a fighter and – with the blessing of the head of his department, who Lord Goodman told me was the best pensions lawyer in the country – he stuck with me for the three years it took[n] to get André Deutsch Limited to honour the guarantee they had given me.

Every step in this marathon is fully documented and I could, without much trouble, pull out some of the ripest plums, like the letter on headed paper seemingly identical[n] to that on which the guarantee had been issued, informing us that the guarantee was invalid because it had been issued by *a different company* . . . This did, indeed, prove to be the case but didn't weaken my claim.

To cut a long story as short as I can – if all this pension stuff hadn't so profoundly affected me then and for ever after (as is the nature of pensions) I would leave it out entirely – what happened was this:

On receiving the money from the sale of the children's list a year or two before, Tom had dissolved André Deutsch Limited, re-birthing it twenty-four hours later, identical in every way except for a few digits and a new name: the charmingly rural Spear-green."

All this became clear when I was sent the relevant pages by Companies House, but it should have been clear a lot sooner, for I had been a signatory to the document which enabled the transaction.

On the day in question, I had been called out of a meeting with one of my authors to add my signature to those of Anthony Thwaite and one or two of the ever-changing cast of directors who were sitting at the table in the dining-cum-boardroom with Tom and two or three men in suits who I didn't recognise.

Reluctant to sign something I hadn't read but embarrassed at appearing mistrustful and holding everyone up (including my author waiting downstairs), I allowed myself to be hurried; but not before Tom had provided a thumbnail sketch of the proceedings and assured me that this way of transferring money through a third company – the incongruously named Speargreen – was strictly kosher: an ingenious but perfectly legal way of saving tax.

I have never doubted that it was legal but why did this 'recap-italising' of the firm, which we were then instructed to tell our authors about in a letter written by Tom thanking them for their loyalty and reassuring them about the future of the firm, make so little difference?

André's answer, which none of us believed – it ranked as the most outrageous of the rumours he was putting about – was that the Scholastic money had never reached the André Deutsch Limited account . . .

Michael House, the Financial Director, was no longer around to shed light on this. He had left to begin a new life in Scotland, taking with him our most dependable editor who, to this day, remains unswervingly loyal to André.

Whether Michael who had been brought in by Tom had anything to do with the selling of the family silver, a process which had begun long before with the dispatch of the Deutsch archive to Tulsa, leaving the firm, as it were, lobotomised, I don't know. But he did introduce the new pension scheme on Tom's behalf, taking special care that the two oldest members of the firm were kept out of it. Why he had not included me, the third oldest, in this rescue operation, I don't know, but once it became obvious that I should have been excluded too, he did what he could to put things right.

One of the many objections that were later made, on my behalf, to these proceedings was the speed with which we employees had to decide whether we wanted to join the new scheme or not. Sceptical by nature – the broker's sales pitch, though delivered in sober tones, had been full of predictions which seemed too good to be true – I would, had I not been about to go on holiday, have looked around for what is now called 'independent advice' but I was told that by the time I got back I would have missed the boat. Reassured by Michael, I signed on, took the dog to his foster parents and set out for Apulia where we had rented the cheapest accommodation in an expensive brochure: a trullo^n on an estate a few miles inland from Bari.

Like so many holidays – I remember waking up in some little town on the estuary of the Somme^n to find that the sea, which we had been able to see from our window, had completely disappeared – this one began badly. The village of San Vito dei Normanni looked, at first, like some derelict frontier town: I remember bursting into tears at the sight of it. So this was the place we were going to stay for a whole week . . . I had finally put my foot down. I was not going to sleep in a different bed every night and see more churches in a day than most people see in a lifetime. I was tired, I wanted a rest.

And I got one. But not in a trullo for when our landlady saw us – by now we had reached the walled estate – she decided that R was too tall to be comfortable in this and put us up in the house itself whose shabby grandeur remains a treasured memory.

There were to be wonders, too, in the week that followed: the cave dwellings of Matera, the hill villages of Basilicata and the dusty little town of Venosa where there had once been a community of Jews and where our hotel room overlooked the main square with its statue of Orazio Flacco whom we didn't recognise as that same Horace who had kept me out of Oxford for a year.

For once, I returned to the office refreshed and got back to work without misgivings, regrets or, indeed, any thoughts at all about the papers I had signed before setting off.

It was at least a year later that studying one of those unintelligible slips from the insurance company more closely than usual, I began to get worried. It looked as though my pension was going not up but down. Michael, unable to make sense of the figures either, called the broker down from Northampton to interpret them. Which he did and, by the end of that summit, at which R as well as Michael was present, the broker had convinced us all that there was nothing to worry about – that I could now expect to retire on a pension or pensions (he was embracing the welfare state in his calculations) of approximately £17,000 per annum . . .

How he arrived at this figure can be pieced together from the notes R made at the meeting. How, after the initial euphoria – £17,000 was more than I had ever earned – I came to have doubts and began to worry away at Michael and Tom till they came up with the 'make good' letter, is a matter of record, as is the yawning gap between what I was told to expect and what I actually get which the hard-won £3,000 goes only a little way to cover.

I have never thought that either Michael or Tom deliberately set out to mislead me, which is why when the bubble broke it was the broker – the only one who really understood the dangers inherent in the scheme – who appeared the real villain and, like the child snapped at by a friendly-looking dog, who remains frightened of all dogs, I am left distrusting all soberly dressed, quietly spoken financial advisers. Now, the only one I trust is the seemingly scatty but radiantly honest lady practitioner who turned up late for our only face-to-face meeting (just as all builders seem to live in Enfield, all financial advisers seem to live in the country) wearing a mini-skirt and showing an impressive cleavage.

Had Tom, at the outset, shown any real concern or, at any time, shown willingness to shoulder the responsibility, I would have focused on the broker, but his deception soon paled beside Tom's indifference. As for Michael, though he had introduced the scheme and took this hitch very much in his stride, he was, like me, an employee and any fall-out from his actions was, ultimately, his employer's responsibility. By the time the lawyers became involved, Tom had become and remained the chief target.

And, what a target. Though cumbersome in person – not unlike those foolish birds that lumber across moorland roads or surge up out of the heather – he proved endlessly adroit in the paper battle and surprisingly resilient considering it was on the grounds of poverty that the company was fighting my claim and it was indeed becoming more and more obvious that, financially, things were going from bad to worse.

There should be a book on how to conduct yourself in a dying firm. Like the handbook I had turned to years before on how to fight bureaucracy after someone appeared at my door and asked me where I would like to be moved to among the several unattractive choices on his list . . .

It turned out that at the tail-end of a planning meeting, at which a thirty-storey office block had been the main issue, a motion had been passed enabling the Council to empty the street I lived in of its inhabitants, prior to tearing it down as they had already torn down the nearby crescent – home in its last blighted years to a Film Co-op and a pleasant community of hippies.

Helping to prevent this, a cause which began in self-interest but became a passionate commitment, meant a lot of strenuous and unfamiliar activity but in this fight to keep people in their homes – many of the residents were council tenants[n] who had lived in the street all their lives – there were no moral ambiguities. There was also a heartening amount of outside support. There was the Neighbourhood Centre where we did our xeroxing and held those meetings at which the larger issues got submerged in stories of missing cats and windows that wouldn't open or wouldn't shut; there was the Law Centre and the Citizens' Rights Office and the 'friendly planner' in lucrative private practice, who lived in leafy Hampstead but came down the hill to give us advice for nothing.

Even if we hadn't succeeded this would have been an experience worth having. But we did. The Council now changed its tune and, loudly advocating 'public participation', decided *not* to pull the street down but to fix it up, so that no one had to move further than from one side to the other during the months of re-hab.

There was nothing rewarding about the Deutsch experience. We couldn't look for outside help in a situation which had, at all costs, to be kept from outsiders, and we were in a constantly false relation to our authors who did not know, as we did, that their books might never come out. In the old days, before it became de rigueur for doctors to tell their patients they are dying whether they want to know or not, the burden of knowing fell on the family. A lesser burden by far, but a burden nonetheless, was the knowledge we carried and could not divulge.

It was pretty obvious that books already in production should be hurried through, and that authors would gain nothing by learning of the dangers. But what about new submissions? If there were no acquisitions, we might as well put the shutters up now. On issues like this, which must beset any business as it struggles for survival, it would have been good to have some open and honest discussion. But there was none and what to do became a constant worry: would this unpublished writer be better off, even if his/her book never came out, to have had a Deutsch contract? The answer was probably yes. But what about writers with a track record, however modest? We had entered a moral minefield and so it was a red-letter day when I came across a novel where we could do the author no harm for she was already dead . . .

Only the other day, I was asked by a prisoner I write to which books I am 'proudest' of having published. Well, Frances Vernon, the gifted young author of that posthumous novel, would be one. Another would be Carol Bruggen, for the quirky tenderness of her imagination, and Jon Elkon[n] for his passionate political convictions (he left South Africa and gave up Business for Teaching) cloaked in gloriously outlandish humour.

I could have added to this list Peter Davies whose *The Farms of Home* was one of the last books I was to work on. Like his earlier books, of which the very first had arrived with a sheaf of somewhat discouraging pencil drawings,[n] it was a lyrical evocation of the English countryside, straying further, but still not far, from the Shropshire village where he – a retired primary school headmaster – had lived as a child.

It was working on manuscripts – *The Farms of Home* among them – that kept me anchored during the year or more that I was both working in the building and at war with my employer.[n] The cracks in the structure of the company – the unpaid bills, the copying machine that stayed out of order for days at a time – no longer needed inside knowledge to be noticed.

Even the most humdrum activities – collating proofs, checking *ibids* and *op cits* – took one's mind off the state of the loos and the fact that we might soon be out of work. Even so, there were lighter moments: the urgent last-minute request from a self-important young author to change his dedication from girl-friend to mother . . . the mystery of the chocolates which arrived from a rejected slush-pile author to whom I had written because I had enjoyed his odd, Herne-the-Hunterish novel: a letter to which first had come a furious reply and then, a week or two later, that slightly battered box of chocolates. We decided to play safe and threw them out.

It has always surprised me that the thousand upon thousand of rejections didn't produce more frequent complaints – but apart from the 'poisoned' chocs there was only a short but disturbing run of dirty phone calls, and one angry letter, addressed to 'the Chairman', about the speed with which a manuscript had been returned. On the contrary, several writers we had to reject stayed in touch for years and one, only recently, sent me a copy of his first book:" an academised version of the magical but uncategorisable offering we had turned down some twenty years before . . .

Although focusing on a text was the best distraction from a situation over which we had no control and about which we were ill-informed, the situation itself required some unprecedented action: if Deutsch were to go out of business or, as was still the hope, and as eventually happened, were sold, our unagented writers would need agents and we would need jobs.

It was reference time. At my age and no better known than at my last job interview more than thirty years before, it was not going to be easy. I wrote for help to those authors whose names carried any weight and their replies warm me still. Among them was Bill Vollmann whose generous two-page response could be used as a primer for beginning editors:

> . . . [She is] *a careful reader . . . has always been honest with me at the risk of hurting my feelings (which has never actually happened) . . . When a disagreement arises, she defers to me if I remain stubborn.*

> *A book is, after all, the author's book . . . An editor can help but the*
> *author must be free to go to hell in his own way . . .*

and this memorable phrase from which I am tempted to lift a title
for this book: '*To disagree with an author is* a thankless task'.

Of their nature, reference letters make pleasant (if questionable)
reading but they are all I have to show for the thirty years spent
bent over other people's productions. (I never saw my schoolboy
son bent over anything except Dungeons and Dragons.) Very occasionally, I will riffle through them or take the books I worked on off
the shelves behind me and feed on the inscriptions:

> *. . . ½ your creation anyway . . .*

from Robert McLiam Wilson, another slush pile 'find' and the only
author with whom I had a terminal falling out;[n]

> *. . . who, alone among editors* [and readers, as it transpired] *gets*
> *the joke . . .*

from Benjamin J. Stein, Republican speechwriter and Hollywood
celebrity whose brilliant novel belly-flopped over here;

> *. . . for not accepting anything but the final effort . . .*

from Frederic Lindsay, the Scottish novelist whose books, like Ian
Rankin's which I have only just discovered and whom he so much
resembles, left me frightened to walk the dog . . .

There are the dedications, too, one of them from someone
whose book we never published, some of them portmanteau-style
and one or two embarrassingly fulsome but the one thing – the two
things – that an editor can't edit however much their fingers may

itch, are an author's dedication and acknowledgements, the latter of which often run on at tedious length. But not Kanan Makiya's:[n] his *'My editor believed in this book before it became all too easy to do so'*, is the one I value most.

The success I had in gathering references wasn't repeated in finding agents for my unagented authors. I hadn't met many agents and the few I knew and trusted worked on their own and couldn't have taken on more than one or two new clients even if they had wanted to. Having exhausted my contacts with a trek to Peckham Rye to offer my wares[n] or, rather, my authors' wares to James Hale, I gave up. But I had found homes for a few of my orphans[n] and had done it without betraying the state of things at Deutsch: as far as anyone knew, I was just preparing for my approaching retirement – which followed sooner than expected, for a short time later I heard from my solicitor that he had had a letter from Tom's solicitor proposing that I take 'gardening leave': not a term I had heard before but what it meant, I was told, was that I would be paid, in full, till I was sixty but that my presence was no longer required: in other words, Get out and Stay out.

My instinct was to refuse but I was persuaded by my solicitor on rational grounds and by friends who had been living this nightmare with me on what might best be called 'health grounds' to accept. Which, reluctantly, I did and at the end of the day on Thursday, 19 August 1993, with a shopping bag full of bits and pieces, and a bunch of flowers, I walked out of Deutsch for the last time.[n]

Epilogue

IN HIS LETTER from prison the other day, Jack asked, half jokingly, had I *really* been an editor when I didn't seem to be able to spell and (he implied) my sentences didn't add up. To which I replied somewhat tetchily (Jack, in for murder, is the same age as my son) that the corrector ribbon on my typewriter is broken and the one in my head is switched off...

I had no idea how difficult it would be to stop correcting things: such a mania does it become that I couldn't read without a pencil in my hand and even writers long dead (Hardy was one) made my pulse race. There was only one way out and my unconscious mind found it. For over two years I did not – could not – open a book.

This block, which took me completely by surprise, did eventually lift and though I don't expect to recover the innocent relation to books I once had, there is less and less static on the line. Manuscripts, however, which I made a conscious decision to avoid, remain firmly out of bounds. Never again will I have to tell anyone that their brain-child, the child of their heart, their soul, was dead at birth which, for all the years of gestation, is most often the case. The only way to be sure not to catch a fish, as I had learnt in Sweden all those years ago, is not to go fishing and, with the one exception of R, whom I still read ahead of his publisher, this is what I have done (or not done) and will continue not to do.

Removed, thus, not only from my job but from the freelancers' arena, I was, though I didn't know it, one step ahead of the game. Editors, like wind-up gramophones (I have just ordered one that will play 45s and 78s from a folksy American catalogue) have become all but obsolete: hence the friend who has been told by her publisher that the book she is working on – a symposium of scholarly essays – must reach them 'ready for the printer'. No wonder that, not too long ago, an author's neatly typed list of corrections appeared in the revised edition of his book as part of the text or that in a book R was reading the other day, published by a reputable publisher, one Renaissance architect 'took his drawings too Rome' while another's youthful dream was 'to bee another Michelangelo' . . . Even literals have lost their flavour. A computer's spell check could come up with 'an interior full of intricate craving' but the 'garden numph' which tripped across a page of *Eccentric Spaces* is, like that 'fashion acorn', Princess Diana, a thing of the past.

So, too, are those visits to the lawyers' offices which, along with the endless legal paperwork and the scheming and plotting (Russellgate was conceived and abandoned at this time) helped to keep me occupied during those fourteen months which, I am told, Tom now refers to as my 'sabbatical', a term that was bandied about at the time, but we all knew what it meant.

On the few occasions that I went to Nab Nat on my own (R was usually with me and, between us, we made embarrassing inroads on the plate of business-class biscuits which were always ready and waiting on the conference room table) I would leave enough time to stop at an old-fashioned coffee-house near Fortnum & Mason, whose wine-coloured booths would later fill with well-dressed ladies on their way to or from the Royal Academy, and sit over my double espresso while I shuffled papers and collected my thoughts. Passing this way now, to meet an ex-Deutsch friend who works in Albemarle Street (but not for much longer) or, like the ladies who lunch, to take in the RA, I think of the days when Nabarro Nathanson was round the next corner and wonder if Peter is still helping the underdog or, like the amusing barrister I met not long ago, 'helping the rich to get richer'.

And here I am reminded of the number of people who, like him, have been surprised, not to say shocked, that I don't share their pleasant memories of André. Whose value as a publisher I wouldn't question. But every time, as now, that I take a run at paying André – the man – his due, my feet slip out from under me. It should help to remember his loyalty, but that was to his mother, to his long-term mistress Gwen, and to his favourites among us, not to me. I can do a little better recalling his endearing weakness for clowns and for owls, stemming from I know not what in his Hungarian childhood, and, when, the other night, an owl, caught in the headlights, rose from the road and flapping its majestic wings settled on the signpost which announces that our churchless, publess hamlet is half a mile away, I felt a twinge of sadness. But, no more than Tom will André ferment in the compost of my mind to emerge a fond memory: as intractable as rose thorns, they belong in another place.

Nostalgia, a mode easier and easier to fall into, is reserved mostly for inanimate things: the smell of paraffin stoves which we used to heat the house before the paraffin van stopped calling because everyone else in the street had central heating; the fox fur rug which arrived, long after our return, from Arakhova, the Greek village where M, my husband-to-be and I had bought it: every foreigner still an event and the beach at Malia on which we slept just a stretch of sand . . . It was lying on that same rug a few years later that I heard the story of R's life and he heard mine while the record player we had bought at the big Boots in Regent Street played our few records: the 'green record' (a Mozart divertimento), the 'water music' (a Haydn quartet), Bellini, 'American Pie' . . . The sound of my barely teenaged son arriving home at two in the morning singing 'What shall we do with the drunken sailor?' at the top of his voice, music to my anxious ears. The dog, in its old age, lying on the floor near where the gas fire had once been . . .

During my 'gardener's leave', we too had central heating installed,[n] along with our first TV aerial and much else that was new. The recurring nightmare of railway sidings, stretching as far as I could see and jammed with manuscripts, sometimes waiting patiently, sometimes clamouring for attention, was a thing of the past. Now my head was full of shopping. Like Rip Van Winkle, I had skipped aeons of time and the household basement at John Lewis was full of surprises. 'You are the proud owner or [*sic*] the Grand Gaggia' announced the leaflet that came with the coffee machine. I had not seen a domestic-sized cappuccino-maker before, nor a 'juicer'. Both proved more trouble than they were worth. But the duvet, we had seen these before in the better B & Bs – the kind that have stacks of *House Beautiful* beside the lavatory – has at least meant fewer arguments about who makes the bed.

The memories crowd in: never more so than this last Christmas when, unwilling to travel far for fear of what we might find[n] on our return (a fear R did not share) we stayed in Yorkshire and spent hours each day worshipping at the memory-laden Christmas tree (substitute for the temples of Orissa) with its shiny metallic baubles brought back from Mexico, silver pasteboard parrot, bought in GUM when it was still covered in patriotic slogans, little wooden sledge from Solvang in California, where it is always Christmas, and Melody's spiky paper ball, constructed with the same care as her public sculptures – in tile, concrete and bronze – which adorn the open spaces of down-town Tucson. The three of us, R, A and I, had strung cranberries, popcorn and sultanas, glued thread to twenty clementines and hung the contents of a whole box of Quality Street by the time that paper ornament was finished. But it has lasted more than twenty years. Best loved of all our lodgers, Melody stayed with us for the four years she studied at St Martin's and the one night a week she was contracted to babysit became, of her own volition, many more. On summer evenings she would disappear for hours at a time, returning way past bedtime with an exultant grass-stained child (they had been rolling down Primrose Hill) and a furiously hungry dog . . .

Every one of the two hundred objects – petals from the garden, seaweed from Pacific Valley, skull of a bird found on the beach at Wells-next-the-Sea – tug at the memory and we sit entranced by this display of our life together. And then we play the list game: Bari, Bijapur, Badami, Borrowdale, Blowing Rock . . . I marvel at the number of places we have been. Most I remember, if I remember them at all, with pleasure; a few (most of these in France: a tribute to that infernal Art Map) for the rows we had (Collioure, Pézenas, Aigues-Mortes) and, fewer still, because in these I had collapsed from exhaustion. In a little town in South Carolina, R actually stepped over me to get a better view of something that might have been something in the distance. He was unlucky. There was *nothing* to see in Sumter where I slept, without waking, for fourteen hours . . .

But we didn't only look at buildings. In Paris we conceived a child. In London I came to my senses. Still, every now and then I think wouldn't it be nice, now, to have another grown up child. But now is now and then was then.

It is nine o'clock. By eleven, maybe before, I will finish this book which I had never planned to write. Why, then, did I? I would like to be able to say that it was finding myself alone and with nothing much to do – R, fuelled as ever by research grants," had gone off to Bolivia but I was saving myself for India, to follow soon after his return. It wasn't this. Nor, though it has perhaps turned out that way, was it meant as therapy like the stuffed pig, streaked with glue, which Effie from across the road, who would sometimes leave her Meals on Wheels on our doorstep for Patch who would eat anything, had given me. She had made it in a class at the Charlie Ratchford Centre. 'Therapy for us old people,' she said.

No, it was reading *Stet*[n] of which someone had sent me a proof and of which Diana was later to give me a copy. Like that molehill in Mexico[n] which grew so quickly into a volcanic mountain that you could see it happening, I, too, exploded. Where had *I* been all that time?

Like the histologist I heard on the radio last night lamenting that the work she and her colleagues do (the programme was about breast cancer), without which the surgeon wouldn't know whether or where to stick his knife, goes largely unacknowledged. Being an editor – not the kind who has to find out what the author looks like before hurrying to meet him or her at some award ceremony – is backroom work. And, like invisible mending, the better done, the less it shows.

So, it began with a question, but in skirting this – best approached, so I thought, as in grandmother's footsteps, one quiet step at a time – something else began to happen . . .

But, back to the lists and the Christmas tree. Some letters are better than others. S is a favourite: Selestun,[n] Sabaudia, Stourhead . . . Stourhead, the first of hundreds of gardens R and I were to visit together and the place where, for the first time, I knew perfect happiness. 'To have met him', to misquote Max Beerbohm, 'is to have lived not in vain.' But, finally, all roads lead back to mothers. On the top spire of the Christmas tree, always uncomfortably close to the ceiling, sits the 'Estonian doll': small, grubby but still king of the castle with her dark blue skirt, white pinny and once flaxen hair. Is my passion for these Yorkshire moors perhaps a throwback to a time, not so long ago, when we weren't city-dwellers and our language wasn't English or even Russian; when having settled my menfolk with their holy texts, I would have set out on a cart with wooden wheels with my barrels of cucumbers[n] . . . It is more than forty years now since I went back to Estonia for the first time with my mother and out walking in the snowy park, was shouted at by a passerby. What he had said, I was told, was 'Get off the grass. You're not in Russia now.' I had been taken, in my headscarf and winter woollies, for the Russian peasant I would once have been.

THE END

Notes

1 Mendel Grozinski or, perhaps, Mendel GRAZINSKI which is how I have just seen it spelt on a certificate from a secondary school in Kilburn which tells me that my father and two of his brothers attended the school between the years 1906 and 1914. It is quite possible that we have been mis-spelling the name for all these years, misled by that chain of bakers' shops so familiar to North London Jews.

1 the George was for St George I have since heard that it was from the king not the saint that our grandfather borrowed his name.

3 Bertha and Freda I had never thought of these as 'Jewish' names but have just come across them in Theo Richmond's wonderful *Konin*, the story of the small Polish town where his parents were born. He, too, had aunts called Bertha and Freda and a father who changed an unpronounce-able Polish name to a solid English place name; in his case, at the sugges-tion of his English teacher, a Mr Richmond, who happened to live there.

It is always a little disconcerting to find that someone with a name that gives no hint of a foreign past is actually a Jew, like the Death Row prisoner I started writing to recently who has the blandest of names but turns out to be a Biblical Zionist, his letters peppered with Hebrew. Of course, in his case, I was misled not only by his name but by his crime. There aren't many Jewish murderers, as he cheerfully agrees.

3 Dublin I have since learnt that the reason the family moved to Dublin was that my grandfather got the job of chief buyer in the fur department of Switzer's, the local Harrods. Among his customers could have been Stanley Price's grandmother. This novelist's recent memoir *Somewhere to*

Hang My Hat: an Irish-Jewish Journey is a delight, but does raise the awkward question of my grandfather's choice of name. How had this orphan from the backwoods heard of St George? The chapter in which Stanley Price unravels the route by which *his* grandfather came by the name of Charles Beresford Price (it had been Moishe ben Bezalel Dov) reads like a detective story without a murder.

4 successful fashion item This was not, in fact, done by my uncle but many years later by Leah and Johnny Hertz, who I was to get to know when Deutsch published Leah's book about successful businesswomen. Nor was this the first time petals had been turned into cash. Apparently Nijinsky's dresser sold each petal off the Bakst costume for *Le Spectre de la Rose* to the dancer's adoring fans, and made enough to buy himself a house with the proceeds.

5 hare-brained scheme More than ninety years after my grandfather took a party, including the Estonian Prime Minister, to inspect the territory he proposed to mine (as reported in the Estonian newspaper *Paewhleht* on 11 August 1927) the rest of the world has caught up. The media now bristles with for and against stories about this novel method of extracting gas (or is it oil?) from shale.

5 a dozen sightings Like that character in Iris Murdoch's *Flight from the Enchanter*, his was a powerful but invisible presence.

6 South Africa had not been safe enough The reason for this, as I have now learnt from a reliable source – Slip's youngest daughter – is that her father had become *persona non grata* with the ruling party in South Africa for reasons of which any liberal-thinking person would approve, and had to leave in a hurry.

6 Blooms is no longer there and the nearby synagogue is now a mosque.

7 couldn't tell him where to find it He could find it easily enough today for, according to a recent article in the *Jewish News*, a splendid new synagogue has recently opened in the centre of Tallinn.

7 nothing about Clive in particular until coming across a speech Nelson Mandela made at Clive's memorial service when I learnt for the first time that Clive and his wife, Irene, were committed philanthropists in the African cause.

8 his wife Pat Another invisible presence to whom this writer owed a great deal but of whose very existence few of his readers knew: this sturdy Englishwoman with her regular job belying the 'lonely-artist-in-a-garret' who was to airbrush her out of his life even more completely when, a short time after her death, he married an effusive Indian lady journalist.

9 never spoke of his origins another story that had become distorted in the telling. Slip *did* at one time conceal his Jewishness but this was because when the family reached the States, shortly after the outbreak of war, without money or possessions, the house they managed to rent was in an area prohibited to Jews. My cousin Monica remembers how the curtains were always drawn on a Friday evening, so no passer-by would see the Sabbath candles.

10 quixotic plan There had been at least one other. Apparently, shortly after Estonia gained its independence, when the country was almost bankrupt, my grandfather came up with the idea of exporting the flax that grew there in abundance. But to do this he needed transport. When the scheme was put to President Påts he endorsed it and before long, a ship or ships carrying Estonian flax landed in Aberdeen and the proceeds of the sale, which was a very considerable sum, was returned to the Estonian government.

10 had invested According to an article in an Estonian newspaper dated 8 March 1921, 'The English Company have agreed to advance up to a million pounds for the necessary installation . . .'

11 one of Jean Rhys's letters The footnote to this letter of 27 March 1964 was to correct Jean's misapprehension about where I had actually gone. 'You must miss EW, though Latvia sounds fascinating. I've often longed for Finland (lakes, forests and so on . . .)' – an understandable confusion, unlike that of the editor who enthused thus about a book of William T. Vollmann's set in Greenland: 'Bill, your book was AMAZING! How EVER did you manage to get to New Zealand?'

12 dropping dead in the foyer of the Marble Arch Odeon Seventy-nine years later – taking a leaf from my grandmother's book in choosing a West End location for a very private event – I had a heart attack while queuing at the Genius Bar in the Apple store on Regent Street.

12 had to have her name It was the custom in Jewish families to pass on the name of the recently dead. I never much liked 'Esther', the name

I inherited, and was amused to see that Madonna, in Kaballah mode, has now adopted it.

12 unpaved roads and . . . dirty-windowed shops A far cry from the attractive little town pictured in the tourist brochure I have just been sent, where the only feature I recognise is the lake. It could be that things have improved beyond recognition during the past fifty years, or maybe we just missed the better parts of town (as we did the castle ruins, churches and lovely country houses) and assumed, as a foreigner might, arriving in London for the first time, that it is all like the Holloway Road or all like Canary Wharf, depending on where he or she first sets foot.

13 audacious scam I may have got things in the wrong order here but there was undoubtedly a scam. It seems that one of the Hoffs, now living in Riga, paid some foolish thug to set fire to a boatload of something or other resting in the harbour while *he* stayed at home eating his dinner. But I have heard, too, that this was to get back at Lloyd's who had failed to honour a genuine claim. Whatever the truth of the matter, the fallout from this affair is almost certainly the reason that this branch of the Hoffs upped sticks and moved to France.

13 the bear hugs that were accepted currency Alas, so English have I become that I am more a Menell than a Gutkin when it comes to displays of emotion, and though not as stony-faced as real Estonians – as so vividly portrayed in Sigrid Rausing's *Everything Is Wonderful: Memories of a Collective Farm in Estonia* – I find it as difficult to express deep feelings as it is easy to skim the surface of life.

15 wouldn't have us because M's wholly English mother had not been *born* Jewish; her gruelling and ultimately successful effort to become a Jew counted for nothing in the orthodox *shul*.

15 the rabbi I have only recently realised that the rabbi was Louis Jacobs of 'the Jacobs affair' and feel lucky to have had this remarkable man, whose intellectual honesty should have been above reproach, officiating at my wedding.

16 never went through that charade again until just the other day when, responding to legal advice rather than parental sentiment, R and I became 'husband and wife' at the local town hall.

18 I am only guessing but having now heard that the Slip Menells also disapproved of Eddie's wife who they referred to as 'that showgirl', I was probably right.

18 the wedding cheque Not to be dismissed lightly for without it, we could not have raised the deposit on the house in which I still live.

19 far gone in his madness He died not long after and thirty years on, two hand-written, unfinished poems found in a barn near the remote cottage in Wales where he had gone to live, have led to the publication of *Fragments of a Lost Voice* in which twenty-two contemporary poets have contributed a verse each, inspired by these remains.

19 rescue from the bankruptcy courts It was, apparently, to the Inland Revenue that my father owed money, a fact which reminds me of the advice I was given by a businessman friend when he heard of my problems with my employer. There isn't a businessman who doesn't dread investigation by the IR, he told me, and advised me to invoke their help. But it seemed too much like blackmail, and I didn't have the nerve.

20 different kettle of fish To be fair to my uncle, he had reason to be annoyed. Some years before, probably when I was given that fifty pounds for helping to win the war, he had, it seems, given my father and his two sisters (i.e. the English Menells) five thousand pounds each, a lot of money then, to buy themselves houses, which none of them had done.

20 could no longer pay the rent I had no idea how bad things were and was almost persuaded by M, my boyfriend then, to go to Greece with him. But the thought of leaving my mother stranded in that seaside town stopped me and I remember that summer as a time of mysterious phone calls, occasional postcards from Greece and Doris Day singing *Che sera sera*.

24 to forgive and forget To quote Saul Bellow, as recorded in James Atlas's superb biography which charts in riveting detail the grievance-filled life and work of this great writer: 'You forgive people too easily. Jews don't forgive.'

25 long line of writers Among them, Philip Roth, Brian Moore, Mordecai Richler, Margaret Atwood and Richard Yates.

25 reading the new novel for offset In those far-off days, all books bought in from America were read through to make sure there were no misprints (there seldom were) and, believe it or not, to alter US spelling to English spelling. This practice stopped, except in the case of children's books, sometime in the '80s.

27 played Goneril Not so, my computer reveals. She played not Goneril but Clytemnestra.

28 her voice was absent I feel pretty sure it wasn't my saying she was the most malicious as well as the most pious of my friends that ended our friendship. It is more likely that she had, to quote Barbara Pym, always thought of me as 'a dim sort of person'. Be that as it may, I was relieved to learn from a sympathetic obituary that she had fallen out with almost everyone she knew, including her agent, Sarah Lutyens, who had all the qualities that Madeleine most admired.

28 roped in Another case of roping in involved me. Whenever the Slip Menells were in town they took a suite at the Ritz. On this occasion I was invited to join my cousin Monica while the rest of her family were away for a few days. So, with a pile of school books, I moved into the Ritz and, as instructed, we ordered all our meals from room service. I can still remember the tables being wheeled in, linen covered and laden with our extravagant choices; also that one of the waiters interested us more than the food.

29 No one else in the large tribe of Menells This is not quite true. My brother would take Victor for outings. Unlike the rest of us, he was not embarrassed by the oddities of our cousin's behaviour.

30 Hindu dancer Ram Gopal died only the other day, in a south London nursing home. I learn this from an obituary in the *Daily Telegraph* which also informs me that he studied two distinct forms of dance – the Bharata Natyam and Kathakali. Whether I have seen the first, I can't be sure, but it may have been what my friend Mavis and I saw performed against the carved rock face at Mahabalipuram while a flock of goats looked on from above. Kathakali we did see, or half see; a violent thunderstorm caused all the lights to go out in the makeshift theatre in the back streets of Cochin.

31 disappeared without trace Alas, if only it had remained so. After visiting the synagogue in Florence recently – a monument of Byzantine appearance and gargantuan size – I discovered she had died when her nightdress caught fire as she was warming a pan of milk in the middle of the night.

36 the only Menell now left in my life 'What about your brother?' I have been asked. The answer is that my brother and I have never been close since those days when we fought over the red wine gums in our parents' sweet ration and (what did I think I was going to do with the money?) he had persuaded me, a gullible but greedy eight year old, to sell all my 'baby books' – something I have regretted ever since.

38 *Judenfrei* is the term I have always known, but *Judenrein*, which I came across only recently – not just free of Jews but *cleansed* of Jews – seems to get closer to the truth and I now use it too.

40 had not . . . recognised herself This is not uncommon. People often fail to recognise themselves when unfavourably portrayed and I have probably wasted a good many hours changing hair colour, birth place, even gender. On this ticklish issue, the publisher is entirely in the author's hands. How could anyone have guessed that the real-life model for a fictional character actually had a metal plate in her hip? I had thought this an ingenious disguise. Nor could I have imagined that the love letters in another novel were actually real love letters and their writer had no idea they were about to appear in a book.

40 now a minor character Another writer who transformed an unpublishable manuscript was Jane Rawlinson (a great favourite of Diana's and mine) who took away the barely intelligible first version of *A Paradise of Fools*, a fictional account of the life of Richard Dadd, and re-cast it so the narrator was no longer the madman but a sympathetic and elderly onlooker, not unlike the narrator in *Wuthering Heights*.

41 the imaginary husband Thanks to Carol's children, her actual husband – or at least a lock of his hair – now rests beside her in that Lancashire churchyard. At the strangest imaginable funeral, this lock of hair (all that Murray's wife would release: understandably, she wanted him near *her*) was solemnly buried in a golden papier-mâché casket, shaped like a tortoise – a memento of Murray's love of amateur theatricals. Although Murray had strayed more than once – his first long-time mistress abandoned for his second – this was surely where he belonged, and the whole village came out to celebrate his return.

41 designing systems The systems were for local government use and his boss, the leader of this team of two, proposed dividing the country between them. He would take place names beginning from A to N, leaving my husband with N to Z . . .

44 novel we had published which was called *Winter Garden* and was to be the first in a long and successful career for Robert Edric who soon abandoned his alter ego.

44 goes soft at the edges I have learnt since from a review of *Jack Holmes and His Friend* that White deliberately abandoned the style of his two earliest novels because they had been so badly received: a change regretted by the reviewer.

45 Lesley Chamberlain One of several writers whom I failed to get taken on at Deutsch. Like Eva Figes, who was another, Lesley went on to better things: her most recent publication *The Philosophy Steamer: Lenin and the Exile of the Intelligentsia*.

46 perhaps I extrapolated I now know that I didn't. Don Walters of the Yorkshire printers Smith Settle, tells me he knew the farmer who grazed his sheep on the hill under which the factory was built.

48 pulsating lights I was lying on the floor on the mattress that was his bed in Bill Vollmann's basement room in San Francisco. The firm had paid my fare to San Francisco from New York, but there expenses stopped so Bill gave me his little apartment and found somewhere else to sleep. By day, the room was a den of books: the whole Library of America, or so it seemed, filled several shelves. At night the books disappeared in the darkness and I became uncomfortably aware of the winking light of his computer (the first that I had seen) which I could find no way to switch off.

49 perhaps the only place In fact, as I find from reading *Heshel's Kingdom*, Dan Jacobson's elegiac reconstruction of his family's Lithuanian past, Estonia was not the only country in which the Germans could rely on the local populace to take the murder of the Jews in their stride.

49 killed on the spot It was not till reading Sigrid Rausing's memoir of the year she spent as a student cultural anthropologist in a remote area of Estonia that I learned that great numbers of Jews were brought to Estonia from elsewhere to be killed. I also learned from *Everything Is Wonderful* that twelve Jews survived in Estonia itself. Many of the original population of 4,000 had, of course, taken refuge in Russia, leaving 'only 1,500' for the Germans to exterminate.

52 a newly erected monument The permanent stone version of that wooden monument is still causing trouble. Not long ago, the Estonian government moved the much-hated monument to a more obscure location which so outraged the Russian Estonians that there were demonstrations in the streets at which Mother Russia came to their aid, launching a mini cyber war against its former satellite and then adding its name to their list of special enemies, alongside the US and the UK.

52 all three lived together No longer. My aunt Leida has died since this was written.

53 its independence In spite of recent history, Estonia still celebrates Independence Day on February 24, the anniversary of the day in 1918 when it first gained independence.

57 have not been seen in their old haunts since I am told there are now some new publications for sale in the 'German church' in Tallinn devoted to the monuments and heraldic devices which cover its walls, which suggests that the Baltic Germans may be coming back, if only as tourists.

57 radio factory and 'conservatoire' have new meaning for me since a recent visit to Strasbourg where I learnt that during her years in the factory she had volunteered to present a half hour music programme to follow the statutory half hour of production talk that was broadcast over the internal radio system each week. In all, she made over a hundred of these programmes and so popular were they that, from time to time, she would be rewarded by her union with a paid outing to some place of cultural interest.

57 who worked in the factory too Fima has since told me that Renata Gutkin, Lena's cousin and closest friend, *didn't* work in the factory (the French in which I conversed with Renata even less reliable than my memory) but as they certainly walked down Narva Maantee together and as she is one of the people I knew and loved the best, here she stays: a happier fate than that of her brother Hermann Gutkin, another committed Communist, who was murdered in the Soviet purge of intellectuals which followed 'liberation'.

58 talk directly to Sasha No longer a problem as learning the language is a basic requirement for immigrants to France and we are able to talk to each other, albeit haltingly, for the first time.

62 dearest friends Among the hundreds of photographs of my mother when she was young, I can find none of Nancy, Paula, Assia or Zippa. My mother is often with girls or young women I do not recognise: perhaps the war had changed these old friends beyond recognition. Most often, though, my mother is pictured with another friend whom I *do* recognise for she, Bounia, had left Estonia before the war and settled in Paris. For her, Tallinn had been too provincial, or so she was to tell me. But there could have been more to it than that: certainly, she was soon to marry another Estonian Jewish émigré, Kolya Sondelevitch, and she may simply have followed in his wake.

62 Nancy, Paula Nancy, stick thin, could not stop shaking. Paula (Powla) short and fat, looked like that character in *Sergeant Bilko* who is the butt of all the jokes. But they and the Katzes and Kamuschers are among the most beautiful people I have known.

64 BBC World Service Someone else who listened to the BBC was the hefty young Estonian, perhaps a farm-worker, who heard us talking in English on the train on the way to Viljandi, and told us that his dearest wish was to have a copy of *Fowler's Modern English Usage*. I sent it to him, of course, but never heard if it had reached him.

67 the way her mother died The news of my grandmother's death had come in a phone call. It was summer and the French doors of the thatched cottage in Kingsbury were open on to the garden which was full of old fruit trees. Here, at weekends, my father tended his strawberry patch – just beyond the hump of the air-raid shelter – putting each strawberry plant into a jam pot to protect it from natural predators. I couldn't hear what was being said but knew something bad had happened. The call ended and my mother went out of the room. I, or so I imagine, went back to bouncing my ball on the paving stones. To this day I don't know whether it was the Foreign Office or the police or the Red Cross who had received news of her mother's death – nor from what source – and passed it on to her. As for the year, each night we were watching and hearing the V1s overhead.

70 *Roots Schmoots* If I hadn't braced myself to buy this, I wouldn't have known that the author had met Rachel Margolis, my distant cousin. Like us, he met her in Vilnius at the Jewish Museum where she works as a volunteer and is a kind of living exhibit. On the walls are pictures of her and her husband, now dead, who had fashioned a key which enabled them to escape from the ghetto, after which they took to the woods.

Like their fellow partisans in Poland, whose memories are recorded in Theo Richmond's *Konin*, they did whatever it took to stay alive. That evening, as we sat in her apartment, drinking tea from porcelain cups, it was hard to believe that this highly civilised elderly lady had once lived like a wild animal. And yet, there was still a spark of that political fire which had helped to keep her and her comrades alive.

70 if anyone wonders They could also read *The Mighty Walzer*, the one *English* Jewish novel of recent years that can bear comparison with the Malamuds, Mailers, Roths and Bellows.

74 less alone It would surely have helped to know that not so very far away, in the Vale of Evesham, where he was working for the Monitoring Service, was another Estonian Jew, Vladimir (Vova) Rubinstein, whose cousin, Kolya Sondelevitch, had married Bounia, now on the run from the Nazis in occupied France.

Vladimir Rubinstein, whom I met for the first time just the other day, was studying at the LSE when war broke out. His maternal grandfather had been my great-uncle's business partner and the two families – Gutkins and Sondelevitches – jointly owned that chunk of central Tallinn.

75 hell-hole by the Solent Disconcerting to have Eversley crop up in an obituary recently and find that Rosemary Verey, described as 'the grande dame of English gardening', had been there. Of course, I can't be sure it was the same Eversley and the fifteen-year difference in our ages could account for her seemingly smooth transition from it to London University. Maybe Fran had not always terrorised her pupils (or this pupil, anyway). How different she was from Battle Abbey's Miss Sheehan-Dare, my next headmistress, a Miss Marple-like character both in appearance and in the hidden sharpness of her mind.

77 my favourite page The caption to this captivating image reads: 'The little white spot on this page is ten times larger than the egg from which you started growing.' The next illustration is a photograph of apple trees in full bloom.

79 Mussolini-like, he affected a huge desk I know one shouldn't speak ill of the dead, but it was not until Tom Rosenthal and I were both nearing eighty (he, reportedly, unwell and I recovering from a heart attack) that I decided to ignore a gagging order he had imposed on me many years before, took the ageing manuscript out of the bottom drawer and allowed it to be published. Like so many books, this one is an attempt to work itself free of its material. I needed to write it, and my only regret is the pain it may cause to others. But history cannot be re-written.

80 and Japanese businessman On a recent visit to Battle Abbey, to attend their centenary celebrations, we were welcomed in the driveway by today's pupils of whom a great number were Chinese. And it was a Chinese male student (both categories unimaginable in the late '40s) who had designed the exquisite cover of the centenary publication.

81 prisoners-of-war Whether this was a figment of our girlish imaginations I will never know but it is a memory shared by my old friend Jennifer, though it does not appear in the little history of the school she has lent me. From this – *Battle Abbey: the story of a school* by June Parker – I now know that Miss Sheehan-Dare (who was Miss Jacoby's aunt, not cousin) was indeed a child psychiatrist (to prevent her reading our minds, we used to think furiously about butterflies whenever she spoke to us) and that Miss Jacoby did, indeed, run the farm. As for their educational qualifications, Miss Jacoby had taught music in the past whilst Miss Sheehan-Dare, like her sister, May Jacoby, who founded the school, was an enlightened educationalist who had stepped in when her sister's health required it. Looking back, I can see that May Jacoby's spirit – she was an early enthusiast for Dalcroze eurhythmics – still permeated the school.

81 neither school had a sixth form At Battle Abbey this omission was put right many years ago. It now has a flourishing sixth form.

82 *The Random Egg* This useful little book by George Bradshaw – *Soufflés, Quiches, Mousses & the Random Egg* – was a lot more typical of what was an excellent but soon to be out of fashion cookery list which valued text above pictures.

85 our only 'scholarship girl' I now know that our 'scholarship girl' was actually the daughter of an immensely wealthy family whose name can be seen on hoardings all over the country. I have discussed this shared false memory with my friend Jennifer and we can only think she must have seemed different in some way. Perhaps she didn't speak as 'nicely' as we did. Whatever the answer, she died young and need never know what little snobs we were.

85 regain the past By a happy quirk of fate, Dierdre has come back into our lives; only last week, she, from her home in Dorset and I, from mine in north London converged on Jennifer, in Surrey, with our near-identical photograph albums and spent a happy few hours catching up on the last fifty years.

87 visited by Bridget Not her real name. And since the school is now thoroughly co-ed, night visitors are more likely to be boys than girls.

89 disgracefully lazy Critchley's autobiography goes a long way to explaining his apparent laziness. The crippling alimony awarded his first wife, for no very good reason that this reader could see, made him take on more commissions than anyone could fulfil and it is a wonder that there was only one dud among them. *A Bag of Boiled Sweets* is a lesson in good humour (and good manners), the more so if read straight after John Osborne's vitriolic *Almost a Gentleman*, when Critchley's lack of rancour and refusal to 'tell all' is especially endearing.

89 would have giggled over at school What I remember giggling over at school – our field was limited for we didn't read the Bible and learning Latin did not constitute a classical education – was the innocuous 'and threw warm gules on Madeleine's fair breast' and the misapprehended 'There's husbandry in heaven, their candles are all out . . .' There was also a verse with an inescapably heavy beat which was so filthy – more Folk Art than Eng Lit – that I cannot bring myself to write it down.

90 punning section titles I am now able to supply a few: 'Holding Your Own', 'Sour Puss', 'Hims to Venus', 'Maidens Over' . . . R ordered me a copy from Amazon. Unfortunately, it hadn't lost its jacket. I had suggested Fragonard's 'Swing', but what the Sales Manager wanted, and got, was a photograph of a pair of legs in fishnet tights, sticking out of a half-open rexine and gold bound book which carries this sticker: 'The book that falls open at every page.'

90 weekly treat Although the restaurant column is no more, there is the several-times-weekly 'Way of the World' to take its place. This is the first thing I turn to after the obituaries, and it seldom disappoints. Being the only *Telegraph* reader I know (and perhaps the only one who voted Socialist

Alliance in the last election), I often find myself syndicating Craig's best pieces among my *Guardian*-reading friends.

98 at his suggestion Though so unlike in manner and appearance, he was a close colleague of Laing and LSD was, at that time, part of the Laingian stock-in-trade.

99 unduly mild in her responses which amounted to murmuring, 'That's about the size of it', as she leant forward to poke the fire or light another cigarette. To my delight, I came across this the other day on the www: 'I was fond of my St Hilda's tutors,' writes Katherine Duncan-Jones, several years younger than me, who went on to edit several of the Arden Shakespeares, 'but the best I could hope for from Anne Elliott [...] was a rather slow and grudging, "Well, Kate; that would be right; that's about the size of it . . . followed by prolonged silences, punctuated by deep inhalations of a Navy Cut cigarette . . .' Thus did generations of Eng Lit students benefit from their privileged one-to-one relationship with their tutors.

99 a syllabus that ended According to the obituary in the St Hilda's College Report, when Anne Elliott was a student at St Hugh's the syllabus ended in 1823, and 'As far as literature was concerned, Anne saw no need to extend her range, or become entangled with non-classical genres such as the novel . . .'

100 uncommissioned translation Also uncommissioned had been *The Real Wagner*, a large, untidy manuscript which had arrived on the reading shelf a few years earlier. Written in slightly odd English (though the English of the translated passages was impeccable) and full of incomprehensible charts and tables, it didn't look promising. But the extraordinary story of Wagner's life, told with such verve and deep understanding, was irresistible. Having fought off the charts, we took the book on, and its modest launch, organised by the author's own students – they took and re-took the evening courses which he continued to give well into his nineties – is one of the happiest I can recall.

102 wasn't written in 'proper English' a complaint that was also made, with no sense of its absurdity, by a member of the public about the excellent American translation of Pagnol's *Jean de Florette*, which was seen to arrive from our warehouse labelled JEAN THE FLORIST.

103 a faceless woman which I had bought as a teenager identifying – long before I became an editor – with that anonymous presence.

104 had saved up to buy me I was wrong about this. I recently came across a very fancy document which I hoped might be my marriage certificate, headed Memorandum of Agreement. It seems that my mother bought the typewriter on hire purchase from Harrods.

104 Deleuze and Lacan Clare, who took this book in its original typed form and re-typed it on her computer, for which I will be for ever in her debt, tells me that she has never heard of Deleuze or Lacan but remains characteristically unruffled and is happy to leave them undisturbed.

105 What would Mrs Hoster have advised? 'Mrs Hoster' was a by-word for gentility. In those days, as we are reminded by Mrs Deborah Bean – the Queen's Correspondence Secretary for forty years and alumna of Mrs Hoster's Secretarial College in the Cromwell Road – girls didn't all go to university. (For nice girls from nice homes, it was nursing or teaching or shorthand and typing.) She is quoted in a delightful piece by Giles Brandreth which can still be found on the www. It first appeared in the *Telegraph* to celebrate Mrs Bean's retirement from royal service.

106 wide-eyed Carol can still surprise me. I had just got back from visiting New York where my son was involved in an alternative-music venue (it was there I heard a conch-shell played for the first time) and was rhapsodising about musicians who will put on the same show for an audience of two as two hundred, when she interrupted to tell me that as a teenager in Paris she had been taken by Sidney Bechet to a club where Louis Armstrong was playing and had listened to them jamming all night.

107 disappeared out of our lives to reappear some years later as the author of several blockbusting film books; as familiar now with Los Angeles and Hollywood as he had once been with the European cities on his salesman's beat.

107 her novel the fate of which, like Penelope's web, is to remain for ever unfinished.

108 Luckily, Diana Athill has pretty well spiked that one Diana Athill is still producing books, writing enviably lucid reviews, broadcasting, and entertaining live audiences in her mid-nineties.

110 penny-pinching The only drinks for which we did not have to pay in the teashop were tea and barley water. At Harrods, I don't remember anything being free except what we now call tap water.

113 that Bryan Kneale portrait I found, on seeking permission to use this, that not only was this the first portrait painted by Bryan Kneale (now in his eighties and long since a sculptor) but that his wife, a picture restorer, had to come to the rescue when the painting was slashed. Obviously somebody didn't like Anthony for, several years later, another portrait, this one by Patrick Proctor, suffered the same fate.

113 *Call It Sleep* was given to me by a friend in New York whose own childhood had not been dissimilar. His father, like the father in the book, had not been pleased when his wife and their brood of children arrived in the New World. Even so, they had one more child, my friend Sol. I remember no other details except that Sol's father was a baker and that his mother's cooking was so awful that when he was called up (Sol Miller is in his eighties, so World War II) he was thrilled by army food.

116 final decline Not final as it turned out: Deutsch still exists as part of ITV.

116 a children's book This book – though not, alas, the cartoons – was to appear on our list and Rhianna became one of Pam Royds' stable of cherished authors.

119 cash transactions There was a time when a customer would be regarded with suspicion or, at least, looked at askance for not wearing a tie, but now it is taken for granted that being unkempt is anyone's privilege and no sales assistant is surprised at someone who looks more like a tramp than a regular tax payer pulling a wad of money out of his pocket.

121 Roger Sale Only a few years older than R, Roger Sale was one of the teachers who made Amherst a more exciting place to be than Cornell. What impresses me, who was never his student, is that he and his wife *chose* to spend a winter sabbatical in a Teesside gîte and know and love Saltburn, that most melancholy of Yorkshire seaside towns.

123 a passion for football To this day, now nearer fifty than forty and living in New York, A disappears at my bedtime to join a game that takes place under arc-lights on a platform beside the river. And, in the morning, I see that familiar-from-childhood sight of discarded football clothes waiting to go into the washing machine.

123 when music took over Most unexpectedly, as piano lessons for me remained a grim memory. But persuaded he really did want to learn, I bought an old upright with a bright, tinny sound and found a football-mad jazz musician to teach him, with consequences none of us could have foreseen for A has made music not only his life but his living and among the happiest memories of my last visit to Brooklyn was hearing him play his own compositions in his basement studio.

124 £300 a week It would have been less still had I not bumped into an acquaintance on the bus – a high earner in the charity field – who told me of a job at an educational trust which she thought I might like and, to my astonishment, thought I might get. I never, in fact, applied for the job but, armed with the advertisement and her confidence in me, pretended that I had and my Deutsch salary was upped by something like 25 per cent.

The discrepancy between what we, at Deutsch, earned and what others earned could be startling. Never more so than during those three days in 1981 spent in Robert Golden's studio photographing those Floris cakes. Robert, one of the very best food photographers, earned something like £500 a day; the cook, the excellent Carol Handslip, something like £300; the stylist (i.e. prop girl) something like £150. And me, £50.

126 turned him down My fear that this would put an end to any interest in books and learning was long ago allayed by his fierce engagement in every kind of political debate. More pleasing still, was finding Blake's *Songs of Innocence and Experience* set to music – the Appalachian mountain music of his wife's childhood – on their latest record, *The Garden of Love*.

126 Hazel Tom Rosenthal was to tell me, years later, that he and Hazel Frame were an 'item' (his word) at about this time. What was never mentioned was the evening when after a Young Publishers' meeting, he had invited me to his Harley Street flat; an occasion as innocent as it was inconsequential and he has probably forgotten it.

126 got them thrown out I had this wrong. It was only the dog that was voted out.

128 conceived and written In a recent obituary of Stratford Johns, Troy Kennedy Martin and Elwyn Jones are credited with being the creators of the Barlow character who dominated the series. I have inflated John's role. He was, I suppose, just one of a team of writers. His success still lay ahead.

128 knew one of them well This was Roger Lonsdale who has remained ever since in both Oxford and the eighteenth century (see his majestic new edition of Johnson's *Lives of the Poets*), and served to restore my faith in 'English' for I had come to share the common view that it attracted only the dullest students.

131 Peter Tegel who went on to produce prize-winning translations and write plays of his own and whose wonderful memoir *Far Away Country* is one of the few that skirts experience rather than dwelling on it – the more astonishing, given the richness of the material: a Sudeten-German childhood and a mother straight out of Tennessee Williams.

131 Gina Conquy Soon to become Mrs Murray Pollinger.

131 business girl was a term used in all seriousness by Kate Caffrey whose *Out in the Midday Sun* – a breathtaking account of the fall of Singapore – had been turned down by seventeen publishers before it reached us: such was the industry of her agent, Ilsa Yardley. More remarkable still was Kate's enrolling in the history faculty of Birkbeck College when she was well into middle age and already an established author.

132 throw off the coils R suggests I go and have another look: I take down Pevsner instead and find this sculpture is called *The Spirit of Brotherhood*.

135 some of the jobs that were thrown at me One of these was to take charge of the jackets, a job I did without ever understanding the technical side of it. I still don't know what a 'colour separation' is but I do remember the embarrassing occasion when Franciszka Themerson, a well-known artist, who was doing something for us as a favour, had to re-do her artwork because one of the three colours she had used was grey (a beautiful silvery grey) and André did not consider grey to be worth paying for.

Some years later, on hearing the price of the Atget photograph which Knopf had used on their edition of *Eccentric Spaces* (also a beautiful silvery grey), he told me to say No thanks and get a photograph from the French tourist board for nothing.

136 and many others who were not all from Africa and the West Indies though many, at the time, were.

137 Penguin bought the paperback rights The success of *Henrietta's War* and *Henrietta Sees It Through* didn't stop there. They have recently been re-issued by Bloomsbury with attractive new jackets.

140 his wife His wife, Joan Hardwick, was now a Deutsch author. When I take my glasses off, I can read the titles of her two books from where I sit: *An Immodest Violet* and *Addicted to Romance* – lives of Violet Hunt and Elinor Glyn.

141 'one of the partners . . . stenographer' Jean Rhys to Selma vaz Diaz in letter of 18 June 1963.

142 been corresponding for years Diana's first letter, enclosing that cheque for £25, had been sent in the summer of 1957. It was now the summer of 1963.

143 during the time I was with her 'I will lay in some drinks and so on, you may be sure . . .' Jean Rhys to EW in letter of 23 July 1963.

144 unsalaried breakdown In fact, Clarice, in union mode, had managed to get me one month's salary (I had been working at Deutsch full-time for five years) and this £80 paid my fares to the ante-natal clinic, bought the knitting wool for those little vests, and covered the cost of the two frozen lamb chops, bought at the corner shop, which I ate every night to satisfy a craving which would more conveniently have been for something less expensive like charcoal.

144 the social whirl of Janet's life which culminated – after many years devoted to worthwhile causes – with a seat in the House of Lords.

145 Anna was Anna Lovell, the 'Anna' of 'Michael-and-Anna' who had seemed so inseparable that I am always surprised by those who link Michael's name with Frances, whom he was to marry and with whom he had a child.

Another painter who, like Anna, lived near us in Ladbroke Grove, was Patricia Gulliver. I still have the artwork she did for a Joseph Singer novel and in our Yorkshire kitchen is the oval wooden panel on which she had painted, on a bright red acrylic background, a contented-looking mother hen in whose belly a bright yellow chick is flapping its wings. Single mother of an adored three-year-old son, Patricia had given me this when she heard I was pregnant. I wish I knew what became of her and her son and the paintings that festooned the walls of her basement room, but it isn't easy to trace someone who called herself after the local telephone exchange.

145 final devastating affair In Sevin, M found what he was looking for. They got married and are still together.

145 What happened was this Gina would disagree. She remembers this episode quite differently and has forgotten having asked me home to meet Molly Keane as a kind of consolation prize. Diana, however, remembers the course of events as I do and says, with characteristic honesty, she would do the same again.

146 the irrepressible Michael Curtin who gave the Deutsch telephone number to a fictional brothel in one of his novels.

147 her appetite for good writing has not diminished. Only the other day, so absorbed was she in re-reading *War and Peace* that she had forgotten to go to bed. It was also no surprise to find that Stefan Zweig's *Life of Balzac* which I took round because I had so enjoyed it, jumped to the head of her reading queue, just as manuscripts had in the old days.

147 *Keine horre!* On the subject of Jews and food, I recently read that some medieval rabbis asked that the boards of their coffins be taken from that holiest of places, the kitchen table.

150 no electricity No road either. The muddy track to this isolated cottage was a driving test I set my son when, after only twelve hours behind the wheel, he was entitled to drive. Looking back, all our holidays alone together, of which this was to be the last, had involved tests of some kind. In Majorca it had been Latin vocabulary; in Tunisia, French irregular verbs. Now, and much more to his liking, it was motorways, country roads and farm tracks. I don't suppose our friends ever expected to see us again as they saw us reversing in the mud, swerving to avoid their free-ranging hens.

152 took pains to hide It was typical of Bill, outcast by his braininess, to take on the colour of his surroundings. So it was that, for a long time, I thought he liked alcohol no more than I do, he having come down to my milk-shake level during the days I spent with him in San Francisco.

152 *Seven Dreams* Four volumes of this monumental series – sub-titled *A Book of North American Landscapes* – have now appeared: most recently, for Bill does nothing like other people, volume 3.

153 sturdy Scottish descent Having visited Selkirk on a wet Sunday morning, it is easy to see why the Harbisons took off, almost four hundred years ago, never to return.

153 underdog himself For more on underdogs, turn to www.martharedbone.com. My daughter-in-law has chosen for her stage name the slang term for a person of mixed African and American Indian descent with which she was taunted as a child. 'Underdog', one of my favourite tracks, has been described as 'an anthem for the underclasses of the world . . .'

154 the weight of his productions To be put in the shade by a book still to come, the 3000-plus page *Rising Up and Rising Down* which Bill hung on to until a publisher appeared who would print it in its entirety. After this he allowed a commercial house to bring out an abridged version. It is hard to imagine how McSweeney's coped with the mammoth original, but anything would be possible that involved both Bill and Dave Eggers (*A Heartbreaking Work of Staggering Genius*) who was, perhaps, already at McSweeney's when they took Bill on.

156 one of my oldest friends I am thinking of Mavis Haut, the friend with whom I first travelled to India and who had, all those years ago, rescued me from the psychiatric ward. Her first book *The Hidden Library of Tanith Lee: Themes and Subtexts from Dionysos to the Immortal Gene* was published when she was already in her sixties.

157 The Violence Initiative TVI was the brainchild of Neil Watson whom A had met during his brief time as a student. A was unusual in having already left home and Neil in being just out of prison. Now a registered charity with an ever-widening field of action, TVI had been funded in the first place by a single individual: this benefactor, a 'captain of industry', and his wife regularly attended the early meetings held variously in a Camden Town coffee bar, a pub under Waterloo Bridge, a council flat in Wood Green and, latterly, the organisation's own premises off Turnpike Lane.

158 Pascoe I have spent a lot of time at the Public Records Office, looking for confirmation of Pascoe's death. I have not found it. Nor have I managed to find the record of his birth. Maybe James Pascoe – for such was his full name – was a pseudonym. Maybe he isn't dead. The only thing I know for sure – for we met several times – is that he did exist.

160 by its author Ellen Meiksins Wood, who inscribed it: 'Enjoy it – even (or especially?) if you don't read it'. The book's title *The Origin of Capitalism: a longer view.*

162 resigning the directorship This wasn't pure moral rectitude. I was also fearful. I had read enough to know that directors were responsible for decisions made in their name whether they knew and approved them or not.

165 How different it would have been On a suburban train, taking us from the airport in Boston to the city centre, we got talking with a charming middle-aged flower child in the seat opposite. Covered with rings and bangles, with discount tags (dog food, cat food) hanging from her woven belt, it was a surprise to learn she had a job at the airport which got her up at four o'clock every morning. 'It's a union job,' she said as though this was explanation enough.

165 a 'new' town Apparently this bit of eighteenth-century social engineering hadn't worked too well. The North Europeans couldn't stand the heat and the Spaniards couldn't stand the Protestants.

166 a friend Caroline Knox (then Owen) now living in Scotland and happily employed promoting local author James Boswell who enjoys an annual festival and the kind of attention many a living author would envy.

167 'a little Hungarian Jew' I have just re-read the *Private Eye* profile in the Westminster Reference Library, to find that the word 'Hungarian' occurs five times; 'Jew' and 'little' not at all: it is easy to see where the latter came from ('dwarf-like') but what about the former? Was André, who wasn't technically Jewish (i.e. he didn't have a Jewish mother) being unduly sensitive?

167 the only Jew Not so. How could I have forgotten Mr Tammer, the Company Secretary, who was even shorter than André, had three splendid daughters and looked askance at my irregular liaison with a goyische man.

173 sent, this time, to give Ilsa the sack … An episode which did little to interrupt a long friendship. Only the other day, arriving for a lunch given in her honour, and at which she was expected to speak, Diana realised she had forgotten her hearing aid. Ilsa, who arrived at the same moment, at once lent her hers, sitting through the long lunch unable to hear a thing, and thus missing Diana's acknowledgement of how she had saved the day.

173 a shouting match to equal Ilsa's Sheila Murphy, whose reading of this manuscript has saved me from many errors (Constance Lambert,

Barley Allison, etc) and who has checked facts for me on her computer, tells me that this isn't what happened. After seven years of shouting matches, she had finally decided to move on and it was she who gave André notice at which he burst into tears and tried to persuade her to stay but she had, wisely, already booked her passage to New York.

177 sees the video Someone else who saw the re-run film was Philip Trevelyan, our Yorkshire landlord and friend. A sheep-farmer for more than twenty years, Philip had once been a documentary film-maker and, as a student, had worked on the lighting at that extraordinary event.

178 hash brownies I must have had about twenty lodgers in all – two at a time – over those few years and their eating and bathing habits, for there was only one bathroom, stick in the mind. There was George Andrews, author of *The Book of Grass*, who lived on pot and brown rice, a serene character who padded about, his greeting always the same: a raised hand and 'Hi, man . . .' There was Jean l'Esperance, an old schoolfriend whose marriage had come unstuck, and who introduced me to feminism (I still have her copy of Kate Millett's *Sexual Politics*) and, more usefully still, to Welsh rarebit. There were those who seemed not to eat (or bathe) and those who ate Lyons individual fruit pies and spent hours in the bathroom which housed the only loo. One of my very last lodgers, now the divorced mother of two grown-up sons, rang not long ago, wondering whether she could stay for a few nights in her old room. But that room is now part of the kitchen, and I had to say no. But her lovely refusenik son, Shimri, now at the LSE, has become a frequent visitor.

179 recently re-issued in Japanese its English title *The Pine Prince and the Silver Birch*, its tale a parable of race and its illustrations by the friend who became my son's stepmother. Sevin had also done some jackets for us, the least successful of which was for *Wide Sargasso Sea*. This Henri Rousseau-like scene of tropical vegetation inhabited by a single figure who looks as though made of wood, would make the book more valuable; a fact I learnt from her husband, my ex-husband, who used his gambling winnings to start an antiquarian book business specialising in first editions of twentieth-century fiction.

180 *The Eden Man* The only novel in which I have appeared as a character: the client in whose newly bricked patio the book's hero Peach O'Hare has inadvertently created an untameable soil-stack-related drain. Luckily, we knew nothing about this at the time.

181 put himself down for Creative Writing instead As I was to learn from Ray, it was the memory of an English teacher who had told him he was good at writing which gave him the courage to add his name to the list: a rare teacher who could see beyond the backward-sloping hand and chaotic spelling. Thirty years later, I was changing Johnathan to Jonathan, enamble to enamel. Now, a spell check would have done it for us.

182 taking three months to reply I have been, am still, at the receiving end of this seigneurial practice. One distinguished editor, whose permission I sought before sending him a friend's manuscript, has still, more than two years later, to reply or return it. Far worse was the case involving a prisoner, serving a 65-year sentence for murder in an American jail, who had written to Carole Blake after finding her address posted in the front of her excellent manual *From Pitch to Publication* which I had sent him. She responded encouragingly to his early letters and the first sight of his manuscript. But it took her the best part of a year to say No, pleading 'a heavy work load' for the long silence! I was ready to throw a brick through her window but Jack was more circumspect and when he did finally land a publisher told me that it was thanks to advice, in her book, that he had been able to negotiate a more favourable contract.

183 issue-filled dramas Faith had deliberately kept 'issues' out. It was only when we met that I found she had been married several times, that Brian wasn't the father of the children in the happy foursome portrayed in her books, and that one of the reasons he and she gave up their first business venture – 'holidays for unaccompanied children' – was because the children had been shoplifting on a fishing trip to Honiton.

183 who charge for them It was a long time before I realised that agents seldom pay for anything. A new low was reached the other day when the least pushy of authors, on asking how his manuscript was faring – it had been with his agent for several years – was told not where it was or had been but about the crippling cost of sending manuscripts out . . .

184 had been surprised as I am now by this exceptional writer having remained unpublished for so long. Six of her novels have been warmly received by her loyal agent, but not one has been sold.

184 writers who stick with their publisher Another writer who stuck with us for a very long time was V. S. Naipaul though there was a short break when he moved to Secker and then moved back again when he found himself described in their catalogue as a 'West Indian writer'.

185 too hastily dismissed Some of the writers I turned down or passed on to other readers without much enthusiasm were, if my memory serves me right, Maggie Gee, Jonathan Coe and Simon Sebag-Montefiore.

186 such harsh power The nature of a book does not always belie its author. A year or two ago, Joan's battle with Totnes Council over what they considered a breach of planning regulations, reached the national press. Now, according to a report in *The Times*, an equally fierce battle rages, this time with a neighbour.

187 more than one meaning Alas, Eva and I are no longer friends. She and I had a terminal falling out after I heard her telling the vast Radio 4 audience words to the effect that if Israel had thought they could get away with it, they would have behaved just as badly as the Nazis. This interview followed the publication of her *Journey to Nowhere*.

189 to the best of my knowledge Although hard to credit, I pass on a story heard since that André did have other liaisons and, at one time, shared a secondary mistress with another publisher, thus cutting the maintenance costs.

191 a venue so familiar for, rather touchingly, Lord Goodman was André's guru-cum-father-figure in whom he had absolute trust and for whom he had infinite respect.

194 geriatric social worker After a stint at *Vogue* for Wendy and in publishing for me, we had decided to become social workers and applied to the LSE. Twice I was offered a place and twice had to turn it down. I have often regretted not spending my working life more usefully.

195 inadvertently circulated a letter It needs to be explained that on his arrival at Deutsch, Tom had initiated a system whereby an extra copy of every letter written by anyone in the building was circulated so that everyone knew what everyone else was doing.

196 'On one side . . . Gorgon' The words – which I badly misremembered – are Shakespeare's. Cleopatra of Antony: 'Though he be painted one way like a Gorgon, / The other way's a Mars . . .'

200 slashed out 'remarkable' Since reading Susie Harries's monumental biography of Pevsner, as entertaining as it is illuminating throughout its 800-plus pages, I see this kind of response from a building's custodians was far from unusual. Thus does 'dull and monotonous' become 'pleasant and dignified'. As for Pevsner's collisions with unhelpful vicars, they are in a class of their own.

201 in midstream because the logo police (apparently all big corporations have a department which does nothing but protect the company logo) would not allow the shell to nestle among the letters of the title as our designer had proposed. It had to be free-standing which is how it ended up in the water.

202 Christobel Christobel Kent wouldn't have stayed there for long for, like Clare Chambers, she was to turn to writing books – leisurely crime novels set in Italy – and having babies herself.

204 plans to move to Cornwall The other morning, to my surprise, I bumped into Gill in our local Safeway, wheeling a baby in her trolley. Gill has changed direction once again and is now the rapturous mother of a two year old. While we caught up with each other's gossip, Zoe was kept happy by the pictures on the dog food tins. More recently still, Gill has been busy getting famous for the sake of the publishers' editors who *love* the book she has written but can't take on anything by an unknown author!

204 television set in Tom's office A recent acquisition (it would have been unthinkable in André's cosy, book-lined room) enabling Tom to watch cricket.

205 our name Faith Addis was one of the writers who came to us by working her way down the list. It was Faith, too, who was said by an interviewer on local radio to be published by 'Andrew Dutch'.

209 there has been no downside This was true until the spring of 2004 when a publishing friend persuaded me to have the manuscript read for libel so I would feel able to try and find a publisher. Unable to contact the libel lawyer who had been so helpful before, I got a list from the local Law Centre and made an appointment with the one firm I could walk to. Surprisingly enough (in retrospect) its terms were much the same as two other firms, carefully chosen because they were definitely not West End.

The net result of plumping for the one I chose, of whom I had not heard at the time, was an instantaneous meeting with a brisk lady lawyer, wearing a girlish cotton frock, who undertook to report on the sixty or so questionable passages before leaving for her holiday in Australia a week or so later.

She kept her word.

Within a matter of days she was ready to meet and having led us into a conference chamber (she and I had sat across a small table in the reception area before) told us (R was now with me) that the problems were so severe that my only course – unless I had the money for a full report and/ or was ready to find myself in court – was to forget about the whole thing. I was not even to show the manuscript to friends though I could send it to agents or publishers, if I really wanted to, as this would be termed a 'privileged read'.

It was not only the substance of what she had to say but the way she said it which made me run for cover. She had taken exception to something I had written about Tessa Jowell – who was no more her business at £5 a minute than André who was dead, but on whom she also wasted time and sympathy. It soon became apparent that she didn't like the book, or me.

What didn't become apparent, until going through her marginal scribbles when we got the pages home, was how bad she was at her job. Apart from jumping to the defence of my dead ex-employer and my ex-neighbour, now Minister of Media, Sport and Culture, she (or someone) had mistaken metaphors for literal truths, had queried copyright on quotations well within the free zone.

And so it went on. But I had been so thoroughly frightened by her version of what was likely to happen if the manuscript ever slipped out of my sight, that I had no appetite to carry on and put it away. As for her bill for £1400, after my detailed letter of complaint had fallen on deaf ears, I sent the money, unable to face the prospect of fighting a whole firm of lawyers.

210 everyone but me It was in similar mode, as I learnt from Stacey Schiff's life of Vera Nabokov, that the Nabokovs – for ever fearful of a return to penury – insisted on a built-in cost-of-living rise in their book contracts.

212 the three years it took Actually, two years and four months between the first letter from Nabarro Nathanson (10 November 1992) and the signing of the Agreement on 1 February 1995. But Peter Ford stayed on during the protracted if sporadic attempts to get André to underwrite this ex-gratia agreement which has, in fact, been honoured by VCI who bought the firm from Tom, Carlton who bought the firm from VCI, and ITV who bought the firm from Carlton.

212 seemingly identical To the innocent eye, identical in every way except for the ever-changing cast of directors.

213 the charmingly rural Speargreen In riffling through the foot-deep pile of papers relating to the pension dispute, before committing them for safe-keeping to a friend's attic, I noticed the name which kept recurring when the Company was dissolved and re-formed was not Speargreen but Thamesdraft. I can't believe I invented the former and assume both names were in play at one time or another.

214 a trullo As I could see from the picture in the brochure, a trullo was a little round house with a pointy roof – a kind of elf-dwelling common in that part of Italy. In the grounds of this crumbling mansion, it had almost certainly been used as a kind of playhouse.

214 the estuary of the Somme Those few days in northern France were the last holiday M and I had together. My mother's illness and the doctor's prediction that she had only months to live made me fearful of leaving her but, at some point during those four years, M persuaded me to go away for a few days and we chose this near-but-foreign destination. Which I was to visit again this spring, touring the Gothic cathedrals of the region and, by chance, happening on the little town, Salins les Bains, where after a train crash in the nearby Alps, some fifty years ago, Sevin and I (on our way to Italy) had found ourselves in hospital.

217 many of the residents were council tenants Not any more. Today the handbook's assumption that every street was bound to yield someone with legal expertise might well prove to be the case. But in the '70s our street was not full of professional people: the foundry where horseshoes had once been made (or so I was told) had only recently shut down; so, too, the piano factories onto which we backed and, three houses down, a truly ancient couple lived, quite contentedly, without electricity. I was one of the few people to have the two essentials in any fight against bureaucracy – a telephone and a typewriter – plus, to my discomfort in all other circumstances, an unmistakably middle-class voice.

218 Jon Elkon was one of two writers who got only the first two books of a trilogy published. *Umfaan's Heroes* and *Laszlo's Millions* which had delighted us, failed to win enough readers for us to be able to continue. Even 'Pirhana Parker', as Jon's agent Imogen Parker (now a prolific writer of romantic fiction) apparently liked to hear herself called, couldn't prevail and *Kruger's Gold* remains an unpublished collector's item; so, too, volume 3 of Lois Lang-Sims's remarkable memoir published many years before.

218 discouraging pencil drawings of which over the years I have become very fond as I receive each Christmas a home-made card from Peter with a delightfully wonky drawing expressive of an innocent joy in life which has never left him.

218 at war with my employer which stopped short at going to court. Tenacious and supportive though my solicitors were, they discouraged this step because I couldn't afford to lose and they were not prepared to underwrite this eventuality as they had everything else.

219 his first book *The World as Information* by Rob Abbott was published by Intellect Books and its author still lives in Nottingham but now with a wife and two teenage daughters and a house full of paintings, almost any one of which I would like to own, for they have retained the untamed spirit of the original manuscript.

220 terminal falling out After the success of *Ripley Bogle* (which a trendier company than ours had kept for a year and then returned to sender), Robert introduced us to a brilliant young photographer called Donovan Wylie (soon to be with Magnum) and proposed their doing a book together on the subject of poverty. We were enthusiastic. The book was commissioned. Both participants received a modest advance, commensurate with the depth of our pocket, the shortness of the text, and the subject of the book.

Donovan's pictures came in on time. Nothing from Robert until a long and plaintive letter, pleading poverty. To cut a long and rancorous story short, the book did eventually come out and Robert's next, pitiful offering came through an agent who broke off relations when we turned it down. To serve up a dud book to sever a writer's connection with his original publisher is a common tactic. In this case, I believe the finished work (we had seen only a fragment) did find a publisher, but I was amused to hear Robert saying how little he now thought of it during an interview on French TV which took place ahead of its re-appearance in a French translation.

221 Kanan Makiya whose *The Monument: Art, Vulgarity and Responsibility in Iraq* published in 1991 under an assumed name – Samir al-Khalil – was an Iraqi dissident whose one previous book, *Republic of Fear*, bravely published by the University of California Press, had fallen on deaf ears. Soon it was to become a bestseller and Saddam Hussein a household name.

221 to offer my wares which included Clare Chambers, who James did take on, and Nadeem Aslam, who he didn't. To my delight, he also took on one unpublished writer – Romana Liddell-Grainger, now Romana Rogoshewska – who remains unpublished to this day but whose extraordinary talent can surely not go unrecognised much longer.

221 a few of my orphans One of these was Nadeem Aslam who hit the jackpot with his second novel *Maps for Lost Lovers* – eleven years in the writing – which was bought by Faber, Knopf and a host of other publishers for large amounts of money. I had sent Nadeem's first novel to Deborah Rogers after asking if she would be prepared to look at it. When, after three months, I had no reply, I sent her a copy of the original letter as a reminder. She never answered, or returned the book.

221 for the last time I realised the other day just how important 'closure' is. My cousin, who had died after a long illness, was interred in the wildflower meadow that had been his pride and joy, while photographs of him rotated on a big screen and his grandchildren sloshed about in the mud and scattered earth and seeds on his grave. At Deutsch, even a temp was given a warm send-off: a bottle of wine in the production department followed by fond farewells was a regular occurrence. To leave as I did, after thirty years, as though it was a day like any other, left an open wound. But, had it been otherwise, this book might not have been written.

226 we too had central heating installed It wasn't just having the time, it was having the money. R had begun his first full-time job for twenty years on his fiftieth birthday, giving us two heady years as a two-income family.

226 what we might find It was only three months since 9/11 when my son and his wife had seen the towers explode, the first on television and the second, across the water, from the end of their Brooklyn street. I was not yet ready to be out of touch and have never seen any point in travelling with one ear cocked to home.

227 research grants When the polytechnics turned, overnight, into universities (about as realistic as Cinderella's pumpkin turning into a golden coach) the great advantage for us was that research grants became available and R was to get a generous share of these for, as ever, they were given to those who had already proved themselves.

228 it was reading *Stet* This is perhaps the place to say that most of my colleagues at Deutsch who appear in this book have had a chance to read it, including Diana who did not ask me to change a thing. Indeed, when we met in a teashop near Primrose Hill for her to return the manuscript, she brought with it that Staffordshire figure. We remain friends.

228 Like that molehill in Mexico the volcano described in Sybille Bedford's enchanting *A Visit to Don Otavio*.

228 Selestun I am told this begins with a 'C' but I don't want to lose the memory of that scruffy little Mexican resort, way off the beaten track, where we could have thrown a pebble into the sea from the window of our room and where, after a night of non-stop drumming, for it was New Year's Eve, we woke to dazzling sunshine and a silent world.

Like so many of the places which meant a lot to us, Selestun (spelt correctly there) appears in *Travels with Bob* (Isle of Wight Architecture Centre, 2009), the beautifully produced catalogue of a bunch of snapshots I took on our travels which an ex-student of R's thought fit to exhibit to accompany the launch of R's book, *Travels in the History of Architecture*.

228 barrels of cucumbers I am indebted to Claudia Roden (*The Book of Jewish Food*) for the description of shtetl life which she has culled from a book by Mark Zborowski and Elizabeth Herzog: *Life is with People: the Culture of the Shtetl*.

Illustrations

1 *The Menell family in Dublin, c.1907. My grandfather, George, and grandmother, Esther, with Arthur between them. My father in top hat, Slip with mortarboard, Bertha behind Freda, both with flowers in their hair, Moos seated. Eddie (Edward Septimus) still to come.*

2 *My grandfather, Boris, with his second wife, Helena (born Łodz) and their children. Stefanie with pearls (a student in Vienna), my mother (still a schoolgirl) and their younger brother, Hermann. Tallinn, c.1920.*

3 *Camborne School of Mines rugby team, 1912. My father seated, middle row, arms crossed.*

4 (Inset) *My father as a young man.*

5 *Estonian Girl Guides group, my mother holding the flag. Directly behind her, at the end of the row, is her best friend, Bounia, who was soon to leave for Paris.*

6 (Inset) *My mother, taken in Reval (as Tallinn was then called) in 1927. She was twenty-two years old at the time.*

7 '. . . in love with her Englishman . . .': my parents before they were free to marry.*

8 *My mother in remission, during her last visit to Tallinn.*

9 *My widower father reading the sports page in our Swiss Cottage flat.*

10 *With my parents in Tallinn, the year before war broke out.*

11 *My tailor grandfather on the site of what would become the Vanamöisa mining complex.*

12 *Down the mine. My father is the one with a cigarette.*

13 *My third birthday party, Tallinn, 1937. Not many years later, all the children in the picture, except my brother (back left) and me (centre front) were in exile or dead.*

14 *My grandmother: one of the many Estonian Jews who were all to die in the same year. With her is my six-year-old brother.*

15 *Ruti, the daughter of my parents' best friends, who was raped and murdered when she was ten years old.*

16 *Taken in Estonia in the early sixties: a street parade with Soviet ikons, the building which housed the synagogue, the radio factory where my cousins Lena and Renata worked, the conservatoire which had been built as a family home by Lena's father, the market.*

17 *My uncle Hermann, back from the war years in Siberia, c.1950.*

18 *Hermann and Leida got married during our first visit in 1964. Here they are signing the register, with Lenin looking on.*

19 *Leida's daughter Aili who was sent to Siberia while still a schoolgirl and Ülo, who she married there. Pictured here in the '80s when back from exile.*

20 *Uncle Slip with Auntie Rae, on shipboard. Probably on their way to or from South Africa.*

21 *My father's youngest sister, Moos, in her Johannesburg garden.*

22 *My father's youngest sibling, Eddie, with his elegant, non-Jewish wife, pictured at their home in Johannesburg.*

23 *My cousin Fima, at this time an English schoolboy, with his parents. Concealing his 'bourgeois origins' was to get him expelled from his beloved Communist Party.*

24 *With Fima, my only English-speaking relative, beside the lake in Viljandi on my first visit to Estonia, 1964.*

25 *My husband with Fima and Lena, a year or two after they had followed their children to live in Strasbourg.*

26 *Variations of this card announcing my birth surfaced recently. We were to live in Eyre Court again after the war.*

27 *The new-born infant in this picture could be either me or my brother. The picture is undated. My grandmother, seen in the background, would have come over for my birth.*

28 *On Bobik, not Bobik then, in a pre-war English garden. With me is my cousin Vicky.*

29 *At school in Ilkley. A photo long-cherished because I look almost skinny.*

30 *In the grounds of Battle Abbey with best friends Dierdre and Jennifer.*

31 *Being led by Anthea (one of our gang of six) during the weekly ballroom-dancing lesson. Miss Silvester instructing.*

32 *A '50s teenager. In Queen's College blazer (with Parker pen).*

33 *With Sevin by the Black Sea. Probably during an Oxford summer.*

34 *Getting married. 3 July 1960.*

35 *This picture of me pregnant was taken during a stay in hospital. Sally Cline was in the next room, expecting her husband Larry Adler's baby.*

36 *With my son and 'the best dog in the world' – taken by Wendy on the beach at Worthing.*

37 *My son and the lodger who was to become my second husband, on Primrose Hill c.1973.*

38 *Diana Athill framed this portrait of Great Russell Street which she had commissioned for use on a catalogue and gave it to me when she no longer had room for it.*

39 *A photo of André which somehow conveys both the best and the worst of him.*

40 *The three arrows that make up the Deutsch colophon are pictured here: Nicolas Bentley, André Deutsch and Diana Athill.*

41 *Tom Rosenthal. Unlike André, Tom smoked a pipe but it would not have been his style, as it was André's, to cadge cigarettes off all the other smokers in the office.*

42 *Editorial meeting, c.1965:* (left to right) *Piers Burnett, me, Ilsa Yardley, Janet Stewart, Ted Collins, Leo Cooper, Diana Athill, Nicolas Bentley (barely visible) and André with his back to the camera. It was Piers Burnett, another long-serving editor,* *who brought in many of the heavyweight non-fiction and natural history books which would never have found their way on to our list without him.*

43 *Clarice, with husband Stan, outside the house in the country that they retired to, seen here calling her cat.*

44 *Pamela Royds who took over the children's list started by Philippa Pearce and became a mainstay of the firm.*

45 *Ilsa Yardley, who came to Deutsch as a secretary, became publicity manager, and was fired twice. Like so many others – Faith Evans, Anne Louise Fisher, Laura Morris among them – she went on to become an agent. André continued to adore her, as does everyone else.*

46 *Mr Tammer, our long-term accountant, with Sheila Murphy, one of our first publicity directors.*

47 *Gill Collins who worked at 105 on and off as a kind of Girl Friday. Missed when she moved on to host a transvestite club in Camden Town.*

48 *Taken by one of my lodgers who remarked that she seldom saw me any other way.*

49 *Bill Vollmann who was to provide me with more to do than anyone else during the last few years of my working life. His handwritten letters (he doesn't use e-mail) are still a part of our lives.*

50 *Carol Filby who I had met while we were both secretaries at Methuen. If only we had heeded her advice and bought* Asterix *– then unpublished in England . . .*

51 *Eva, for many years a close and valued friend. No one was better to have on one's side in a verbal skirmish, as with the car rental company when we once holidayed together in Portugal.*

52 *Madeleine St John who wrote one perfect novel but wasn't good at lasting friendship.*

53 *Leah Hertz, a businesswoman who wasn't satisfied with just making money. She died tragically young, on the threshold of a career in politics.*

54 *Nadeem Aslam, a waif-like youngster who had to borrow the fare to come down and see us, is now published around the world.*

55 *Robert Edric, who after wondering if he would ever get published was published by Deutsch and Secker & Warburg simultaneously . . .*

56 *Clare Chambers whose irresistibly witty first novel we published while she was still our secretary.*

57 *The manuscript of* The Monument *was handed in at Reception with no return address and no picture of the monument among its many illustrations. It was some time before I met the author: not Samir al-Khalil, as appeared on the title page, but Kanan Makiya, an Iraqi dissident who was still living undercover at that time, and who, only with the greatest difficulty, managed to get a photograph, taken by a British tourist, of the monument which was the subject of the book and which we were to use on its jacket.*

58 *Jane Rawlinson, whose youngest son thought she had written six different novels when her complimentary copies arrived.*

59 *Bella Aronovitch, whose life was transformed by publication.*

60 *I not only treasure Joyce's books but also one of the pastel drawings which she was doing in her nineties. To celebrate the publication we arranged an exhibition of these in André's office and I have always feared I may have underpriced them for every one was sold.*

61 *Faith Addis, whose books were fought over when they arrived in the office and, long after publication, rediscovered and turned into a popular television series.*

62 *Rudolph Sabor, whose home-made productions were to become standard works of Wagnerian scholarship.*

63 *Michael Curtin, the Limerick printer, whose two-line submission letter in a backwards hand, heralded the arrival of an outlandish talent.*

64 *Paul Lyons – Cambridge drop-out and lifelong hippy – in his own garden.*

65 *Carol Bruggen, who wrote at her kitchen table and took medication to keep madness at bay.*

66 *Murray Bruggen, the one husband who encouraged his wife's writing.*

67 *Gwendolyn Mary Parkinson, Carol's mother, who did not recognise herself in her daughter's novel.*

68 *Tom Bruggen, Carol's son, on a recent anniversary of his mother's death. Beside him is the grave enclosing a lock of his father's hair.*

69 *Kate Harris who, after seven years in a comfortable and caring home for the old, decided enough was enough and opted out. She often said to me that old people were just clutter and that the world should be left to the young. But perhaps she didn't realise how much she would be missed.*

Bookcover *It was Madeleine St John who suggested patchwork that summer when I found myself jobless, and showed me how to do it. The habit, begun as therapy – like Effie's pig – long outlasted those few grim months and on quiet Yorkshire evenings I would stitch away so contentedly that the squares, if laid out side by side, would now carpet a room and I am hoping that one day, when I am long gone, they may be stitched together and used as insulation on the walls of my son's Brooklyn studio.*

But for me, they remain like the leaves of this book, a memory vault: bits of long-ago bathroom curtains, cotton scraps from the market at a Gambian beach resort, pretty off-cuts from my friend Jennifer who still makes her own dresses, the occasional cheat: a packet of ready-cut squares from some country church where, while my husband inspects the building, I flip through the parish magazine and check out the home-made articles for sale. This heap of memories, still backed with old newspapers, will remain just as they are but now, by some miracle, also decorate this book.

Acknowledgement is made to the following for their kind permission to reproduce illustrations: **39**, **40**, **42** and **46**, Oxford Brookes Special Collections (and for their help, Eleanor Possart and Chris Fowler); **41** and **51**, Nigel Sutton; **49**, Ken Miller; **56**, Richard Mason; **57**, Mike Lovett, Brandeis University; **64**, Camilla Baines; **65**, Dookie Clunies Ross; **68**, Linus Bruggen. And particular thanks to Bryan Kneale for allowing us to reproduce in black and white his stunning portrait of Anthony Blond – originally, of course, in colour.

Acknowledgements

✑

Most of those who matter to me the most are already named and often pictured in these pages, but there are those who have slipped the net and my thanks to them too for what their friendship has meant to me: Jane and Juliet (only memories now), Carole, Margaret, Nicky, Yvonne . . .

There are also those who patiently helped to turn this memory bank into a book. Without my publisher, editor and friend, Howard Davies, it would never have happened and I would never have known what being 'the author' is like. So my very special thanks to him. My thanks too to Janette Revill who designed the book, Cliff Webb for his help with the photographs and Julia Brown and Caroline Westmore for their generous advice. Also to Philip and Nelly Trevelyan, overlooking whose farmyard much of the book was written.

It only remains to thank my husband, Robert Harbison, who has lived through so much of this with me, and my son, Aaron, whose birth, not long after my mother's death, gave my life meaning again.

Index

References to my parents, husband, ex-husband and son, also to André Deutsch and Tom Rosenthal, occur throughout and are often fleeting. To avoid the irritation of long lists of page numbers or sub-heads inappropriate to the rambling nature of the text, I have resorted to *passim* for these; so too for Diana Athill and William T. Vollmann who both make many appearances. The references to my parents occur most often in Chapters 1 and 2. The others will be found scattered throughout but with greatest frequency in Chapters 5, 6 and 7. One other anomaly: there are times where a name appears in the Index but not in the text. Those concerned will be able to find themselves if they want to. No one else, I hope, will be bothered by this.